D0090269

The Browser's Dictionary
of Foreign Words
and Phrases

The Browser's Dictionary of Foreign Words and Phrases

Mary Varchaver and Frank Ledlie Moore

CASTLE BOOKS

This edition published in 2006 by
CASTLE BOOKS ®
A division of Book Sales, Inc.
114 Northfield Avenue
Edison, NJ 08837

This edition published by arrangement with and permission of
John Wiley & Sons, Inc.
111 River Street
Hoboken, New Jersey 07030

This publication is designed to provide accurate and authoritative
information in regard to the subject matter provided. It is sold with the
understanding that the publisher is not engaged in rendering professional
services. If professional advice or other expert assistance is required, the
services of a competent professional person should be sought.

Library of Congress Cataloging-in-Publication Data:

Varchaver, Mary.
The browser's dictionary of foreign words and phrases /
by Mary Varchaver and Frank Ledlie Moore.
p.   cm.
1. English language—Foreign words and phrases—Dictionaries. I. Moore,
Frank Ledlie. II. Title.
PE1582.A3 V37 2001
422'.4'03—2001017921

ISBN-13: 978-0-7858-2156-4
ISBN-10: 0-7858-2156-2

Printed in the United States of America

Foreword

At last we are given a bright and sprightly dictionary that is not only useful but a joy to read. Veteran reference book compilers and editors Mary Varchaver and Frank L. Moore, who are known especially for their recently published *Dictionary of the Performing Arts,* have turned their talents to enlightening us on the meanings of foreign words and phrases we meet in our daily lives. This is not a dictionary of academic terms you might have been expected to learn in school. Nor is it a dictionary directed to travelers in foreign lands from which you are supposed to learn scores of terms about ordering your dinner in restaurants, or learning to get about in a train station, or arguing with concierges about the state of your hotel room or the high amount of your bill. It is, rather, a dictionary to help you elucidate what you come across every day in newspapers or hear on television. Its choice of terms and directness of style reflect the immediacy of everyday discourse. Thus it is a unique and exceptionally useful addition to the genre of special dictionaries.

What are its other features? First, it guides you to the correct pronunciation of foreign words, using transcriptions from ordinary English. Most other dictionaries of foreign words and expressions use elaborate phonetic symbols unfathomable to most persons, or, even worse, have no pronunciation guides at all.

Second, the definitions are a model of clarity, and the meanings are illustrated by hundreds of sentences. Consider these entries, given in their entirety:

afflatus *(ah-FLAH-tus)* [Latin: a breathing on] An inspiration; an irresistible understanding that comes into the mind as a fresh breeze. ⟨He goes at the canvas with all the *afflatus* of a silkworm eating its phlegmatic way across a mulberry leaf.⟩—*Time,* April 13, 1998.

smorgasbord *(SMOR-ges-bord)* [Swedish: sandwich table] A buffet table that presents a great variety of hot and cold dishes. By extension, any situation that offers many choices. ⟨Here, in the sunny Southern Caliphate, they make up a *smorgasbord* of least-favored nations.⟩—*The New York Times Book Review,* July 18, 1993.

Third, the entries focus on those words that an American reader will recognize as truly foreign. Thousands of words in American English have foreign sources, such as *dollar* or *ketchup,* but their meanings have become so thoroughly absorbed into our everyday language that they are no longer classified as foreign. In this *Browser's Dictionary of Foreign Words and Phrases,* the authors have stressed foreignness by choosing words that are relatively recent additions to the language. They have also included some older adopted words that have different or expanded meanings in current usage.

I learned early on in my career as an editor and writer of reference books that a really useful dictionary is one that contains the information you need, in a form you can easily use. This dictionary is, in short, a book you will want to keep at hand year in and year out. You will not be disappointed if you approach it with that expectation in mind.

Gorton Carruth, former editor in chief
of Funk & Wagnalls, coeditor of the
Oxford American Dictionary, and
editor of *The New York Times
Crossword Puzzle Dictionary*

Acknowledgments

Grateful acknowledgment is made to our agents and friends Nicholas Smith and Andrea Pedolsky, who provided the impetus for this project, and to the fine editors at Wiley & Sons: Chip Rossetti, Mark Steven Long, and Jim Gullickson. Special thanks also to Gorton Carruth, Yola Coffeen, André Varchaver, and Nicholas Varchaver for their help and encouragement. Without the invaluable assistance of Gabi Moore, this dictionary would not have seen the light of day.

Dedicated to the memory of Frank Ledlie Moore.

*H*ow to Use This Dictionary

1. The entry word or phrase appears in **boldface.**
2. Pronunciation appears next in *italics* in parentheses, with the stressed syllables in uppercase type. In some cases where the original pronunciation of the foreign word differs from that of modern or standard English, both pronunciations are given.
3. The etymology and/or language origin of the words appears in brackets.
4. The definition follows.
5. Cross-references appearing within or at the end of the entries are in SMALL CAPITAL letters.

Pronunciation Guide

ah   the sound of (a) in *father.*
ay   the sound of (a) in *day, ace.*
eh   the sound of (e) in *met, edge.*
eye   the sound of (i) in *ice, write.*
ih   the sound of (i) in *it, give.*
oh   the sound of (o) in *go, over.*
ow   the sound of (o) in *cow, now.*
uh   the sound of (u) in *but, up.*
zh   the sound of (s) in *vision, treasure.*

Foreign Sounds

au   as in German *auf,* Latin *laude,* Spanish *gaucho:* the sound of (ou) in *out.*

eu   as in French *deux,* German *schön:* the sound of (e) in *get* or *let,* pronounced with the lips rounded or pursed.

kh   as in German *ach* or Scottish *loch:* made by pronouncing a strong, aspirated (h) with the tongue in position for (k), as in *keel* or *cool.*

ü   as in French *rue*, German *über:* the sound of (e) in *feet*, pronounced with the lips rounded or pursed.

nh   Indicates the heavy nasalization of a preceding vowel. (The symbols *n* and *h* are not pronounced.) Nasalization means that more of the sound comes through the nose than through the mouth. Thus:

anh   heavily nasalized sound of the (a) in *father*, as in French *piquant (pee-KANH)* or *nuance (nü-ANHS).*

enh   heavily nasalized sound of the (a) in *cat*, as in French *vin (venh)* or *point (point).*

onh   heavily nasalized sound of the (o) in *order*, as in French *tontine (tonh-TEEN)* or *marron (mah-RONH).*

Note: In some words, such as the German *verboten (fehr-BOH-tn)*, no vowel appears in the unstressed syllable because the (tn) is closest in sound to the entire syllable. Many languages do not use stress in the manner of English. In some transliterations of Japanese words that have high and low tones rather than accents, we have chosen to indicate a syllable that the Japanese pronounce with a low tone, as if it were a stressed syllable.

à bas *(ah BAH)* [French] Down with, as in *à bas le roi:* down with the king. The opposite is VIVE.

abbatoir *(ah-bah-TWAHR)* [French] A slaughterhouse.

abbé *(ah-BAY)* [French, from Latin] An abbott. In France, a title given to a priest or member of the clergy.

abogado *(ah-boh-GAH-doh)* [Spanish] An advocate; an attorney; a lawyer.

ab origine *(ahb oh-RIH-jeh-neh)* [Latin] From the beginning. Not the same as the single word ABORIGINE.

aborigine *(ah-boh-RIH-jeh-nee)* [Latin] One of the original people (of a country). ⟨The Maoris are the *aborigines* of New Zealand.⟩

ab ovo *(ahb OH-voh)* [Latin: from (the) egg] From the very beginning.

abrazo *(ah-BRAH-soh)* [Spanish] An embrace; a hug.

abri *(ah-BREE)* [French, from Latin] A shelter; a place of refuge.

absinthe *(AB-sinth)* [French, from Latin and Greek] A green, bitter, licorice-flavored liqueur distilled from wormwood and other aromatics; like OUZO, it turns milky white when water is added. Because of its extremely high alcohol content (70 percent to 80 percent) and toxicity, it has been banned in most countries.

a capella *(ah kah-PEL-ah)* [Italian: in chapel] A musical term describing choral music that has no instrumental accompaniment.

accablé *(ah-kah-BLAY)* [French] Overwhelmed; physically or mentally overcome by fatigue or sorrow; crushed.

accolade *(ah-koh-LAID)* [French: around the neck] Originally, the embrace around the neck by which the king bestowed knighthood, later the touch of a sword on the shoulder. Recently, any award, honor, or praise. ⟨The highest *accolade* honored two officers killed in the line of duty⟩

accouchement *(ah-koosh-MANH)* [French, from *accoucher*: to give birth, to be delivered] Childbirth; confinement; lying-in.

achtung *(AHKH-toong)* [German] Watch out! Attention! Pay attention.

acme *(AK-mee)* [Greek: point, edge] The highest point; the greatest achievement.

actualités *(ahk-tyoo-ah-lee-TAY)* [French] Current or recent events; the news of the moment; a newsreel.

adagio *(ah-DAH-zhyoh)* [Italian, from *ad agio*: at ease] In music, slowly. A slow piece of music or dance. ⟨In ballet, the slow, sustained movements of an *adagio* form the first section of the classical PAS DE DEUX.⟩

addenda (plural); **addendum** (singular) *(ah-DEHN-dah, ah-DEHN-dum)* [Latin] Something added; additional information. ⟨thousands of clumsy, awkward amateurs, whose *addenda* to this "course" of study make the schools ridiculous⟩—*The Atlantic Monthly,* March 1999.

addio *(ah-DEE-oh)* [Italian, from *a Dio*: to God] Good-bye.

à deux *(ah DEU)* [French] For or of two people; for two people only; between two people in a close relationship; intimate.

ad hoc *(ahd HOHK)* [Latin: for this] For a particular purpose or thing; up to this time. Usually applied to small groups or committees whose work will continue only as long as a specific problem is under discussion. ⟨This *ad hoc* group of five investigators . . . published a report.⟩—*The New York Review of Books,* April 22, 1999.

ad hominem *(ahd HOM-ih-nehm)* [Latin: to the man] Founded on or appealing to the interests, passions, or prejudices of an individual, rather than to his or her argument. By extension, casting doubt on an opponent's character rather than responding to the question posed. Also, an argument that fails to prove a point under discussion by failing to address it directly. ⟨There is a difference between satire and spiteful, *ad hominem* playground insults.⟩

adieu *(ah-DYEU)* [French, from *à Dieu:* to God] Good-bye; farewell.

ad infinitum *(ahd in-fih-NYE-tum)* [Latin] To infinity; forever. ⟨The list could be extended *ad infinitum.*⟩—*The New York Times,* November 30, 1941.

adios *(ah-DYOHS)* [Spanish, from *a Dios:* to God] Good-bye; farewell.

ad libitum *(ahd LIB-ih-tum)* [Latin] At liberty; at will.

ad nauseam *(ahd NAW-zee-um)* [Latin] To the point of nausea; to a sickening degree.

adobe *(ah-DOH-bee)* [Spanish] A yellow silt found in the U.S. Southwest, used to make sun-dried bricks for building. ⟨The community houses of the Pueblo Indians were built of *adobe* or stone.⟩

Adonai *(ah-doh-NYE)* [Hebrew] A phrase meaning "the name of God," used in Orthodox Jewish services to avoid speaking the actual name in accordance with the commandment not to take the Lord's name in vain.

ad valorem *(ahd vah-LOH-rehm)* [Latin] To the value; according to (its) value. ⟨With recent *ad valorem* taxes the figure is higher.⟩— *The Guardian,* February 4, 1999.

aegis *(EE-jiss)* [Latin, from Greek: the shield of Zeus] Protection; sponsorship. ⟨To complicate the bureaucracy even further, Europe-only actions would be carried out under the *aegis* of the Western European Union.⟩—*Time,* April 12, 1999.

affaire de cœur *(ah-FAIR deu KEUR)* [French] An affair of the heart; a love affair.

affaire d'honneur *(ah-FAIR don-NEUR)* [French] An affair of honor; a duel.

affiche *(ah-FEESH)* [French] An official notice or an advertisement posted in a public place; a poster.

afflatus *(ah-FLAH-tus)* [Latin: a breathing on] An inspiration; an irresistible understanding that comes into the mind as a fresh breeze. ⟨He goes at the canvas with all the *afflatus* of a silkworm eating its phlegmatic way across a mulberry leaf.⟩— *Time,* April 13, 1998.

aficionado *(ah-fee-syoh-NAH-doh)* [Spanish] An enthusiast; a fan, especially a devotee of bullfighting. ⟨This is the domain of *aficionados,* and categories rapidly ramify.⟩—*The New York Review of Books,* April 22, 1999.

à fond *(ah FONH)* [French] To the bottom; fully; thoroughly. See also AU FOND.

agal *(ah-gahl)* [Arabic] A cord wound around an Arabic man's head to hold his KAFFIYEH in place.

agent provocateur *(ah-zhanh pro-vok-ah-TEUR)* [French: instigator] A paid undercover agent who abets activities directed against the state or against society, or one who incites people under suspicion to commit illegal acts that result in their downfall or punishment. ⟨The novel follows the misfortunes of a double-dealing *agent provocateur* in the former Soviet Union.⟩

agità *(AH-jee-tah)* [Italian] Agitation; annoyance; trouble.

à gogo *(ah GOH-goh)* [French] As much as you want; galore; to your heart's content.

agon *(AH-gon)* [Greek: a struggle or contest] In drama, the struggle or tension between principal characters that precipitates the action of the play ⟨In Shakespeare's *Othello* the *agon* can be felt in every evil insinuation as Iago goads Othello into murderous jealousy.⟩

agora *(AH-go-rah)* [Greek] A marketplace in ancient Greece; a popular place of assembly. ⟨And nothing really happens that isn't older than the forum, more ancient than the *agora* in Athens.⟩—*The New York Times*, May 5, 1962.

aide-de-camp *(ehd deu KAHN)* [French: camp helper] A military or naval officer acting as a personal assistant to a senior officer.

aide-mémoire *(ehd-mehm-WAHR)* [French: an aid to the memory] A memorandum recounting a proposal, discussion, agreement, or action.

aikido *(eye-KEE-doh)* [Japanese: way of spiritual harmony] A method of self-defense, designed to subdue rather than injure an opponent, that uses throwing and twisting techniques to turn the opponent's impetus and strength against him or her. ⟨Her mother is a student of homeopathy and a teacher of the Japanese martial art *aikido.*⟩—*Time*, August 14, 1995.

aioli *(eye-oh-LEE)* [Provençal, from Portuguese and Latin: garlic and oil] A garlic-flavored mayonnaise popular in southern France, often served with cold fish, chicken, or cold boiled potatoes.

à la carte *(ah lah KAHRT)* [French: by the card] According to the menu. With each item on the menu having a separate price; the opposite of PRIX FIXE or TABLE D'HÔTE. ⟨that offer a range of menus, from prawn cocktails to *à la carte*⟩—*The Guardian,* March 20, 1999.

alameda *(ah-lah-MAY-dah)* [Spanish] A public walkway shaded with poplar trees.

à la mode *(ah lah MOHD)* [French] In the style of; according to the fashion. Fashionable. In the United States, describing a dessert served or topped with a scoop of ice cream.

albergo *(ahl-BEHR-goh)* [Italian] An inn or hostelry. ⟨Our room at the *albergo* had a small, private terrace shaded by grapevine.⟩

alembic *(ah-LEM-bik)* [Arabic: a cap on a still] A device or a method that tests, transforms, or purifies.

alfresco, al fresco *(ahl-FREHS-koh)* [Italian] In fresh air; out of doors, as in "an *alfresco* supper on the terrace." See also EN PLEIN AIR, FRESCO, PLEIN AIR.

algorithm *(AL-goh-rithm)* [Arabic, a variant of *algorism*] A procedure for analyzing or solving a particular kind of problem in a finite or measurable number of steps. Any method of computation based on the Arabic system of arithmetical notation. ⟨National Weather Service Doppler radars use *algorithms* to analyze radar data for determining accumulated rainfall, storm motion, etc.⟩

alibi *(AL-lih-bye)* [Latin: in another place] An excuse; a story that would, if proven true, exonerate an accused person. ⟨People who cannot do mental arithmetic may have been given a new *alibi.*⟩—*The Guardian,* May 7, 1998.

à l'improviste *(ah lemh-proh-VEEST)* [French, from Italian] All of a sudden; in an unexpected, sudden, or spontaneous manner.

aliyah, aliya *(ah-lee-YAH)* [Hebrew: ascent] The immigration of Jewish individuals or groups to Israel. In a synagogue, the act of going to the lectern to read the weekly selection from the Torah.

alkali *(AL-kah-leye)* [Arabic: from ashes] Any of several base chemicals that neutralize acids or form caustic solutions in water. Soap, for example, is an *alkali.*

allegro *(ah-LEH-groh)* [Italian] Light; lightly. In music, a directive to play briskly, at a fairly rapid pace.

allemande *(ahl-MAHND)* [French: German] A 16th-century German dance in duple meter. In music of the 17th and 18th centuries, a section of an instrumental suite, often in moderate 4/4 time.

alma mater *(ahl-mah MAH-ter)* [Latin] Benign, nourishing mother; originally an epithet of several goddesses in Greek mythology, now used almost exclusively in reference to one's college or university. ⟨He has contributed lavishly to Princeton, his son's *alma mater.*⟩

almanac *(AHL-mah-nak)* [Arabic: the calendar] An annual publication that provides tables of astronomical and meteorological information for the year. *Almanacs* for the general public typically contain the times of sunrises and sunsets, the beginnings and endings of seasons, holidays, predictions of weather, and general advice for living.

aloha *(ah-LOH-hah)* [Hawaiian] Greetings; hello; good-bye.

altiplano *(ahl-tee-PLAH-noh)* [American Spanish: high plain] Any plateau or large area of level land at a high elevation. ⟨this Andean snow-fed lake is, in fact, a remnant of an ancient inland sea that covered much of what is now the Bolivian *Altiplano*⟩— *The New York Times,* January 10, 1999.

alto *(AHL-toh)* [Italian: high] In music, formerly, the highest male voice, now generally restricted to the lowest female voice. Having the tonal range of an alto, between tenor and soprano.

amah *(ah-MAH)* [Portuguese] A female servant who takes care of the children; a nanny. See also AYAH.

amandine *(ah-manh-DEEN)* [French] In French cooking, prepared or served with almonds.

amanuensis *(ah-man-yoo-EHN-sis)* [Latin, short for *servus amanuensis:* servant at hand] A personal secretary who writes down everything that is spoken; a literary assistant. ⟨More than that, she became an acolyte at the foot of the sage, an *amanuensis* chronicling his every word.⟩—*Time,* August 12, 1996.

ambience, ambiance *(ahm-bee-ANHS)* [French] The character, pervading atmosphere, mood, or quality of the surroundings or the MILIEU. That which encompasses; the environment. ⟨Even the lowliest diner has its particular *ambience.*⟩

ambuscade *(ahm-büs-KAHD)* [French, from Portuguese] An ambush. To lie in wait to attack from a hidden position.

ami (m)**, amie** (f) *(ah-MEE)* [French] A friend; a lover.

amicus curiae *(AH-mee-kus KYOO-ree-ay)* [Latin: friend of the court] A person who advises or is invited to advise the court upon a matter to which he or she is not a party. ⟨Douglas N. Letter, Attorney, U.S. Department of Justice, argued the cause for *amicus curiae*⟩—*The New York Times,* July 28, 1998.

amiga (f)**, amigo** (m) *(ah-MEE-gah, ah-MEE-goh)* [Spanish] Friend; comrade.

amok *(ah-MOK)* [Malay] In parts of Southeast Asia, a psychic disorder in which depression is followed by frenzied or murderous behavior; used in the phrase "to run *amok*." ⟨Against a relatively tame attack Lara ran *amok*, hitting 111—and South Africa out of the series.⟩—*Time*, May 17, 1999.

amontillado *(ah-mon-tee-YAH-doh)* [Spanish: from (the town of) Montilla] A type of matured, medium-dry Spanish sherry.

amoretto *(ah-mor-REH-toh)* [Italian] A little *amor*; a cupid.

amor vincit omnia *(ah-MOR VIN-sit OM-nee-ah)* [Latin] Love conquers all. Also written as OMNIA VINCIT AMOR.

ancien régime *(anhs-YEHN ray-ZHEEM)* [French] The old government, particularly that of France before the revolution of 1789. See also REGIME. ⟨straight talk that pierces the pretensions and propaganda of an oppressive and antidemocratic *ancien régime*⟩—*The Atlantic Monthly*, March 5, 1997.

andante *(ahn-DAHN-teh)* [Italian] In music, moving along; at a comfortable walking pace.

angst *(ahnkst)* [German] Anxiety; dread; psychological tension. ⟨all three rather passive actors notable for exuding *angst* and spiritual injury⟩—*The Guardian*, May 16, 1999.

anima *(AH-nee-mah)* [Latin: breathing being] The soul or spirit; vital force. In Jungian psychology, the inner person that is in contact with the subconscious. ⟨When asked about the source of his strong *anima*, he said it might have developed from his position as the only male in a family of many women.⟩

anomie *(AN-oh-mee)* [French, from Greek: lawlessness] A social or personal condition characterized by a lack of social values and standards. ⟨a story of existentialist *anomie* tricked out in real gold⟩—*The Guardian,* April 25, 1999.

antebellum *(AN-tee-BEL-lum)* [Latin: before the war] In existence before the war; usually used in reference to the period before the American Civil War of 1861–1865. ⟨Many of the elegant plantation houses in the deep South are preserved as examples of *antebellum* grandeur.⟩

ante meridiem *(AN-tee meh-RIH-dee-em)* [Latin] Before noon; before the sun reaches the meridian. Abbreviated A.M.

antipasto *(ahn-tee-PAH-stoh)* [Italian: before the meal] Appetizers consisting of anchovies, olives, artichoke hearts, various sausages, etc., served before the main course of a meal.

apartheid *(ah-PAHR-tayt)* [Afrikaans: apartness] The rigid government policy of racial segregation and discrimination against nonwhites in the Republic of South Africa, abolished in the early 1990s. By extension, any policy or system that segregates people according to their race or social class. ⟨With the Olympics increasingly mired in political controversy—whether as anti-*apartheid* protesting ground or cold-war proxy battle⟩—*Time,* May 10, 1999.

aperçu *(ah-pehr-SÜ)* [French: perceived] A quick glance; a glimpse. An immediate estimate, insight, or understanding. A summary exposition; a view of the whole.

aperitif *(ah-pay-ree-TEEF)* [French, from Latin] A drink of wine or liquor taken before a meal to stimulate the appetite. See also DIGESTIF.

aplomb *(ah-PLONH)* [French, from *à plomb:* by the lead; as straight up and down as the plumber's lead weight] Confidence; dignity; poise; self-assurance. Also, the vertical position. ⟨He answered personal questions from the press with great *aplomb.*⟩

apocalypse *(ah-POK-ah-lips)* [Greek] When capitalized, the last book of the New Testament: the Revelation of Saint John the Divine. A prophecy, revelation, or disclosure, especially one concerning a conflict between the forces of good and evil. Also, a catastrophic event; universal destruction; the end of the world, as in "the *apocalypse* of nuclear warfare."

à point *(ah PWENH)* [French: to the point] Cooked just right; done to a turn.

a posteriori *(ah poh-steh-ree-OH-ree)* [Latin: to the back] Going back to what came before; based upon facts that were known before. An *a posteriori* theory is one that has been derived from the evidence of its result.

apotheosis *(ah-poth-ee-OH-sis)* [Greek: from a god] Deification; the elevation of a human being to godhood or divine rank; the glorification of a person or principle. Also, the epitome or perfect example, as in "the *apotheosis* of creativity." ⟨I love paper—a good book is the *apotheosis* of which every tree dreams.⟩—*The Atlantic Monthly,* February 1997.

apparat *(ah-pah-RAHT)* [Russian] A machine or system; a power structure; a political organization.

apparatchik (singular); **apparatchiki** (plural) *(ah-pah-RAHT-chik, ah-pah-RAHT-chih-kee)* [Russian] An agent or member of the APPARAT or power structure within an organization or political party. The word was introduced into English in the early 1940s. ⟨The speech catapulted him from *apparatchik* obscurity to political prominence as a Serb nationalist.⟩—*The New Yorker,* April 19, 1999.

appassionato *(ah-pah-syoh-NAH-toh)* [Italian] In music, with passion; to be played passionately.

appellation contrôlée *(ah-peh-lah-SYONH konh-troh-LAY)* [French: controlled appellation] A designation given to those French wines for which the government guarantees the origin, the variety of grapes used, and the quality of the finished product. The designation appears on wine labels as, for example, *Appellation Côtes du Rhône Contrôlée.*

appliqué *(ah-plee-KAY)* [French: applied; fastened] In quilt making or sewing, a piece of fabric cut to a certain shape or design and sewn onto a backing; the piece of work so formed. To apply such pieces to a quilt, a dress, a wall-hanging, etc. ⟨She wore a handsome velvet jacket with silk *appliqués* in art deco style.⟩

après moi le déluge *(ah-pray MWAH leu day-LÜZH)* [French] After me, the deluge: attributed to Louis XV, referring to evidence of the coming revolution.

a priori *(ah pree-OH-ree)* [Latin: from before] Already known to be valid. A fact known *a priori* requires no analysis. ⟨Logic and *a priori* assumption, not empirical research, led to Sennett's insight⟩—*The Atlantic Monthly,* February 1998.

apropos *(ah-proh-POH)* [French, from Latin] As an adverb: to the purpose; pertinently; at the right time. As an adjective: opportune; pertinent, as in, for example, "an *apropos* comment." *Apropos of:* with regard to; with respect to, as in "*apropos* of the latest news." When used to introduce a noun: incidentally, by the way. ⟨the amusing congruity of Lola Young's remarks (*apropos* the Orange Prize short-list⟩—*The Guardian,* May 11, 1999.

aquarelle *(ah-kwah-REL)* [French, from Italian, from Latin] A painting done in watercolors. A printed picture on which watercolors have been applied by hand, using stencils.

aquavit *(AHK-wah-veet)* [Danish, Norwegian, Swedish] A distilled drink similar to vodka, flavored with caraway seeds.

arbitrage *(AHR-bih-trahzh)* [French, from Latin: to regulate; arbitrate] The simultaneous buying and selling of the same stocks, bonds, commodities, etc., in different markets to profit from unequal prices. ⟨It means the government ought to practice colossal *arbitrage* with irrational private savers.⟩—*Fortune*, November 25, 1996.

arcana *(ahr-KAH-nah)* [Latin] Mysterious or hidden things; profound secrets. ⟨The general reader can immediately appreciate the architecture of its orchestration with little or no grounding in Yeatsian *arcana* or the "Irish question."⟩—*The Atlantic Monthly*, February 1998.

arête *(ah-REHT)* [French, from Latin: a bristlelike ear of wheat] A sharp mountain ridge or rugged spur, created by the action of glaciers.

argot *(AHR-goh, ahr-GOH)* [French] The jargon, slang, or specialized vocabulary used by a particular group or class of people; the jargon or idiom of a trade or profession. ⟨I thought at first it might be a piece of Welsh *argot*⟩—*The Guardian*, April 28, 1999.

aria *(AH-ree-ah)* [Italian: air] An extended song for solo voice, often with orchestral accompaniment, usually part of an opera or choral work.

arigato *(ah-ree-GAH-toh)* [Japanese] Thank you.

Armageddon *(ar-mah-GEHD-don)* [Hebrew] The name of a great battle that was prophesied to occur on the plains (now called Megiddo) in the Valley of Jezreel near Mount Carmel in northern Israel. In modern parlance, the final conflict that will destroy the world, or any battle that results in utter devastation. ⟨Of course, in thinking about the financial implications of doomsday, don't overlook stockpiling and other standard *Armageddon* preparations.⟩—*The New York Times*, April 12, 1998.

armoire *(ahr-MWAHR)* [French, from Latin] A large, movable cupboard, cabinet, or wardrobe. Formerly a place for storing arms;

an armory. ⟨Our spacious hotel room also boasted an *armoire* in lieu of a closet.⟩

arpeggio *(ahr-PEH-jyoh)* [Italian] In music, the notes of a chord played in succession, with an upward or downward sweep, rather than simultaneously.

arrière-pensée *(ah-ree-EHR panh-SAY)* [French: backward thought] A mental reservation; a concealed motive.

arriviste *(ah-ree-VEEST)* [French] A person who uses any means available to realize his or her desires. In current usage, one who attains sudden social or financial success through underhanded or dishonorable practices rather than hard work. ⟨They were distressed when their only child married an *arriviste*.⟩

arrondissement *(ah-ronh-dees-MANH)* [French: a rounding out] The largest subdivision of a French *département,* made up of several cantons or smaller administrative districts. A municipal district in some larger French cities, such as Paris.

arroyo *(ah-ROY-oh)* [Spanish] In the southwestern United States, a gorge with relatively steep sides and a flat floor, usually dry except during infrequent rains.

art deco *(ahrt DEH-koh)* [French, from a shortening of *arts déco-ratifs*] A style of decorative art and industrial design introduced in the 1920s and 1930s, since revived in the 1970s, that uses geometric motifs, long, sleek forms, and synthetic materials to evoke or express modern technology. ⟨City planners hope to preserve at least the facade of this *art deco* building.⟩

artiste *(ahr-TEEST)* [French: artist] An entertainer; a public performer, as a singer, dancer, actor, mime, etc.

art nouveau *(ahrt noo-VOH, ahr noo-VOH)* [French: new art] A style of decorative art popular in the late 1880s and early 1890s.

Lavishly ornamental, it made use of exotic and dreamlike forms, strong symbolism, and a linearity reminiscent of natural forms such as plant tendrils. ⟨The jewelry of designer René Lalique was considered one of *art nouveau*'s most elegant expressions.⟩

ashram *(ASH-ram)* [Sanskrit] In India, a secluded place of religious retreat and learning, sometimes the home of a GURU. ⟨Since the Beatles' flirtation with meditation in the 1960s, *ashrams* in India have been frequented by celebrity ascetics.⟩— *Time*, July 6, 1998.

assegai *(AH-seh-gheye)* [Portuguese, from Arabic] A wooden spear carried by the original warriors of the Bantu-speaking tribes of South Africa.

atelier *(ah-teul-YAY)* [French, from Latin] A workshop, especially of an artist, artisan, printmaker, or designer; a studio. ⟨The *atelier* served as a living space as well as a work area.⟩

atrium *(AY-tree-um)* [Latin] The main room of an ancient Roman house, at the center of the house, and open to the sky. In a modern house, a small, not necessarily skylit room near the entrance, where guests may be received before they enter the main living room.

attaché *(ah-tah-SHAY)* [French] A diplomatic or military official attached to a diplomatic mission or staff in a specific field of activity, as a cultural *attaché* or army *attaché*. ⟨He was the U.S. defense *attaché* in Paris during the Nixon administration.⟩

auberge *(oh-BEHR-zh)* [French, from Provençal] An inn or hostelry.

aubergine *(oh-behr-ZHEEN)* [French] Eggplant, or the dark purple color of eggplant.

au contraire *(oh kon-TRAIR)* [French] On the contrary; on the opposite side. ⟨I am not prepared to say that all American husbands are untrue to their wives. *Au contraire,* I think most husbands are faithful in their fashion.⟩—*The New York Times,* September 20, 1998.

au courant *(oh koo-RANH)* [French: in the current] Up-to-date; well-informed; fully aware. ⟨your company will become more flexible, more profitable, more *au courant*⟩—*The Guardian,* February 7, 1999.

au fond *(oh FONH)* [French] At bottom; to the bottom; essentially; thoroughly; in actuality. See also À FOND.

auf Wiedersehen *(owf VEE-dehr-zay-en)* [German] Until we meet again; good-bye for now.

au gratin *(oh grah-TENH)* [French: with the scrapings from the bottom of the pan] In French cooking, a baked dish sprinkled with buttered breadcrumbs and/or grated cheese.

au jus *(oh ZHÜ)* [French] As applied to cooked meat: served with its natural juices or gravy.

auld lang syne *(awld lang ZINE)* [Scottish: old long since] Days of long ago; old times or friendships fondly remembered. The title and theme of a Scottish song by Robert Burns. ⟨It was the occasion of our *auld lang syne* to the fine old stadium, soon to be torn down.⟩

au naturel *(oh nah-tür-EHL)* [French] In the natural state; in the nude. Also, plainly cooked; ungarnished; raw.

au pair *(oh PAIR)* [French: even; equal (exchange)] A foreign young person employed to help with housework and child care, in exchange for room and board. Relating to or employed under such an arrangement. ⟨The highest court in Massachusetts upheld a reduced sentence for British *au pair* Louise Woodward on Tuesday⟩—*The New York Times,* June 17, 1998.

au revoir *(oh reu-VWAHR)* [French] Until we see each other again; good-bye for the time being.

aurora australis *(aw-ROH-rah aw-STRAH-liss)* [New Latin] The southern lights; the *aurora* of the Southern Hemisphere. See also AURORA BOREALIS.

aurora borealis *(aw-ROH-rah boh-ray-AH-liss)* [New Latin] The northern lights: great waves and streamers of colorful light seen at night in the northern sky at high latitudes. They are caused by the flow of solar particles from the Sun as they meet the forces near Earth's magnetic poles.

auteur *(oh-TEUR)* [French, from Latin: author; originator] The chief creator of a motion picture, especially one belonging to the French "new wave" movement of the 1950s and 1960s; a filmmaker with control over all the elements of production. ⟨All right, any *auteur* can replay his greatest hits, exploiting even the youngest viewer's need for nostalgia.⟩—*Time,* April 26, 1999.

autobahn *(OW-toh-bahn)* [German] In Germany, a main high-speed highway.

auto-da-fé (singular); **autos-da-fé** (plural) *(aw-toh-dah-FAY)* [Portuguese: act of the faith] Public condemnation of a religious heretic by the court of the Spanish Inquisition, and the execution of the religious verdict by civil authorities, usually by burning at the stake.

autoroute *(aw-toh-ROOT)* [French] In France and French-speaking Canada, a main highway or expressway.

autostrada *(aw-toh STRAH-dah)* [Italian] In Italy, a main highway or expressway.

avant-garde *(ah-vanh-GAHRD)* [French: advance guard] The van-guard; the innovators and experimenters, especially in the arts, noted for their willingness to use daring or unorthodox techniques. Pertaining to or belonging to the advance guard. ⟨The painting introduced a technique that was considered *avant-garde* in its time.⟩

avatar *(AH-vah-tar)* [Sanskrit: descent] In Hindu mythology, the personification or spirit of a god, the embodiment of a principle or idea. In computer jargon, the digital identity a person takes when corresponding with others on the Internet. ⟨Mayor Daley was the unapologetic *avatar* of "The City That Works," once known as "The Windy City."⟩

aviso *(ah-VEE-soh)* [Spanish, from Latin] A message or notice, or the boat or vehicle that carries it.

avoirdupois *(ah-VWAHR-dü-PWAH)* [French, from Latin: to have weight] A system of weights in the United States and Britain, based on the pound of 16 ounces and the ounce of 16 drams. Informally, corpulence; heaviness of body.

à votre santé *(ah voh-treu sahn-TAY)* [French] A toast: to your health.

ayah *(AH-yah)* [Hindi] A female servant who takes care of children; an AMAH.

ayatollah *(ah-yah-TOH-lah)* [Persian, from Arabic] Among Shiite Muslims, a chief religious leader with profound knowledge of Islam and its laws.

Ayurveda *(ah-yoor-VEH-dah)* [Sanskrit: life knowledge] The ancient Hindu system of medicine, based in part upon natural substances. ⟨He practices yoga and teaches a course in *Ayurveda*, an ancient holistic discipline from India.⟩

azan *(ah-ZAHN)* [Arabic] The Muslim call to prayer, chanted by a MUEZZIN from a minaret, or other high place in a MOSQUE, five times a day.

baba *(BAH-bah)* [French, from Polish: old woman; grandmother] A small, spongelike cake made with yeast and steeped in rum syrup. Also called *baba au rhum.*

baba ghanouj *(BAH-bah gah-NOOZH)* [Origin uncertain] In Middle Eastern cooking, a salad or dip of pureed roasted eggplant, garlic, olive oil, lemon juice, and TAHINI. Also called *eggplant caviar.*

babka *(BAHB-kah)* [Polish] A sweet yeast cake, often in the form of a cylinder and sometimes flavored with rum.

babu *(BAH-boo)* [Hindi] A Hindu term of polite address, equivalent to sir or mister.

babushka *(BAH-boosh-kah)* [Russian] An old woman; a grandmother. A woman's scarf folded into a triangle and used as a head covering, with two of the ends tied under the chin.

bacalao *(bah-kah-LAH-oh)* [Spanish, from Basque] Salt cod, or a dish made with salt cod, tomatoes, olives, garlic, etc.

baccarat *(bah-kah-RAH)* [French] A gambling game in which two or more players bet against the banker; winnings are calculated by comparing the banker's cards with those of the players.

bacchanal *(bah-kah-NAHL)* [Latin, from Greek] A tumultuous celebration in dance and song with a good deal of drinking, named after the orgiastic festivals in honor of the Greek god Bacchus; a carousal; a debauch.

badinage *(bah-dee-NAHZH)* [French, from Provençal and Latin] Banter; raillery; good-humored teasing. ⟨One can find endearment in the lame *badinage* of C-3PO⟩—*Time,* February 10, 1997.

bagasse *(bah-GAHS)* [French, from Spanish] The dry, fibrous refuse of sugarcane that remains after pressing, used to make paper.

bagatelle *(bah-gah-TEHL)* [French, from Italian] A trifle; something of little importance or worth. A short musical composition, usually for piano. Also, a game similar to billiards. ⟨Compared to that book, "An Equal Music" is a *bagatelle*⟩—*The Guardian,* March 28, 1999.

bagel *(BAY-gl)* [Yiddish, from German] A ring-shaped yeast roll with a firm texture, simmered in water and then baked.

baguette *(bah-GEHT)* [French] A small gem or crystal cut in a rectangular form, or the form itself. A long, narrow loaf of French bread. In architecture, a small, bead-shaped molding. ⟨Chirac didn't specify whether this helps to bake a better *baguette.*⟩—*The New York Times,* September 23, 1997.

baklava *(BAHK-lah-vah)* [Turkish] An intensely sweet Turkish pastry consisting of layers of PHYLLO, butter, and ground nuts; after baking it is drenched in honey or sugar syrup.

baksheesh *(BAHK-sheesh)* [Persian: gift] Money; a tip in cash. ⟨With his country on the verge of economic meltdown, he is back in line for American *baksheesh.*⟩

balaclava *(bah-lah-KLAH-vah)* [Russian, after Balaklava, a port on the Black Sea, site of a British attack during the Crimean War, immortalized by Tennyson's poem "The Charge of the Light Brigade"] A knitted, helmetlike cap that fits closely over the head, neck, and tops of the shoulders.

balalaika *(bah-lah-LYE-kah)* [Russian] A stringed instrument with a triangular body and a short neck, played (usually by strumming) like a guitar, sometimes solo but more frequently in bands.

balletomane *(bah-leh-toh-MAYN)* [back formation from French, *ballet,* and Greek, *mania*] A ballet enthusiast.

ballon d'essai *(bah-LONH deh-SAY)* [French] A trial balloon, one released to gather information on meteorological conditions. By extension, an experiment, often a program or statement issued to test public reaction.

bandanna *(ban-DAN-nah)* [Hindi] A large, colorfully dyed handkerchief, sometimes folded into a triangle, worn over the head and tied under the chin; often worn around the neck by horsemen in the American Southwest with the wider part in back to protect the neck from sunburn.

bandeau *(banh-DOH)* [French] A headband; a narrow band of fabric, sometimes elasticized, worn over the forehead or about the hair.

banlieue (both singular and plural) *(banh-LYEU)* [French] A suburb; the suburbs. A *banlieusard(e)* is someone living in the suburbs; a suburbanite.

banshee *(BAN-shee)* [Irish] In Irish legend, the spirit of a woman whose wailing was thought to foretell a death.

bantam *(BAN-tam)* [Dutch, from Indonesian] Any of several varieties of small domestic fowl noted for their combativeness. A small, belligerent person. Diminutive; miniature; tiny.

bar mitzvah *(bahr MITZ-vah)* [Hebrew] A ceremony, usually held in a synagogue, by which a thirteen-year-old boy who has successfully learned the fundamentals of Judaism is admitted to adulthood. See also BAT MITZVAH.

baroque *(bah-ROHK)* [French, from Portuguese: a rough pearl] Characteristic of a 17th-century European style of art and architecture, notable for its extravagant ornamentation and theatrical effects. Of or resembling music of the period after the Renaissance; ornate, florid, or fantastic in style. Anything lavishly ornamented, particularly when it goes beyond the borders of good taste. An irregularly shaped pearl is referred to as a "*baroque* pearl." Compare ROCOCO. ⟨Guest acts include the Canadian *baroque* troupe⟩—*Time,* May 31, 1999.

barrage *(bah-RAHZH)* [French: a blocking off; a barring] A barrier of artillery fire designed to protect one's own troops or to stop enemy movements; a massive attack or concentration of firepower. By extension, an overwhelming amount of words, questions, blows, etc.; a torrent, burst, or storm. ⟨She faced a *barrage* of questions from reporters and interested citizens.⟩

barrette *(bah-REHT)* [French] A small bar with a clasp, used to hold a girl's or a woman's hair in place.

barrio *(BAH-ree-oh)* [Spanish: a district; a quarter] An urban ghetto; the densely populated area of a big city where mostly Spanish-speaking people live. In New York City, the *barrio* on the Upper East Side of Manhattan Island came into existence after World War II, as Hispanic people from Puerto Rico and South America moved into the area. ⟨The graceful atmosphere of *Barrio* Norte is at the heart of what makes Buenos Aires a supremely pleasant and civilized city.⟩—*The Atlantic Monthly,* September 1998.

bas-relief *(bah reh-LEEF)* [French, from Italian] A type of sculpture in which the figures and decorative elements project slightly from the background. Also called *low relief.*

basso continuo *(BAH-soh con-TIN-yoo-oh)* [Italian] A continuous bass accompaniment in a piece of 17th- or 18th-century chamber music, often played by a harpsichord and a cello, with the harpsichordist improvising chordal embellishments.

bastion *(BASS-tee-yun)* [French, from Italian] A projecting part of a rampart or fortification; a bulwark, stronghold, or fortress. Anything seen as defending or preserving a position, quality, or condition. ⟨They see themselves as the last *bastion* of unadulterated and intelligible French speech.⟩

batik *(bah-TEEK)* [Javanese: painted] A method of applying designs to fabric by first applying wax for a negative image, then dyeing it and when the dye has set, removing the wax with boiling water.

batiste *(bah-TEEST)* [French] A fine, plain-woven fabric, now made of cotton but originally linen.

bat mitzvah *(baht MITZ-vah)* [Hebrew] A ceremony, usually held in a synagogue, by which a thirteen-year-old girl who has successfully learned the fundamentals of Judaism is admitted to adulthood. See also BAR MITZVAH. ⟨The family showed guests a videotape of their daughter's *bat mitzvah*.⟩

batterie de cuisine *(bah-TREE deu kwee-ZEEN)* [French] The ensemble of (mostly metal) utensils used in cooking, such as pots and pans, spoons, whisks, graters, etc.

bayadere *(bye-yah-DAIR)* [French, from Portuguese: dancer] A professional dancing girl of India, especially one serving in a temple. A fabric or pattern of brightly colored horizontal stripes.

bayou *(BYE-yoo)* [Louisiana French, from Choctaw *bayuk*: a small stream] A marshy inlet, outlet, or arm of a lake or a river; a stagnant creek. Any sluggish, boggy, or still body of water.

bazaar *(bah-ZAHR)* [Persian] A marketplace, particularly a large public market in a Middle Eastern city. A sale of miscellaneous items to raise money for a charitable cause. ⟨The widowed mother of two lost her life savings to looters ushered in by men who arrived in trucks and broke open the steel doors of the *bazaar*.⟩—*Time,* May 31, 1999.

beaucoup *(boh-KOO)* [French] A large number; a considerable quantity; a lot; much. Sometimes used informally in English, as in "He won *beaucoup* dollars in the lottery."

beau geste *(boh ZHEST)* [French: beautiful gesture] A display of magnanimous conduct; a fine, noble, or gracious gesture, sometimes futile or made only for effect.

Bedouin *(BEH-doo-in)* [French, from Arabic: desert dweller] A member of a nomadic Arab people living in the desert in Africa and the Near East. ⟨Once a desert roamed by *Bedouin* nomads, dubiously carved into a hatchet-shaped country by Winston Churchill after the defeat of the Ottoman Empire⟩—*Time,* February 22, 1999.

beguine *(beh-GHEEN)* [West Indies French: an unimportant love affair] A ballroom dance originally from Martinique, based on the rhythm of the BOLERO, or the music for such a dance.

behemoth *(beh-HEE-moth)* [Hebrew: beast] A huge animal; a machine or organization of enormous size and power. ⟨America is beginning to see itself less and less in the tall image of Lincoln or even the robust one of Johnny Appleseed and more and more as a dazed *behemoth* with padded shoulders.⟩—*The New York Times,* May 13, 1990.

beignet *(bayn-YAY)* [French] A fritter or doughnut, sometimes with a fruit or other filling; anything dipped in batter and deep-fried.

bel canto *(bel KAHN-toh)* [Italian: beautiful singing] In music, a vocal style in which the melody is sung smoothly and gracefully. ⟨But (the part of) Aron . . . should and must sing with all the florid *bel canto* roulades he can muster.⟩—*The New Criterion,* May 1999.

bella figura *(BEH-lah fee-GOO-rah)* [Italian: handsome face] An impressive or dashing presence; a grand effect. A personal style characterized by a high standard of dress and mannerly behavior. The opposite of *bruta figura* (ugly face). ⟨he was a great favorite with the fighting men, who had their nation's love of *bella figura*.⟩—*The New York Review of Books*, March 4, 1999.

belles lettres *(behl LEH-treu)* [French: fine letters] Literature that has aesthetic rather than informational value, such as fiction, poetry, or drama; literature characterized by elegance, refinement, and the "light touch." ⟨The struggle, as Bloom famously conceived it in "The Anxiety of Influence," is a *belles-lettres* re-enactment of Freud's 'family romance'—the sons in Oedipal revolt against their poetic fathers.⟩—*The New York Times*, September 25, 1994.

beluga *(beh-LOO-gah)* [Russian: white] A white sturgeon found in the Black and Caspian Seas, prized as a source of high-quality caviar. Not to be confused with the white whale, an aquatic mammal sometimes called *beluga*.

bento, obento *(BEHN-toh, oh-BEHN-toh)* [Japanese, from Chinese] A complete meal served in a lacquered box divided into sections that keep the various dishes apart.

beret *(beh-RAY)* [French, from Latin] A soft, flat, woollen cap of Basque origin, with a close-fitting headband and a round top.

bergère *(behr-ZHEHR)* [French: shepherdess] A large, deep armchair of the 18th century.

bête noire *(beht NWAHR)* [French: black beast] A bugaboo; a bugbear; a person or thing that arouses hatred or fear. ⟨Everyone has his or her personal nightmare or *bête noire*.⟩

bêtise *(beh-TEEZ)* [French: foolishness] A stupid or nonsensical act or remark; an absurdity. Something of no consequence; a trifle.

beurre blanc *(beur BLANH)* [French: white butter] In French cooking, a sauce made from a reduction of vinegar and shallots, beaten with butter until thickened.

beurre manié *(beur mahn-YAY)* [French: kneaded butter] In French cooking, a paste of butter and flour, usually blended with the fingers and used to thicken sauces, soups, etc.

beurre noir *(beur NWAHR)* [French: black butter] In French cooking, a dark-brown butter sauce often flavored with vinegar, capers, or herbs.

bhakti *(BUK-tee)* [Sanskrit: devotion] In Hinduism, personal devotion to a god in the hope of reaching enlightenment.

bhang *(bang)* [Sanskrit: hemp] MARIJUANA or HASHISH made from the Indian hemp plant, used as a narcotic.

bibelot *(beeb-LOH)* [French] A small decorative object; a pretty, curious, or rare trinket.

bidarka *(bee-DAHR-kah)* [Russian: a little coracle] An Alaskan Eskimo boat made of sealskin.

bidet *(bee-DAY)* [French] A low washbasin that can be straddled for washing the genital and anal areas.

bidonville *(bee-donh-VEEL)* [French, from *bidon:* metal drum, and *ville:* city] A shantytown, in which abandoned metal drums are used as building material; a poor section of a city or a suburb composed of hastily built, ramshackle dwellings.

bien entendu *(byenh anh-tanh-DÜ)* [French: well understood] Of course; naturally.

bienvenu *(byenh-veh-NÜ)* [French] Welcome.

bijou (singular); **bijoux** (plural) *(BEE-zhoo, bee-ZHOO)* [French, from Breton] A jewel; a trinket; something small, delicate, and beautifully made.

bildungsroman *(BIL-doongs-roh-MAHN)* [German: portrait novel] A type of novel that recounts the formative years and character development of a young protagonist; a classic example is Goethe's *Wilhelm Meister's Apprenticeship* (1796). ⟨This romantic fable is part classical riff, part homoerotic *Bildungsroman.*⟩— *Time,* February 22, 1999.

billet-doux *(bee-yay-DOO)* [French: sweet note] A love letter; a note from a lover.

biretta *(bih-REHT-ah)* [Italian, from Latin] A brimless, square cap with three or four upright projections on its crown, worn by clerics in the Catholic hierarchy.

bis *(beess)* [French] Again; a second time; twice. In France, the equivalent of ENCORE.

bisque *(beesk)* [French] A thick cream soup, especially one of pureed shellfish. Also, an unglazed ceramic having a pinkish tan color.

bistro *(bee-STROH)* [French, from Russian: quickly] Informally, a small, unpretentious bar, restaurant, or nightclub. The term came into use in France after the battle of Waterloo in 1814, when Russian troops who had helped conquer Napoléon spent their free time in Parisian bars and expressed their impatience with the service by shouting *"bistro!"*

bivouac *(BIH-voo-ak)* [French, from Swiss German] A temporary encampment for soldiers in the field, often without protection from enemy fire. To assemble or rest in such a place. ⟨Some hardy fans, undeterred by the rain, set up a *bivouac* outside the stadium ticket office.⟩

blanc de blancs *(blanh deu blanh)* [French: white of whites] In France, a champagne made from a single variety of white grape, the Pinot Blanc. Also, a white table wine that may be mildly effervescent.

blancmange *(blanh-MANHZH)* [French: white food] A whitish, sweet pudding made with milk, gelatin, eggs, and various flavorings; it has a jellylike consistency.

blanquette *(blanh-KEHT)* [French] A meat stew, often of veal *(blanquette de veau)*, prepared in a white sauce.

blasé *(blah-ZAY)* [French, from *blaser:* to make indifferent] World-weary; bored or indifferent due to overindulgence in worldly pleasures; jaded; unimpressed.

blintze, blintz *(blints)* [Yiddish, from Byelorussian: small pancake] In Jewish cooking, a thin pancake folded over a filling of pot cheese, potato, jam, etc., usually fried and served with sour cream.

blitz *(blits)* [German, short for *blitzkrieg:* lightning war] Any swift, overwhelming attack, particularly the massive air attacks by the Germans in Poland that opened World War II. In football, to charge directly at the passer as soon as the ball is snapped; to red dog. ⟨During World War II, the *blitz* caused great devastation and loss of life in London.⟩

bloc *(blok)* [French: block] A group or coalition of politicians, businesses, countries, etc., that share common interests and act together to promote or protect those interests. The Organization of Petroleum Exporting Countries (OPEC) is an example.

bobeche *(boh-BEHSH)* [French] A glass or metal collar that fits over the socket of a candlestick to catch the wax drippings.

boccie *(BAW-chee)* [Italian] An outdoor game of bowling on a dirt surface between low wooden curbs, popular among Italians everywhere. Also written *bocce, bocci.*

Boche *(bosh)* [French: blockhead] A derogatory slang term for a German soldier during World War I.

bodega *(boh-DAY-gah)* [American Spanish] A grocery store, wine-shop, or storeroom, usually in a Spanish-speaking area. ⟨Several Hispanic leaders and city officials met outside a *bodega* in Washington Heights.⟩

bodhisattva *(boh-dih-SUHT-vah)* [Sanskrit: enlightenment being] In Buddhism, the compassionate and altruistic one who has achieved enlightenment, but renounces full entry into NIRVANA until all beings can be saved.

boiserie *(bwahz-REE)* [French: woodwork] Wainscoting; wood paneling, sometimes carved, used often in 18th-century French interiors.

boîte de nuit *(bwaht deu NWEE)* [French: night box] A nightclub or CABARET.

bok choy *(BOK choy)* [Chinese] A mild-tasting Chinese cabbage with dark green leaves and white stems and ribs.

bolero *(boh-LEH-roh)* [Spanish] A moderately slow Spanish dance for a soloist or a couple to an intricately syncopated measure of three beats (in Spain) or two (in Cuba).

bolillo *(boh-LEE-yoh)* [Spanish, from Latin] In Mexican cooking, a hard roll, or a sandwich made with such a roll.

bolo *(BOH-loh)* [Philippine Spanish] A large, single-edged knife, or MACHETE, used in the Philippines.

Bolshevik *(BOHL-sheh-vik)* [Russian: larger, greater] A member of the radical majority of the Social Democratic Party that seized control in Russia in 1917. A member of the Communist Party. By extension, any radical or revolutionary. ⟨The *Bolshevik* Cheka, or secret police, was founded by the man known as Iron Felix.⟩

bombe *(bohmb)* [French: bomb] A dessert molded in the form of a ball, especially one made of ice cream or frozen MOUSSE.

bombé *(bohm-BAY)* [French] In describing furniture, swelling or curving outward.

bona fide *(BOH-nah fied)* [Latin: with good faith] Legitimate; authentic; done or made in good faith. See also MALA FIDE.

bona fides *(BOH-nah fiedz)* [Latin: good faith] Demonstrable trustworthiness; freedom from intent to mislead; sincerity; honest intention. Not a plural form of *bona fide,* thus: "Our chairman's *bona fides* was subject to intense scrutiny." See also MALA FIDES.

bon appétit *(bon ah-pay-TEE)* [French] (May you have) good appetite; enjoy your meal. ⟨The point is to find combinations that fit your palate and your schedule. *Bon appétit!*⟩—*Time,* October 12, 1998.

bonbon *(bonh-bonh)* [French nursery word: good-good] A piece of candy.

bonhomie *(boh-noh-MEE)* [French] Good-heartedness; geniality; friendliness. ⟨an office lawyer full of contrived *bonhomie*⟩—*The Guardian,* May 2, 1999.

bon mot *(bonh MOH)* [French: good word] An elegant expression; the right word at the right time; a compliment. ⟨Ideally he would like to die while gardening, and he would like it to be quick, although not so quick as to deny him the opportunity of uttering his final *bon mot.*⟩—*The New York Times,* April 24, 1999.

bon ton *(bonh TONH)* [French] Good style or breeding; elegant form. Something considered fashionably correct.

bon vivant *(bonh vee-VANH)* [French] A person who enjoys good food, good drink, and luxurious living; an EPICURE.

bon voyage *(bonh vwah-YAHZH)* [French] (Have a) good trip.

bonze *(bonz)* [Japanese, from Chinese] A Japanese Buddhist monk.

boondocks *(BOON-doks)* [Tagalog: mountain] A slang term for rough, uninhabited backcountry; the backwoods; "the sticks." ⟨and where by March we feel dull and flat and lost in the *boondocks*⟩—*Time,* March 24, 1997.

bordello *(bohr-DEL-oh)* [Italian] A house of prostitution. ⟨A woman alleged to have operated a local *bordello* pleaded guilty to charges of prostitution.⟩

borscht *(borsht)* [Russian] In Russia and eastern Europe, any of a variety of soups based on cabbage, beets, potatoes, meat stock, etc., served hot or cold and sometimes topped with sour cream.

borzoi *(BOR-zoy)* [Russian: swift] The Russian wolfhound.

bossa nova *(BOS-sah NOH-vah)* [Portuguese: new bag] A couple dance, similar to the SAMBA, that combines Brazilian rhythms and North American cool jazz. The music for such a dance.

bouclé, boucle *(boo-KLAY)* [French: curled; buckled] A yarn with loops or knots that produce a nubby, curly surface on knitted or woven fabric; the fabric itself.

boudin *(boo-DENH)* [French] A sausage made with pig's blood *(boudin noir)* or with a mixture of chicken, pork, and veal *(boudin blanc).*

boudoir *(boo-DWAHR)* [French, from *bouder:* to sulk] A lady's bedroom or private sitting room.

bouffant *(boo-FANH)* [French: swelling] Puffed out or flaring, as a skirt. A hairstyle in which the hair is teased to form a puffed, rounded shape over the forehead and temples, or over the entire head. ⟨The role called for bleached-blonde *bouffant* hair and rhinestone-studded jeans.⟩

bouillabaisse *(boo-yah-BEHSS)* [French, from Portuguese] In French cooking, a soup or stew made with a variety of fish and shellfish, flavored with saffron and served with ROUILLE.

bouillon *(boo-YONH)* [French, from *bouillir:* to boil] A clear broth made by simmering together meat or chicken, vegetables, and seasoning.

boulangerie *(boo-lanh-ZHREE)* [French] A bakery, especially one that produces and sells bread.

bouquet *(boo-KAY)* [French] A bunch of flowers. The distinctive aroma of wines, liqueurs, etc.; a delicate odor. Also, a compliment.

bourgeoisie *(boor-zhwah-ZEE)* [French] The middle class. In the class struggle of Marxist theory, the group opposed to the working class; those not engaged in manual labor, whose primary concerns are personal comfort and property values. Critic H. L. Mencken referred to this class, which he saw as uncultured and complacent, as the "booboisie."

bourrée *(boo-RAY)* [French] A 16th-century peasant dance from the French Auvergne, in duple time, or a musical form based on that dance.

bourse *(boorss)* [French: purse] A stock exchange or money market of some European cities. ⟨Soon after Lindbergh landed an employee of the *Bourse* telegraph office arrived with more than 700 cablegrams for him⟩—*The New York Times,* May 22, 1927.

boutique *(boo-TEEK)* [French] A small retail shop selling clothes and other items of the latest fashion. Within a larger store, a shop that carries a special selection of merchandise. Any exclusive small business that provides customized service. Of or relating to such a business.

boutonniere *(boo-ton-YEHR)* [French: buttonhole] A small BOU-QUET or flower worn in the buttonhole of a man's jacket lapel.

bouzouki *(boo-ZOO-kee)* [Modern Greek, from Turkish] A modern Greek stringed instrument similar to a lute, with a long neck and fretted fingerboard. ⟨We found a Greek nightclub with live *bouzouki* music and the added attraction of good food.⟩

boyar *(boy-YAHR)* [Russian] In Russia and other Slavic countries before Peter the Great, a member of the old nobility or privileged class. ⟨In the traditional Russian *bylina,* or folk epic, a dashing warrior in shining armor rescues the good Czar from the evil influence of his scheming *boyars.*⟩—*Time,* July 1, 1996.

bracero *(brah-SAY-roh)* [Spanish] A migrant worker from Mexico, admitted legally for seasonal labor in the United States.

Brahman, Brahmin *(BRAH-min)* [Sanskrit] A member of the highest of the four Hindu castes in India, the priestly caste.

Brahmin *(BRAH-mahn)* [Sanskrit, a variant of Brahman] Informally, in the U.S. Northeast, a person of high intellectual or social status, especially an aloof, snobbish, or conservative one. ⟨After earning an MBA at Harvard, the young Boston *Brahmin* astounded his family by joining the Peace Corps.⟩

brasserie *(brahs-REE)* [French: brewery] An unpretentious tavern or restaurant that serves simple food and drinks, especially beer. ⟨the sandwiches and beer sent up from the neighboring *brasserie*⟩—*The New York Times,* August 4, 1975.

bratwurst *(BRAHT-woorst)* [German: roasted sausage] A sausage made of pork with herbs and spices.

bravado *(brah-VAH-doh)* [Italian] A show of bravery, often unsupported by real strength; boastful defiance.

bravura *(brah-VOO-rah)* [Italian] In music, a show of brilliance in creating or performing a technically difficult passage. Any performance that displays brilliance and daring. ⟨It was both an example of *bravura* playing and an endurance test for the cellist.⟩

bric-a-brac *(BRIH-kah-brak)* [French: at random] A collection of miscellaneous old or interesting objects, often those of little value; knickknacks; trinkets.

brioche *(bree-UHSH)* [French, from Norman dialect: to knead] A soft roll or small pastry made with flour, yeast, butter, and eggs, baked in a mold.

briquette *(brih-KEHT)* [French: small brick] A small block of compressed coal dust or charcoal used as fuel for outdoor cooking.

bris, brith *(briss)* [Hebrew: covenant] The ritual circumcision of Jewish infant males. ⟨The statistics do not include infant boys circumcised in the Jewish ritual of the *bris*.⟩—*The New York Times,* March 2, 1999.

brise-soleil *(BREEZ-soh-LAY)* [French: sun breaker] A louvered screen placed outdoors to protect the windows of a house from direct sunlight.

brochette *(broh-SHEHT)* [French] A skewer used in roasting or barbecuing. *En brochette* refers to anything cooked on a skewer or a small spit.

brochure *(broh-SHOOR)* [French: a stitched book] A pamphlet or booklet containing information.

broderie anglaise *(broh-deh-REE anh-GLEHZ)* [French: English embroidery] A style of fine white cotton fabric with embroidered eyelets laid out in a pattern or a flowerlike design.

brouhaha *(BROO-hah-hah)* [French] An uproar; a commotion; a hullabaloo; a clamor; an incident involving turmoil or confusion, especially a disagreement or fight over something unimportant. ⟨The twenty-fifth is called "Silk Stockings" and will open Thursday in a fashionable *brouhaha*⟩—*The New York Times,* February 20, 1955.

brusque *(brusk, broosk)* [French, from Italian, from Latin] Abrupt and offhand in manner; curt; blunt; rough.

brut *(broot)* [French: raw; unpolished] In describing champagne: very dry; not sweet.

bubkes *(BUB-kehs)* [Yiddish: beans] In slang, something worthless; a trifle; zilch; "peanuts," as in "he sold his grandmother's brooch for *bubkes.*"

bulgur, bulghur *(BULL-ger)* [Turkish, from Arabic] Whole-grain wheat that has been dehusked, parboiled, cracked, and dried; sometimes used in place of rice or potatoes.

bulmus *(BULL-mus)* [Hebrew, from Greek *boulimos:* hunger] A ravenous hunger; a faintness caused by prolonged fasting. By extension, an exaggerated eagerness; an avidity; a mania.

bungalow *(BUNG-ah-loh)* [Hindi: of Bengal] A small house of one floor and often only one room, surrounded by a wide VERANDA.

bunraku *(boon-RAH-koo)* [Japanese] In Japan, the traditional puppet theater since the 1600s, with almost life-size puppets operated by puppeteers who are fully visible; the chief handler wears period costume, while the assistants are dressed and hooded in black.

burka, burqa *(BOOR-kah)* [Urdu] The long, dark, featureless cloak that Muslim women in Pakistan and Afghanistan are required to wear in public to conceal their bodies. See also CHADOR.

burlesque *(ber-LESK)* [French, from Italian] A literary or dramatic work that uses comic or mocking imitation in its treatment of a serious or dignified subject. Any broad satire, parody, or grotesque caricature. Characterized by ridiculous incongruity. Also, a vaudeville show often featuring striptease acts, slapstick humor, and bawdy songs. Such luminaries as Al Jolson, Mae West, and Bert Lahr began their careers in *burlesque.*

burnoose, burnous *(ber-NOOS)* [French, from Arabic] An Arab or Moorish cloak with a hood. ⟨The cloakroom displayed everything from fur jackets and ten-gallon hats to a checkered *burnoose.*⟩

burrito *(boo-REE-toh)* [Mexican Spanish: young donkey] In Mexican cooking, a stuffed TACO, using a TORTILLA made from wheat rather than corn flour.

burro *(BOO-roh)* [Mexican Spanish] A small donkey used in Mexico and the southwestern United States as a pack animal.

Bushido *(boo-SHEE-doh)* [Japanese] The strict military code of conduct, honor, and loyalty of samurai warriors in feudal Japan.

bustier *(büst-YAY)* [French] A woman's corsetlike, sleeveless, strapless top, either reinforced with facing or supported by stays to give it shape. Originally an undergarment.

Butoh *(BOO-toh)* [Japanese] A modern style of Japanese theater developed shortly after World War II, characterized by a general sense of despair and pessimism. ⟨and Dairakudakan, one of Japan's oldest *Butoh* dance companies⟩—*Time,* May 31, 1999.

C

cabal *(kah-BAHL)* [Latin, from Hebrew] A secret plot, conspiracy, or intrigue. A small group of people that meet secretly for some private purpose, such as the inner group of advisers that strongly influenced court policy during the reign of Charles II of England; a faction, league, or JUNTA.

caballero *(kah-bah-YEH-roh)* [Spanish] In Spain, a gentleman; a cavalier. In the southwestern United States, a horseman or a woman's escort.

cabana, cabaña *(kah-BAH-nah)* [Spanish] A cabin, especially a little cabin on the beach or beside a swimming pool, large enough for changing one's clothes in private. A cottage.

cabaret *(kah-bah-RAY)* [French] A restaurant or nightclub that offers food, drink, and entertainment featuring skits, humorous improvisation, and songs of political satire, with much of the material drawn from current events; any similar form of theatrical entertainment. ⟨to be presented in the Algonquin's intimate Oak Room, where *cabaret* singers usually perform⟩—*The New York Times,* September 17, 1997.

cabochon *(KAH-boh-shon, kah-boh-SHONH)* [French, from Latin *caput:* head] A highly polished hemispherical or oval-cut gem with a smooth, unfaceted surface.

cabriolet *(kah-bree-oh-LAY)* [French: a leap; caper] A two-wheeled, doorless, one-horse carriage with a folding top, with space for two passengers, popular in the 18th century. Later the word was shortened to "cab" and used to designate any carriage for hire.

cacciatore *(kahtch-yah-TOH-reh)* [Italian: in the style of hunters] In Italian cooking, a dish of poultry or meat prepared with mushrooms, tomatoes, olive oil, herbs, etc.

cache *(kahsh)* [French] A secret place for storing or hiding food, ammunition, equipment, treasure, etc., especially one in the ground. The things hidden in such a place. ⟨The police uncovered a vast *cache* of arms and ammunition on Tuesday.⟩

cachepot *(kahsh-POH)* [French] A decorative container used to cover an ordinary flowerpot.

cachet *(kah-SHAY)* [French] Originally, an official stamp or seal that validated a document. Currently, a sign of consent or approval given by an important person. By extension, a distinctive mark, or sign of originality. ⟨Revelatory films by New Wave directors gave French cinema an unprecedented *cachet.*⟩

cadenza *(kah-DEN-zah)* [Italian, from Latin] In music, an elaborate solo passage, sometimes improvised, that interrupts a piece often just before the end; it consists of variations on the themes of the work.

cadre *(KAHD-ree, KAH-dreh)* [French, from Italian and Latin: frame; framework] The core group of officers and men needed to organize and train a new military unit; a nucleus of qualified personnel or leaders in politics, business, religion, etc. A framework; a skilled workforce. In Communist countries, a cell of trained and conscientious workers. ⟨bright New Labourites . . . who can be brought on quickly and help sustain a Blairite *cadre* of ministers⟩—*The Guardian,* May 12, 1999.

caduceus *(kah-DOO-see-us)* [Latin, from Greek] The herald's staff, consisting of two snakes wound around a staff with the wings of an eagle on top, carried by the mythical Greek god Hermes (Mercury) to symbolize his position as the messenger of the gods. It is the emblem of the medical profession and the medical corps.

café *(kah-FAY)* [French: coffee] A coffeehouse; a small restaurant, often with a sidewalk section; a barroom.

café au lait *(kah-FAY oh LAY)* [French] Coffee with an equal amount of hot milk. A light-brown color.

caffe latte *(kah-feh LAH-teh)* [Italian] Coffee mixed with an equal part of hot milk.

caftan *(KAHF-tan)* [Russian, from Turkish] A traditional Middle Eastern garment consisting of a full-length cloak with long sleeves, bound with a girdle at the waist. ⟨Slaves stand at attention along the mosaic-covered walls, while concubines glide to and fro in sumptuous *caftans.*⟩—*Time,* March 29, 1999.

ça ira *(sah ee-RAH)* [French] It will go; it will succeed; it will be enough.

caisson *(KAY-son)* [French, from *caisse:* box; chest] A watertight chamber that makes it possible to work on underwater structures such as a bridge pier; a device to raise sunken ships. Also, a two-wheeled vehicle for carrying artillery ammunition.

calaboose *(KAH-lah-booss)* [Creole, from Spanish] A jail.

calamari *(kah-lah-MAH-ree)* [Italian] Squid, especially the small squid used in Italian cooking.

calash See CALÈCHE.

calèche, calash *(kah-LEHSH)* [French, from German and Czech] A light carriage of two or four wheels with a folding top, pulled by one or two horses. ⟨A line of *calèche* drivers waits at the Place de Foucauld.⟩

caliph *(KAH-lif)* [Arabic] The head of state and spiritual leader in a Muslim state.

calpac See KALPAK.

calumet *(KAHL-yoo-met)* [French, from Latin] Among northern Native American tribes, a long, straight, highly decorated pipe ceremoniously passed around and smoked by negotiators, each in turn, who have arrived at an agreement; a peace pipe.

calzone *(kahl-ZOH-neh)* [Italian: trouser leg] In Italian cooking, a type of turnover made with PIZZA dough and a filling of cheese, sausage, herbs, etc., baked or deep-fried.

camaraderie *(kah-mah-RAH-deh-ree)* [French, from Spanish] Comradeship, brotherhood; good fellowship; conviviality. ⟨The *camaraderie* is awkward—they have to shout to be heard.⟩— *Time,* March 22, 1999.

cambio *(KAHM-bee-oh)* [Italian, Spanish] Change (money). An exchange; a place to convert money from one currency to another.

camera lucida *(kah-meh-rah loo-SEE-dah)* [Latin: bright chamber] An optical device that projects an image from a microscope to a piece of paper so that it can be traced.

camera oscura *(kah-meh-rah oh-SKOO-rah)* [Italian: dark chamber] A box or a room where no light is admitted except that coming through a small hole in one wall; it produces an image on the opposite wall showing something outside the room.

camino real *(kah-MEE-noh ray-AHL)* [Spanish: royal road] A highway or main road.

camisole *(KAH-mih-sohl)* [French, from Spanish] A woman's short sleeveless shirt or underwaist, worn under a sheer bodice; a short NEGLIGEE. Also, a long-sleeved straitjacket.

camouflage *(KAH-moo-flahzh)* [French] A method or the materials used to conceal or disguise objects, military installations, equipment, etc., by coloring or screening so that they blend into the background or natural surroundings. To obscure or conceal under a false appearance. By extension, any disguise or stratagem used for concealment. ⟨The natural *camouflage* of some big cats makes them almost invisible in the African grasslands.⟩

campanile *(kahm-pah-NEE-leh)* [Italian] A bell tower, particularly one that stands free, apart from its church. ⟨Will a British professor be the one to save the legendary *campanile* with his high-risk underground strategy?⟩—*The Guardian,* April 19, 1999.

campesino *(kahm-peh-SEE-noh)* [Spanish] A peasant; a farmer.

canaille *(kah-NYE)* [French, from Latin: a pack of dogs] Rabble; riffraff; a mob.

canapé *(kah-nah-PAY)* [French: covering; spread] A thin piece of toast or bread topped with savory paste, cheese, caviar, etc., often served as an appetizer. Also, an 18th-century French sofa.

canard *(kah-NARD, kah-NAHR)* [French: a duck] A story, often disparaging and usually false, based upon rumor or innuendo and used to discredit someone or something; a hoax. ⟨a speech for Secretary McNamara which would, INTER ALIA, once and for all dispose of the *canard* that the Vietnam conflict was a civil war⟩—*The Atlantic Monthly,* April 1968.

cannoli *(kah-NOH-lee)* [Italian] A small roll of pastry filled with sweetened ricotta cheese or pastry cream.

cantata *(kahn-TAH-tah)* [Latin: sung] A piece of religious or secular music for voices, often accompanied by an organ or other instruments.

cantatrice *(kahn-tah-TREESS)* [French, from Italian, from Latin] A professional woman singer, especially an opera singer.

cantina *(kahn-TEE-nah)* [Spanish] A place where food and drinks are sold; a saloon.

canto *(KAHN-toh)* [Italian, from Latin *cantus:* song] A division of a long poem.

capo *(KAH-poh)* [Italian: chief] A slang term for an underboss in a MAFIA organization. ⟨St. Martin serves as the hide-out of choice for all kinds of unsavory types, including an aged Mafia *capo* under F.B.I. protection.⟩—*The New York Times Book Review,* September 21, 1997.

capotasto *(kah-po-TAHS-toh)* [Italian] A steel bar that can be clamped at different positions along the fingerboard of a guitar to change its tuning; often shortened to *capo* and pronounced *KAY-poh.*

cappuccino *(kah-poo-CHEE-noh)* [Italian: little Capuchin (friar)] Italian coffee and steamed milk topped with whipped cream and a dash of cinnamon. A white cowl over a simple brown robe was the style of dress that marked the Capuchin friars of the Franciscan order, who were sworn to a life of poverty and good works.

carabiniere (singular)**; carabinieri** (plural) *(kah-rah-been-YEH-reh, kah-rah-been-YEH-ree)* [Italian] A member of the Italian police, so called because they used to carry short rifles, called carbines. The mountain passes are guarded by the Alpini, but the *Caribinieri* guard the ports and the highways.

carafe *(kah-RAHF)* [French, from Arabic] A bottle for holding and serving beverages, especially wine, with a wide mouth and a neck narrower than its base.

carbonade *(kahr-boh-NAHD)* [French] In France, meat grilled over charcoal. In Belgium, *carbonade Flamande* is a beef stew made with vegetables and beer.

carillon *(KAH-rih-lon, kah-ree-YONH)* [French, from Latin] A set of church bells mounted in an open tower, played by means of a keyboard installed in a room just below.

carioca *(kah-ree-OH-kah)* [Brazilian Portuguese] A form of SAMBA made suitable for ballroom dancing. Not to be confused with KARAOKE.

caritas *(KAH-ree-tahss)* [Latin] Charity; kindness.

carnitas *(kahr-NEE-tahss)* [Mexican Spanish] A Mexican snack consisting of crisp bits of diced or shredded roast pork.

carpe diem *(KAHR-peh DEE-em)* [Latin: seize the day] Enjoy the present; take advantage of today's opportunities; make hay while the sun shines. ⟨*Carpe diem*—you need good planning and analysis.⟩—*The Guardian,* January 9, 1999.

carrefour *(kahr-FOOR)* [French, from Latin] A crossroads; the junction of several streets or roads. Also, a public square or plaza.

carte *(kahrt)* [French] A menu; a bill of fare.

carte blanche *(kart BLANHSH)* [French: white card] A blank paper signed by one person and given to another, allowing its bearer to write in his or her own conditions. Also, permission or authority to act as one thinks best; unrestricted authority or access. ⟨Hollywood misused him . . . by giving him *carte blanche* to run wild with the Rat Pack in vanity productions.⟩— *The Atlantic Monthly,* September 1998.

carte du jour *(kahrt du JOOR)* [French] The menu of the day.

cartel *(kahr-TEL)* [French, from Italian] An international trust or syndicate formed with the aim of controlling a specific market. A coalition of political groups with a common interest or cause; a BLOC. An official agreement between hostile governments, often for the exchange of prisoners. Formerly, a written challenge to a duel.

cartouche *(kahr-TOOSH)* [French, from Italian] A rounded surface bearing an image, such as the little sculptures of cherubs that decorate the inner corners of some ceilings in old Italian buildings, or the stark pictographs contained in oval outlines carved in ancient Egyptian tombs. ⟨Something more easily found is a *cartouche,* usually a pendant in gold or silver with the wearer's name in Pharaonic hieroglyphics.⟩—*The New York Times,* December 13, 1998.

casino *(kah-SEE-noh)* [Italian: little house] A public dancing hall where food and drink may be served and, usually, where gambling is permitted.

cassareep *(KASS-ah-reep)* [Carib] In West Indian cooking, a syrup or condiment made from the juice of cassava roots.

cassis *(kah-SEESS)* [French] The European black currant, or a cordial made from black currants.

cassoulet *(kah-soo-LAY)* [French, from Provençal] A rich French stew containing white beans, preserved goose or duck, mutton, and sausage.

castanet *(kah-stah-NET)* [Spanish: little chestnut] One of a pair of small wooden shells held in the palm of the hand and clapped together with the fingers to produce a hollow clicking sound as a rhythmical accompaniment to dance.

caste *(kast)* [Portuguese, Spanish: race; lineage] In India, one of the hereditary social divisions of Hindu society. A distinct social group consisting of people of the same or similar background, customs, and status.

casus belli *(kah-sus BEHL-eye)* [Latin] An act or event that justifies war, or one seen as a reason for declaring war.

catafalque *(KAH-tah-fahlk)* [French, from Italian] A platform that supports the coffin of a distinguished person during a funeral, or one mounted on a carriage on which the coffin is drawn in a funeral procession.

catalogue raisonné *(KAH-tah-log ray-soh-NAY)* [French: reasoned catalog] A list of items, such as works of art, with descriptive notes or commentary.

catamaran *(kah-tah-mah-RAHN)* [Tamil: tied wood] In some parts of India, South America, etc., a long raft made of logs lashed together. Also, a sailboat with twin hulls held apart by a frame above them.

catharsis *(kah-THAHR-siss)* [Greek: a cleaning out; a purification] The feeling of relief and satisfaction that comes with the resolution of any deeply felt period of stress and change. Aristotle called *catharsis* the principal experience to be sought in any performance of a great tragic drama. ⟨The punishment will be sufficient to satisfy the need not only for moral satisfaction and justice but also for some measure of emotional satisfaction, a *catharsis.*⟩—*Time,* March 8, 1999.

cauchemar *(kohsh-MAHR)* [French] A nightmare; an experience that arouses feelings of dread, helplessness, or sorrow.

caucus *(KAW-kus)* [poss. Algonquian] A preliminary or private meeting of political party leaders to choose candidates or convention delegates. Within a legislative body, a meeting of party members to shape policy and choose leaders. To hold or meet in a *caucus.* ⟨The latest *caucus* includes some of the more Internet-literate members of Congress.⟩

caudillo *(kow-DEE-yoh)* [Spanish, from Latin] The leader of a government, especially a military dictator such as General Franco of Spain. Also, the mayor of the town; the chief of the village.

cause célèbre *(kohz say-LEH-breu)* [French: famous case] A highly controversial matter that becomes the focus of public attention; a famous trial or lawsuit, especially one involving broad legal or social issues. ⟨The Simpson case became a nationwide *cause célèbre.*⟩

causerie *(kohz-REE)* [French, from Latin] An informal, easy conversation; a chat. A brief, informal piece of writing.

cavatina *(kah-vah-TEE-nah)* [Italian: little thing drawn out] A short song, usually composed on a single sentence without repeats.

caveat *(KAH-veh-aht)* [Latin: let him beware] A caution or warning. In law, a formal notice to an officer or a court to stop a proceeding until the notifier can be heard. ⟨each country still trailing along its own special *caveats* and reservations⟩—*The Guardian,* May 18, 1999.

caveat emptor *(KAH-veh-aht EMP-tor)* [Latin] Let the buyer beware.

cerise *(seh-REEZ)* [French] A cherry. Usually used as an adjective meaning cherry red; cherry-colored.

cerveza *(sehr-VAY-sah)* [Spanish] Beer.

cesta *(SESS-tah)* [Spanish: basket] In the game of JAI ALAI, the racket used for catching and throwing the ball. It has a narrow, curved wicker basket at one end and a glovelike fitting at the other.

c'est-à-dire *(seht ah DEER)* [French] That is to say.

c'est la guerre *(say lah GAIR)* [French] That's war; such is war.

c'est la vie *(say lah VEE)* [French] That's life; that's the way it goes.

cha *(chah)* [Chinese] Tea.

chacun à son goût *(shah-KUNH ah onh GOO)* [French] Each according to his or her own taste.

chador *(CHUD-er, CHAH-der)* [Hindi, from Persian] A long, dark-colored traditional garment of Hindu and Muslim women that covers the entire body and part of the face. See also BURKA, YASHMAK. ⟨I wanted the anonymity and protection a *chador* would bring.⟩—*The New York Times*, February 8, 1998.

chaise longue *(shehz LONH-geu)* [French] A sofalike lounging chair, with the seat extended to allow the sitter to stretch out.

chalet *(shah-LAY)* [French, from Swiss French] A Swiss hut or cottage built of wood, with a projecting roof and wide eaves, common in Alpine areas; a small villa or ski lodge in this style. ⟨The steeply pitched roof of the *chalet* prevents excessive accumulation of snow.⟩

champlevé *(shanh-leu-VAY)* [French] In the decorative arts, the ancient process of cutting away or hollowing areas in a metal plate, and filling the hollows with enamel. An enamel object made by this method.

chanoyu *(CHAH-noh-yoo)* [Japanese: tea ceremony] A traditional Japanese ceremony, both simple and meticulous, in which tea is prepared with carefully chosen utensils and served and consumed in a quiet ritual.

chansonnier *(shanh-son-NYAY)* [French] A writer or singer of satirical songs; a CABARET entertainer who performs in a style that blends singing and speech.

chantage *(shahn-TAHZH)* [French] Blackmail; extortion.

chanterelle *(shanh-TREHL)* [French, from Latin: drinking cup] A wild, mustard-yellow, edible mushroom, much in demand in France.

chanteuse *(shanh-TEUZ)* [French] A female professional singer, one who performs in CABARETS and nightclubs. ⟨The rakish secret agent. A blond *chanteuse.* Cameras masquerading as bow ties.⟩—*Time,* May 10, 1999.

chapati *(chah-PAH-tee)* [Hindi] In northern India, a staple flatbread often made of whole-wheat flour and baked on a hot griddle.

chapeau (singular); **chapeaus, chapeaux** (plural) *(shah-POH)* [French, from Latin] A hat. Also, in France, a congratulatory expression, short for "Hats off!"

charcuterie *(shahr-kü-TREE)* [French] A shop where pork sausages, hams, PÂTÉS, etc., are sold; the pork products themselves.

chargé d'affaires *(shahr-ZHAY dah-FAIR)* [French: one in charge of things] The deputy in charge of a diplomatic mission during the temporary absence of its ambassador or minister. An envoy to a foreign nation to which an ambassador or minister is not accredited. ⟨After the recent impasse, they withdrew their *chargé d'affaires* from Baghdad.⟩

charisma *(kah-RIZ-mah)* [Latin, from Greek] A spiritual gift or talent, as the ability to heal. A personal quality or presence that allows an individual to influence others and to inspire devotion; magnetism. ⟨Forest Whitaker brings presence and *charisma* to the part.⟩—*The Guardian,* May 20, 1999.

charlatan *(SHAHR-lah-tn)* [French, from Italian] A person who claims more expertise than he or she possesses; an imposter; a quack; a phony. ⟨He was an accomplished *charlatan,* from a long line of itinerant patent medicine salesmen.⟩

charlotte *(SHAHR-let)* [French, from a woman's name] A rich dessert; a mold lined with cake or bread and filled with a mixture of fruit, whipped cream or custard, and gelatin.

charpoy *(CHAHR-poy)* [Urdu, from Persian] In India, a light bedstead or cot with a wooden frame.

chasse gardée *(shahss gahr-DAY)* [French] A private hunting ground.

chaud-froid *(shoh-FRWAH)* [French: hot-cold] A cooked dish, often of fowl or game, that has been glazed with aspic and chilled.

chauffeur *(shoh-FEUR)* [French: stoker] A person hired to drive a car or limousine. To drive as a chauffeur; to transport by car.

chauvinism *(SHOH-vih-nism)* [French, after Chauvin, a soldier in Napoléon's army] Extreme zeal or patriotism; loudly expressed enthusiasm for a group or cause. Biased admiration for one country or ideology to the exclusion of all others. More recently, the tendency to treat members of the opposite sex as inferiors. ⟨he was taken to task for his *chauvinism.*⟩—*The St. Louis Post-Dispatch,* January 31, 1999.

chauvinist *(SHOH-vih-nist)* [French] A person whose chief characteristic is CHAUVINISM. ⟨You gotta love a self-described "female *chauvinist* sow" who writes like Walt Whitman crossed with Erma Bombeck.⟩—*Time,* March 8, 1999.

chazan See HAZAN.

chef *(shehf)* [French, short for *chef de cuisine:* head of the kitchen] The chief cook in a restaurant or hotel, whose responsibilities include planning menus, buying ingredients, and supervising the preparation of food. More generally, any cook.

chef d'oeuvre (singular)**; chefs d'oeuvre** (plural) *(shay DEU-vreu)* [French] A masterpiece; a matchless or outstanding work, often a work of art. ⟨The string quartets, taken as a whole, may well be Shostakovich's *chef d'oeuvre.*⟩

chenille *(sheh-NEEL)* [French: caterpillar; silkworm] A velvety yarn of cotton, rayon, or silk used for bedspreads, curtains, and sometimes for clothing; any fabric with a protruding pile.

cher (m)**, chère, chérie** (f) *(shair, shay-REE)* [French] Dear; beloved.

cherchez la femme *(shehr-shay lah FAHM)* [French] Look for the woman: used to suggest that a woman is the motive behind a specific action, or the clue to solving a mystery. ⟨In this romantic comedy written and directed by John Walsh, a Midwesterner plays *cherchez la femme* in New York.⟩—*The New York Times,* September 8, 1996.

cheroot *(sheh-ROOT)* [Tamil] A cigar, particularly one with open, untapered ends.

chèvre *(SHEH-vreu)* [French: goat] In full: *fromage de chèvre.* A cheese made from goat's milk.

chiaroscuro *(kee-ah-roh-SKOO-roh)* [Italian, from Latin: clear-obscure] The treatment and distribution of light and shade in a painting or drawing, used to enhance character traits and/or dramatic effects. Also called *clair-obscure.* ⟨the *chiaroscuro* use of light and shadow⟩—*The St. Louis Post-Dispatch,* May 10, 1998.

chic *(sheek)* [French, from German *Schick:* skill] Stylish; fashionable and elegant. Good taste and stylishness in dress.

chicanismo *(chee-kah-NEES-moh)* [Spanish] The values, traditions, and culture of Mexican Americans, or the pride taken by Mexican Americans in their background.

chichi *(SHEE-shee)* [French] Trendy in a pretentious or ostentatious way; fussily elegant; showy; in an affected manner. ⟨There is nothing *chichi* about the sweaters, skirts, pants, jackets and coats.⟩—*The St. Louis Post-Dispatch,* April 5, 1999.

chiffonade *(shih-foh-NAHD)* [French, from *chiffon:* a rag] A mixture of greens or herbs sliced in fine ribbons, used in soups or salads.

chiffonier *(shih-fon-EER, shih-foh-NYAY)* [French] A tall chest of drawers mounted on short legs, often with a mirror on the top.

chignon *(sheen-YONH)* [French, from Latin] A woman's hairstyle: long hair dressed in a knot or roll at the back of the head or the nape of the neck. ⟨But that was four makeovers ago and before Washington hairdressers, previously known for keeping the *chignon* alive, had p.r. agents.⟩—*Time,* April 13, 1998.

chili con carne *(chee-lee kon KAHR-nay)* [Spanish] A Mexican-style dish consisting of hot peppers or chili powder, ground meat, onions, tomatoes, and kidney beans.

chili verde *(chee-lee VAIR-day)* [Spanish] A stew containing beef or pork, flavored with hot green peppers.

chimera *(kee-MEH-rah)* [Latin, from Greek] A grotesque, fire-breathing monster of the imagination. ⟨She may not be the *chimera* your anxiety has made of her.⟩

chinoiserie *(sheen-wahz-REE)* [French: Chinese trinket] An example of Chinese art; something decorated in the Chinese style or with Chinese motifs. By extension, something needlessly complicated; red tape.

cholo *(CHOH-loh)* [Mexican Spanish: MESTIZO; peasant] Among Mexican Americans, a youth who belongs to a street gang. Also, a disparaging term for a half-breed or half-civilized Indian.

chorizo *(choh-REE-zoh)* [Spanish] A Mexican or Spanish pork sausage flavored with garlic and chilis.

chotchke See TCHOTCHKE.

chutney *(CHUT-nee)* [Hindi] A spiced, sweet-and-sour condiment of East Indian origin, often served with curry.

chutzpah *(HOOTS-pah)* [Yiddish] Effrontery; impudence; audacity; brazen boldness. ⟨a manic-eyed showgirl with the curls of Shirley Temple and the *chutzpah* of Barbra Streisand⟩—*Time,* November 2, 1998.

cicerone *(sis-eh-ROH-neh)* [Latin, after the Roman orator Cicero] A guide, one who shares his or her knowledge of antiquities and historical curiosities with sightseers. ⟨A bad egg, he has made his dubious living by writing leaders for *The Daily Beast,* by selling champagne and by acting as a bored and wicked *cicerone* to humdrum tourists.⟩—*The New York Times,* May 30, 1942.

cineast, cineaste *(see-nay-AHST)* [French: filmmaker] A film producer or director. A devotee or AFICIONADO of moviemaking. Also written as *cinéaste.*

cinema verité, cinéma vérité *(see-nay-mah veh-ree-TAY)* [French] A style of motion picture, prevalent in the 1940s and 1950s, that avoided any hint of prepared staging, and used handheld cameras to photograph the characters of the story (who were not always actors) in seemingly real, completely unprepared situations. ⟨Just like Frederick Wiseman is *cinéma vérité,* David Isay is audio vérité.⟩—*The New York Times,* November 8, 1998.

cinquecento *(ching-kway-CHEN-toh)* [Italian] In Italy, the 16th century; usually used with reference to prevailing attitudes in art and literature of the 1500s.

circa *(SEER-kah)* [Latin] About; around. Used before an approximate date or figure and often abbreviated as *c., ca., cir.*

cirque *(seerk)* [French, from Latin: circus] A bowl-shaped mountain valley with steep walls; a circular hollow, sometimes with a small lake at the base.

clairvoyance *(clair-VOY-ans)* [French: clear seeing] The supposed ability to perceive hidden or distant things, or to see future events; insight that goes beyond the range of normal perception. Second sight; vision. ⟨Lack of *clairvoyance* comes with the territory.⟩—*Time,* June 2, 1997.

claque *(klahk)* [French, from *claquer:* to clap] A group of people in an audience who have been hired to applaud a performer or act; a group that applauds an actor who is either a friend or an employer. ⟨He entertained the journalistic elite and had them applauding as if he had hired a *claque.*⟩

claves *(KLAH-vays)* [Spanish: keys; keystone] In music, a pair of short hardwood sticks, played by striking them together to produce a dry clacking sound of indeterminate pitch.

clavier, klavier *(klah-VEER, KLAH-vee-er)* [German, from French, from Latin] A keyboard of a musical instrument; an instrument that has a keyboard, as a piano or harpsichord.

cliché *(klee-SHAY)* [French, from *clicher:* to stereotype] A trite phrase, idea, action, plot, etc., that has lost its impact through overuse. Hackneyed; stereotyped; commonplace. ⟨Soon I'm a *cliché* in sunglasses and rolled-up pant legs.⟩—*The Washington Post,* February 28, 1999.

clique *(kleek)* [French] A small, exclusive, or clannish group of people; a narrow COTERIE; a set. ⟨The small, sectarian world of mainstream poetry has never been free of *cliques.*⟩—*The Guardian,* May 20, 1999.

cloche *(klosh)* [French, from Latin: bell; bell-jar] A woman's bell-shaped, close-fitting hat. A glass cover in the shape of a bell, used to protect young plants from frost, or one placed over a plate to keep food warm.

cloisonné *(klwah-zoh-NAY)* [French: partitioned] Decorative enamel-ware in which the colors of the design are separated by metal strips or wires laid edgewise. Pertaining to or made by such a method.

cloture *(KLOH-cher)* [French, from Latin: barrier; cloister] A maneuver to stop debate in a legislative body in order to have an immediate vote on a question. ⟨He had a greater task remaining before him than cobbling together a Republican majority for a *cloture* vote.⟩—*Time,* May 27, 1996.

cocotte (1) *(koh-KOT)* [French, from Latin] A small cast-iron or porcelain cooking pot with handles and a lid.

cocotte (2) *(koh-KOT)* [French: a child's word for hen] A woman of easy virtue; a prostitute.

coda *(KOH-dah)* [Italian, from Latin: tail] The closing section of a piece of music, a ballet, or a literary or dramatic work, particularly a concluding passage that contains themes or motifs from preceding sections. Anything that serves to bring a composition to a formal, complete ending. ⟨This book ends with a *coda,* sustained but puzzling.⟩—*The New York Review of Books,* March 4, 1999.

cognac *(KON-yahk)* [French] Brandy made in the area around the French town of Cognac. Any good brandy.

cognoscenti *(kon-yoh-SHEN-tee)* [Italian, from Latin: *cognoscere:* to know] Those people with exceptional inside knowledge and appreciation of a particular field, most often in the fine arts, literature, and fashion. ⟨Whisk wizard Marty Kaplan . . . serves up scrumptious goodies to the *cognoscenti.*⟩—*The St. Louis Post-Dispatch,* March 7, 1999.

coiffeur (m), **coiffeuse** (f) *(kwah-FEUR, kwah-FEUZ)* [French] A hairdresser or hairstylist.

coiffure *(kwah-FÜR)* [French] A style of dressing or combing the hair. Also, a headdress or head covering.

cojones *(koh-HOH-nes)* [Spanish: testicles] Courage; nerve; "guts."

collage *(koh-LAHZH)* [French: pasting; gluing] An artistic work, often abstract, made by gluing newspaper, bits of cloth, tickets, labels, etc., onto a flat surface, with or without painting around them. By extension, a collection of diverse or seemingly unrelated elements presented without transition, as in an abstract film or play. Picasso introduced *collage* in 1912, when he glued a piece of printed oilcloth to a cubist painting.

coloratura *(koh-loh-rah-TOO-rah)* [Italian, from Latin: coloring] Describing a style of singing characterized by rapid, florid passages that require great vocal agility, usually composed for the highest soprano voice. Also, a soprano who specializes in the *coloratura* style.

comanchero *(koh-man-CHAY-roh)* [American Spanish] In the southwestern United States, an Indian trader.

commando *(kah-MAN-doh)* [Afrikaans, from Portuguese: a group commanded] Describing any specially trained fighting unit used for quick, deadly raids behind enemy lines; a member of an assault team that uses hit-and-run tactics in extremely dangerous situations.

comme il faut *(kom eel FOH)* [French] As it should be; correct; fittingly. ⟨How many candidates have violated the *comme il faut* of campaign finance?⟩

communiqué *(kom-myoo-nih-KAY)* [French: communicated] An official bulletin or announcement that reports to the public or the press on a meeting or conflict. ⟨(He) was working on an unrelated computer-security problem when the *communiqué* first unfolded on a colleague's screen.⟩—*The Atlantic Monthly,* April 1999.

compadre *(kom-PAH-dray)* [Spanish: godfather] A male friend, companion, or crony.

compañero (m), **compañera** (f) *(kom-pahn-YEH-roh, kom-pahn-YEH-rah)* [Spanish] Companion; partner; coworker.

compos mentis *(KOM-pohs MEHN-tiss)* [Latin] Of sound mind; sane.

compote *(kom-POHT)* [French, from Latin: composite] Fruit that has been cooked or stewed in sugar syrup, often served in a dish called a *compotier*.

con amore *(kon ah-MOH-reh)* [Italian] In music, with love; to be played lovingly; with tenderness.

concerto *(kon-CHEHR-toh)* [Italian] In music, an orchestral work featuring one or more instrumental soloists.

concerto grosso *(kon-CHEHR-toh GROH-soh)* [Italian: big concert] In music, an instrumental work in which several soloists play individually and together with an orchestra.

concierge *(konh-see-AIRZH)* [French, from Latin] In France, the doorkeeper and janitor of a building; the person charged with screening visitors, etc., who often occupies a ground-floor apartment in the building. In a hotel, a staff member responsible for special services for guests, such as obtaining theater tickets, arranging for tours, or providing special equipment.

concordat *(kon-KOHR-daht)* [French, from Latin] An official agreement. A contract between the pope and a national government for the regulation of church matters. ⟨Once it has approved the *concordat,* the assembly can go on to debate the issue in Wales.⟩—*The Guardian,* April 13, 1999.

concours *(kohn-KOOR)* [French] A contest; a public competition. See also HORS CONCOURS.

confetti *(kon-FEHT-tee)* [Italian: confections] Small bits of colored paper, thrown or dropped from above to add merriment to a festive occasion such as a wedding or a parade.

confidant (m), **confidante** (f) *(KON-fih-dant)* [French, from Italian, from Latin] A person with whom one can discuss private matters or to whom secrets can be confided. ⟨the toast of Hollywood during the 1930s and 1940s—the *confidant* of Aldous Huxley and a friend to Charlie Chaplin⟩—*Time,* March 29, 1999.

confit *(konh-FEE)* [French, from Latin] In French cooking, goose or duck that has been cooked and preserved in its own fat. Any food preserved in vinegar or sugar.

confiture *(konh-fee-TÜR)* [French] Fruit preserves; jam.

congé *(konh-ZHAY)* [French] Leave-taking; departure. A temporary permission to leave one's employment, as a leave of absence.

con moto *(kon-MOH-toh)* [Italian] In music, with animation; to be played in an active or lively manner.

connoisseur *(kon-neh-SEUR)* [French, from Latin *cognosciter:* knower] A person with thorough knowledge of any of the arts or of matters of taste, whose expertise qualifies him or her to make critical judgments in such matters. ⟨*Connoisseurs* will encounter some old Vidal favorites⟩—*The New York Review of Books,* April 22, 1999.

conquistador *(kon-KEES-tah-dor)* [Spanish] A conqueror, especially one of the Spanish conquerors of Mexico and Peru in the 1500s.

consigliere *(kon-seel-YEH-reh)* [Italian: counselor] One who closely advises a MAFIA leader; a counselor of considerable power and influence. ⟨One of those convicted of conspiring in that plot was Louis "Bobby" Manna, who prosecutors say was the *consigliere*—or No. 3 man—in the Genovese family under Gigante.⟩—*The New York Times,* July 11, 1997.

consommé *(KON-soh-may, konh-soh-MAY)* [French, from Latin: to add up; finish] A clear broth made with meat or chicken, vegetables, bones, and seasonings, boiled in water.

consortium *(kon-SOR-tee-um)* [Latin: partnership] A coalition or combination of nations, corporations, banks, or other groups, for the purpose of launching a venture that requires vast financial resources. Any association, union, or fellowship. ⟨industry-wide concerns, like leading a *consortium* called Sematech to stave off foreign competition⟩—*Time,* March 29, 1999.

conte *(konht)* [French] A short story.

contrejour *(konh-treu-ZHOOR)* [French: against the daylight] In photography, an image taken with the main light source behind the subject; with the camera aimed at, or almost at, the strongest light.

contretemps *(KON-treu-tanh, konh-treu-TANH)* [French: against time] A mischance; an unfortunate or unforeseen event that interferes with one's plans; an inopportune incident. ⟨After a tape of the Pfeiffer pilot got out, it set off yet another over-heated racial *contretemps* in Los Angeles.⟩—*Time,* October 12, 1998.

coq au vin *(kok oh VENH)* [French: cock in wine] A traditional French stew containing chicken, vegetables, diced bacon, seasonings, and red wine.

coquette *(koh-KEHT)* [French] A woman who flirts in a casual manner; one who attracts the attention of men by flirting.

corazón *(kor-ah-SOHN)* [Spanish] The heart; affection; sympathy; courage or spirit.

cordillera *(kor-dee-LAIR-ah)* [Spanish] A system of mountain ranges within a large landmass. The *Cordilleras* is the system of mountain ranges lying parallel to the Pacific Coast, extending from the Andes to the Rocky Mountains.

cordon bleu (singular)**; cordons bleus** (plural) *(kor-donh BLEU)* [French: blue ribbon] The blue ribbon once worn by the highest-ranking knights of the (French) Bourbon monarchy. A person who has achieved great eminence in his or her field, especially an outstanding cook. Any high distinction. At the highest level of excellence in cooking. ⟨In recent years, the only women I know who got as much of a creative kick as men out of cooking are a few whose *cordon bleu* expertise now gets public acclaim⟩—*The New York Times,* January 5, 1977.

cordon sanitaire *(kor-donh sah-nee-TAIR)* [French] A guarded line or barricade around a quarantined area, designed to prevent the spread of infectious disease. Also, a group of buffer states surrounding a potentially dangerous nation, or forming a barrier between two hostile nations.

corniche *(kor-NEESH)* [French, from Italian: rock ledge] A narrow, winding road cut into the face of a cliff or a steep hill, especially one that follows a coastline. A famous example is the *Grande Corniche* on the French Riviera.

cornuto *(kor-NOO-toh)* [Italian: one who is horned] A cuckold.

corps de ballet *(kohr deu bah-LAY)* [French] The company of ballet dancers of a particular theater, or the ensemble of nonsoloists in a ballet company.

corpus delicti *(KOR-pus deh-LIK-tye)* [Latin: the body of the offense] In law, the essential fact of a crime; in a murder case, the discovery of the body of the murder victim. The object of a crime, such as a murder victim's body, that provides evidence that the crime was committed.

corral *(kor-RAL)* [Spanish, from Latin] Formerly, a circular enclosure made of wagons, for protection against attack. More recently, an enclosed space; a pen for cattle or horses. Informally, to capture, seize, or secure.

corrida *(kor-REE-dah)* [Spanish: course; race] Short for *corrida de toros:* running of the bulls. A bullfight.

corrigendum (singular) *(kor-ee-JEHN-dum)* [Latin] Something to be corrected, as an error in print. In the plural, *corrigenda:* a list of corrected errors in a printed book or publication.

cortege *(kor-TEHZH)* [French, from Italian] A ceremonial procession, as in a "funeral *cortege.*" A train of attendants accompanying an important person; a RETINUE. ⟨The *cortege* will travel slowly from the church to the cemetery.⟩—*The Guardian,* May 15, 1999.

corvée *(kor-VAY)* [French, from Latin] Formerly, the unpaid peasant labor required by a feudal lord. More recently, unpaid or underpaid labor, usually for repairing roads.

coterie *(KOH-teh-ree)* [French, from earlier *cotier,* an association of tenant farmers] A small group of people with common interests and pursuits; a CLIQUE.

cotillion *(koh-TIL-yon)* [French, from *cotillon:* a petticoat] An elaborate French dance usually executed by four couples; the ancestor of the square dance. In modern usage, a formal ball for young women being introduced to society. ⟨No more would it summon folks to come and read how kids' crepe-paper birthdays rivaled royal *cotillions.*⟩—*Time,* August 4, 1997.

coulee *(KOO-lee)* [French, from *couler:* to flow] In the western United States and western Canada, a deep gulch or dry ravine formed by rainfall or melting snow. Also, a small, intermittent flow of water.

coulisse *(koo-LEESS)* [French: flowing] A groove or narrow space through which something slides or flows. In theater, a narrow space between the wings. In landscape painting, a view through dark valleys toward distant light.

coup *(koo)* [French: a blow with the fist; a sudden shock] An unexpected, telling blow, act, or move; a brilliant accomplishment; a masterstroke. See also COUP D'ÉTAT. ⟨He was arrested and ac-

cused of instigating a palace *coup* designed to unseat the reigning monarch.⟩

coup de foudre *(koo deu FOO-dreu)* [French: thunderbolt] Informally, love at first sight.

coup de grâce *(koo deu GRAHSS)* [French: a stroke of mercy] A
death blow; a mortal stroke delivered to end the suffering of a
wounded enemy. By extension, any decisive action taken to fin-
ish or put an end to something.

coup de main *(koo deu MENH)* [French: a blow from the hand] A
vigorous and unexpected stroke; a surprise or sudden development. Informally, a helping hand; temporary assistance.

coup d'état *(koo day-TAH)* [French: a stroke of state] The sudden
and illegal overthrow of those in power; a sudden and often
violent takeover of a government by rebel forces. See also JUNTA.

coup de théâtre *(koo deu tay-AH-treu)* [French] A surprising or
sensational twist in the plot of a play; a successful dramatic device that excites the audience.

coup d'oeil *(koo DEUY)* [French: a stroke of the eye] A quick
glance; a comprehensive view of a landscape, building, etc.

courgette *(koor-ZHEHT)* [French] Zucchini; green summer squash.

couscous *(kooss kooss)* [French, from Arabic] In North African
cooking, a form of semolina, usually steamed and served with
a light stew of meat and vegetables.

couture *(koo-TOOR, koo-TÜR)* [French: sewing; seam] The art and
action of sewing, dressmaking, and tailoring; clothing created
by fashionable designers or COUTURIERS. See also HAUTE COUTURE.
⟨Ferragamo has also purchased the Paris *couture* house of
Emanuel Ungaro.⟩—*Time,* October 19, 1998.

couturier (m), **couturiere** (f) *(koo-too-ree-AY, koo-too-ree-AIR)* [French: one who scws] A dressmaker, one who designs and makes high-fashion clothing. ⟨The fabrics were made by skilled artisans, something like those who work in a *couturier's* atelier⟩—*The Baltimore Sun,* April 9, 1999.

crèche *(krehsh)* [French: crib; cradle] A group of figures representing the scene at the stable in Bethlehem when Christ was born, often displayed at Christmastime. Also, a home for foundlings or, in Britain and France, a day nursery.

credenda *(kreh-DEN-dah)* [Latin] Matters or articles of faith; things to be believed, as opposed to *agenda:* things to be done.

credenza *(kreh-DEN-zah)* [Italian, from Latin] A buffet or sideboard, often without legs; a closed cabinet used to store office supplies.

crème anglaise *(krehm anh-GLEZ)* [French: English cream] A sweet custard sauce that may be flavored with liqueur.

crème brûlée *(krehm bru-LAY)* [French: burned cream] A rich custard dessert that is sprinkled with sugar just before serving and run under the broiler to caramelize the sugar.

crème de la crème *(krehm deu lah krehm)* [French: cream of the cream] The very best; the most select. ⟨what you see will definitely not be the *crème de la crème.*⟩—*The Guardian,* May 7, 1999.

crème de menthe *(krehm deu MANHT)* [French: cream of mint] A sweet, green or white liqueur strongly flavored with mint.

crème fraîche *(krehm FREHSH)* [French: fresh cream] A thickened, flavorful form of cream, slightly fermented, similar to but milder than sour cream.

crepe, crêpe *(krehp)* [French, from Latin *crispus:* crinkled] A thin pancake, rolled around a filling or served with a sauce. Also, a dress fabric; see CREPE DE CHINE.

crepe de chine, crêpe de chine *(krehp deu SHEEN)* [French: crepe from China] A thin, soft, silk dress fabric with a finely crinkled surface.

crêpes suzette *(krehp sü-ZEHT)* [French] Thin pancakes, folded and warmed in a sauce of butter and orange-flavored liqueur, and served FLAMBÉ.

crescendo *(kreh-SHEHN-doh)* [Italian] In music, growing louder; increasing in volume of sound. The opposite of DECRESCENDO.

cri de coeur *(kree deu KEUR)* [French: cry from the heart] A cry of distress, resentment, or exasperation.

crime passionel *(kreem pahs-yoh-NEL)* [French] A crime of passion, one directly caused by feelings of love, hate, or jealousy. ⟨Although it involved homicide, this unpremeditated *crime passionel* inspired some sympathy for the accused among jury members.⟩

crise *(kreez)* [French, from Greek] A crisis.

crise de conscience *(kreez deu konh-SYANHS)* [French] A crisis of conscience; an ethical or moral dilemma.

critique *(krih-TEEK)* [French, from Greek] A critical review of an artistic or literary work; a detailed commentary on a specific subject or problem. Often misused as a verb: to review critically. ⟨Its allegorical *critique* of paternalism obviously still has special resonance.⟩—*The Guardian*, May 20, 1999.

croquette *(kroh-KEHT)* [French, from *croquer:* to crunch] A small cake or patty of finely chopped food, often coated in batter or breadcrumbs and fried in deep fat.

croupier *(kroop-YAY)* [French] An attendant in a gambling house who rakes in chips or money at a gaming table and pays the winners.

crouton *(kroo-TONH)* [French] A small square of toasted or fried bread, used to garnish soups or salads.

cru *(kroo, krü)* [French: growth] In France, a vineyard that produces wine of excellent quality. See also GRAND CRU.

crudités *(krü-dee-TAY)* [French, from Latin *cruditas:* indigestion] An appetizer consisting of small, raw vegetables, served with or without a dressing or dip.

cui bono *(kwee BOH-noh)* [Latin] For whose benefit? Who profits by it?

cuisine *(kwee-ZEEN)* [French, from Latin: kitchen] The style or quality of cooking, as that of southern France or Indonesia. ⟨eating seasonal foods and safeguarding regional *cuisines* and producers who cultivate them⟩—*Time,* May 17, 1999.

cul-de-sac *(kül-de-SAK)* [French: bottom of the bag] A street or passage open only at one end; a dead-end street; a blind alley. By extension, any situation in which one cannot make further progress, or from which one cannot escape. ⟨But now the horror of winter storms in Southern California is a Seattle occurrence: water runs down fresh-paved *cul-de-sacs* and crushes everything below.⟩—*The New York Times,* December 29, 1996.

culotte *(kü-LOT)* [French: breeches] A woman's trousers that are cut loosely to resemble a skirt. Often used in the plural, *culottes.*

cum laude *(kum LAU-deh)* [Latin] With praise; with honor. Used on diplomas to denote academic achievement above the average. See also MAGNA CUM LAUDE, SUMMA CUM LAUDE.

curé *(kü-RAY)* [French] In France, a parish priest.

curettage *(kyoor-TAHZH)* [French] The process of scraping with a CURETTE.

curette *(kyoo-REHT)* [French] A small surgical instrument in the shape of a scoop or spoon, used to scrape tissue or growths from body cavities.

Curia *(KYOOR-ee-ah)* [Latin] The papal court; the body of officials of the Vatican. ⟨uses this thread which she follows through the labyrinthine, protean structure of the papal *Curia*⟩—*The New York Review of Books,* March 4, 1999.

curriculum (singular)**; curricula, curriculums** (plural) *(kuh-RIK-yoo-lum)* [Latin: course of action; race] The complete range of studies available at a school, a college, or a university; a particular or regular course of studies. ⟨The university is reducing its core *curriculum* and increasing recreational facilities to attract more students.⟩

curriculum vitae (singular)**; curricula vitae** (plural) *(kuh-RIK-yoo-lum VEE-tay)* [Latin] The course of one's life; one's career. A short biographical summary of a person's education, training, and work experience, usually prepared when applying for a job. See also RÉSUMÉ.

cynosure *(SYE-noh-shoor)* [Latin, from Greek: dog's tail] A focus or center of attraction and attention; something that invites admiration. Also, something that provides guidance or direction. ⟨So it's more of a shock to discover children who are not the *cynosure* of all eyes.⟩—*The Guardian,* January 4, 1999.

czar, tsar *(tzahr)* [Russian, from Latin *Caesar*] An emperor or king; the former emperor of Russia. An absolute ruler, or any person in a position of supreme power or authority. ⟨Formerly the Defense Department's export *czar,* he knows every sinkhole in the regulatory swamp.⟩—*Time,* May 24, 1999.

czardas *(CHAR-dahsh)* [Hungarian] A Hungarian folk dance dating from the Middle Ages, with a slow, melancholy section followed by a fast, lively one.

da capo *(dah KAH-poh)* [Italian: from the head] In music, from the beginning; an instruction to the player to go back to the opening of the piece, or the section just played, and repeat it.

d'accord *(dah-KOR)* [French] Informally, (I am in) agreement; (I) accept.

dacha *(DAH-chah)* [Russian] A villa or house in the Russian countryside; a summer weekend cottage once available only to aristocrats and party officials. ⟨he met with Stalin in the Kremlin and then at a *dacha* outside the city.⟩—*The New York Review of Books,* March 4, 1999.

dacoit *(dah-KOYT)* [Hindi] In India and Burma, one of a gang of criminals engaged in organized theft and murder.

Dada *(DAH-dah)* [French nursery word: horse; hobbyhorse] In the early 20th century, a nihilistic movement in art and literature that flouted artistic convention and declared a program of protest against bourgeois values. A popular means of expression among *dadaists* was photomontage, which combined pasted bits of photographs with printed messages or slogans. ⟨*Dada* evaporated because its original revolutionary spirit could not be sustained⟩—*The New York Times,* June 5, 1977.

daikon *(DYE-kon)* [Japanese, from Chinese: big root] In Asian cooking, a long, white, winter radish used raw (grated or shredded), or pickled.

daimyo, daimio *(DYE-myoh)* [Japanese, from Chinese: great name] Formerly, a title given to the hereditary feudal lords of Japan.

Dalai Lama (*DAH-lye LAH-mah*) [Mongolian] The title of the highest-ranking monk of Tibet, said to be a reincarnation of the BODHISATTVA known as Avalokitesvara. Until the Chinese Communist takeover in 1959, the *Dalai Lama* was the temporal as well as spiritual ruler of Tibet. See also LAMA.

dan (*dahn, dan*) [Japanese, from Chinese: grade] In the martial arts, the highest ranks of proficiency in JUDO, KARATE, etc., symbolized by the wearing of a black cloth belt.

danke schön (*DAHN-keh SHEUN*) [German] Thanks very much.

danse macabre (*dahnss mah-KAH-breu*) [French] A scene in a medieval mystery play, in which the figure symbolizing Death leads his victims in a dance to the netherworld. The French word MACABRE may derive from celebrations of the biblical battle of the Maccabees.

danseur (m), **danseuse** (f) (*danh-SEUR, danh-SEUZ*) [French] A dancer.

daruma (*dah-ROO-mah*) [Japanese, from a Chinese transliteration of the Sanskrit: DHARMA] A large Japanese doll made in the image of a seated Buddhist monk, a symbol of the Indian monk Bodhidharma, who founded the Zen sect of Buddhism; it is thought to be a good-luck charm.

dashiki (*dah-SHEE-kee*) [Yoruba] A loose-fitting pullover garment, usually made of brightly colored printed cotton, worn by some African men. ⟨While Barry is fond of *dashikis* and rambling rhetoric, Brimmer is as precise and exacting as the cut of his charcoal-gray suit.⟩—*Time*, August 18, 1997.

daube (*dohb*) [French] In French cooking, a stew made by braising meat and vegetables, i.e., simmering with a small amount of liquid in a tightly covered pot.

dauphin *(doh-FENH)* [French, from *Dauphiné,* a former province] The eldest son of a king of France, a title in use between 1349 and 1830.

dayan (singular); **dayanim** (plural) *(dah-YAHN, dah-YAHN-ihm)* [Hebrew] In Judaism, a judge in a religious court. Also, a person who advises rabbis on matters of Talmudic law.

debacle *(day-BAH-kl)* [French, from *bâcler:* to act hastily and carelessly] An abrupt change resulting in disorder or ruin; utter collapse; a sudden, disastrous breakdown.

debauchee *(day-boh-SHAY)* [French] A person given to debauchery or immoral conduct; one addicted to the pleasures of the flesh.

debonair *(deh-boh-NAIR)* [French, from *de bon air:* of good mien] Having an urbane and nonchalant manner; charming and sophisticated; gracious and self-confident. ⟨Fred Astaire has to have been the most *debonair* entertainer of his generation.⟩

de bonne grâce *(deu bun GRAHSS)* [French] With good grace; willingly.

débrouillard *(day-broo-YAHR)* [French, from *débrouiller:* to untangle] Cleverly resourceful; adept at coping with a tricky situation. One who is skilled at managing his or her own affairs.

debut *(day-BYOO)* [French, from *débuter:* to begin] A first public performance or appearance on the stage, or the formal introduction to society of a young woman. The beginning, as of a profession or career. As an adjective: pertaining to a first appearance.

debutante *(DEH-byoo-tahnt)* [French] A young woman who is being formally introduced to society.

decathlon *(dih-KATH-lon)* [Greek] An athletic competition in which each contestant participates in a series of ten track-and-field events.

déclassé *(day-klah-SAY)* [French] Lowered or diminished in rank; reduced in position or social status. ⟨Are the Hamptons becoming *déclassé* as a summer gathering place?⟩

décolletage *(day-kohl-TAHZH)* [French, from *décolleter:* to uncover the neck and shoulders] A low-cut neckline in the front or back of a dress, one that may bare the shoulders as well.

décolleté *(day-kohl-TAY)* [French] Used to describe a garment cut low in front or in back; with the neck and shoulders bare.

decor *(day-KOHR)* [French] The style of decoration used in a home, a room, or a building; the furniture, fabrics, objects, etc., that serve to convey the style. In the theater, the decorative style of a stage set; the scenery and set dressing. ⟨The elegant *decor* of this restaurant does not excuse the haughtiness of its service.⟩

decorum *(deh-KOHR-um)* [Latin] Correctness and dignity of behavior and dress; propriety of manners. In the plural *(decorums),* the requirements of good taste or social convention.

decoupage *(day-koo-PAHZH)* [French: a cutting out] The art of decorating a surface with cutouts of paper and lacquering over them; a piece produced in this manner.

decrescendo *(deh-kreh-SHEN-doh)* [Italian] In music, decreasing; gradually becoming softer in volume. The opposite of CRESCENDO.

de facto *(deh FAK-toh)* [Latin] According to fact; in reality. Compare DE JURE. ⟨So long as poverty persists, *de facto* if not de jure⟩— *The Guardian,* May 19, 1999.

dégringolade *(day-grenh-goh-LAHD)* [French: a precipitous descent] A rapid deterioration or breakdown; a falling apart; ruination.

de gustibus non est disputandum *(deh GOO-stee-bus non ehst dih-spoo-TAHN-dum)* [Latin] About taste there is no disputing. One cannot argue about matters of taste.

Dei gratia *(deh-ee GRAHT-syah)* [Latin] By the grace of God.

déjà vu *(day-zhah VÜ)* [French: already seen] The illusion that something seen or encountered for the first time has been experienced before. Often used incorrectly to describe a situation that one already experienced.

déjeuner *(day-zheu-NAY)* [French, from Latin] Lunch; luncheon.

de jure *(deh JOO-reh)* [Latin] According to the law; according to a specific decision. Compare DE FACTO. ⟨but any citizen whatever whose *de jure* equality was a facade for de facto enmity and injustice.⟩—*The New York Times,* December 20, 1987.

delicatessen *(deh-lih-kah-TEH-sen)* [German: delicacies] Prepared, ready-to-serve foods such as cooked meats, salads, pickles, cheeses, etc., or a store that sells such foods.

delirium tremens *(deh-LEER-ee-um TREH-mehnz)* [Latin] A violent form of mental disturbance caused by excessive drinking, exhaustion, some infectious diseases, etc., characterized by terrifying hallucinations, tremors, and acute emotional distress. Also called *d.t.'s.*

deluxe *(deh-LUKS, deu LÜKS)* [French] Elegant and expensive; of the highest quality; luxurious. In a sumptuous manner.

demagogue, demagog *(DEHM-ah-gog)* [Greek: a leader of the people] A political leader, orator, or agitator who gains popular support by appealing to people's emotions and prejudices; an unscrupulous politician.

démarche *(day-MAHRSH)* [French: a step; gait] A diplomatic or political action, especially one introducing a change in policy; a formal diplomatic protest or appeal. A manner of approach; a way of proceeding.

démenti *(day-menh-TEE)* [French: contradiction] An official statement issued by a government that denies actions or policies attributed to it.

demimondaine *(deu-mee-monh-DEHN)* [French] A woman of the DEMIMONDE; of or about the demimonde.

demimonde *(deu-mee-MOHND)* [French: half world] The class of women no longer considered respectable because of their immoral or licentious behavior; courtesans or prostitutes. Also, a fringe social group, such as the criminal or bohemian underworld.

demi-plié *(deu-mee-plee-AY)* [French] In ballet, a movement in which the dancer keeps the feet flat on the floor and bends the knees halfway. See also PLIÉ.

demi-pointe *(deu-mee-PWENHT)* [French] In ballet, a position on the toes but not on the tips of the toes; on the balls of the feet.

demi-sec *(deu-mee-SEHK)* [French] In describing wines: medium dry; sweeter than SEC.

demitasse *(deu-mee-TAHSS)* [French: half cup] A small cup in which strong after-dinner coffee is served; the coffee itself.

démodé *(day-moh-DAY)* [French] Out of fashion; outmoded; dated; "old hat." ⟨a part of human history . . . has become merely *démodé*⟩—*The New Criterion,* May 1999.

demoiselle *(deu-mwah-ZEL)* [French] An unmarried girl or young woman.

de nada *(day NAH-dah)* [Spanish] It's nothing; you are welcome; don't mention it; not at all (in answer to "thank you").

denouement, dénouement *(day-noo-MANH)* [French: an untying or unraveling] In a novel or drama, the final untangling of a complicated plot, or the moment in the story at which such a resolution takes place. More generally, the outcome of a perplexing or intricate series of events. 〈But Ronald Christ's oil on linen, "Interval (From Umbertide)," serves as the proper *dénouement* for this exhibit.〉—*The St. Louis Post-Dispatch,* August 21, 1998.

de profundis *(deh proh-FOON-dis)* [Latin] Out of the depths (of sorrow, misery, etc.): the first words of Psalm 130 in the Bible.

derailleur *(dih-RAY-ler, day-rye-YEUR)* [French: derailer; disengager] On a bicycle, a gear-shifting device that moves the drive chain from one sprocketed wheel to another.

de rigueur *(deu ree-GEUR)* [French] Strictly required by custom, fashion, or etiquette. 〈A tuxedo is *de rigueur* for the occasion.〉

dernier cri *(dehrn-yay KREE)* [French: the last cry] The newest trend or thing; the most up-to-date fashion. 〈This interpretation of the lurid tale of a Hollywood star and her gigolo is the *dernier cri* in adult drama.〉

derriere, derrière *(deh-ree-AIR)* [French] The buttocks; the rear.

desaparecido *(dehs-ah-pah-ray-SEE-doh)* [Spanish, Portuguese] One who has disappeared, especially a Latin American secretly imprisoned or executed during a government's campaign of repression, as in Chile and Argentina in the 1970s. 〈who claimed responsibility for as many as 5,000 *desaparecidos* (disappeared ones) during his tenure as police chief〉—*Time,* September 5, 1994.

descamisado *(dehs-kah-mee-SAH-doh)* [Spanish: shirtless] Formerly, a liberal extremist of the Spanish revolution of 1820–1823. More recently, a poor factory worker or laborer, especially in Argentina.

deshabille *(dis-ah-BEEL, day-zah-BEE)* [French: undressed] A state of being untidily or partially dressed; the negligent style of clothing worn in this state. By extension, a disorganized or careless way of thinking.

desideratum (singular)**; desiderata** (plural) *(deh-see-deh-RAH-tum, deh-see-deh-RAH-tah)* [Latin] Something desirable or required that is lacking in a situation. ⟨Transparency in the arms trade is the first *desideratum*.⟩—*The New York Review of Books*, March 4, 1999.

désolé *(day-soh-LAY)* [French] Greatly distressed; afflicted; upset.

desperado (singular)**; desperadoes** (plural) *(dehs-per-AH-doh)* [Spanish, from Latin] A desperate, reckless outlaw or criminal. ⟨the kind of dingbats and *desperadoes* who are currently destroying our railway system⟩—*The Guardian*, May 13, 1999.

détente *(day-TANHT)* [French: relaxation] An easing of tension in relations between countries, particularly through diplomatic negotiations. ⟨Kissinger's goal in this was to reassure the Chinese that the *détente* with the Soviet Union was in no way designed to isolate China.⟩—*The New York Review of Books*, March 4, 1999.

detritus *(dih-TRY-tus)* [French, from Latin] Loose particles or fragments of rock or other material, separated or washed away from an exposed surface by erosion, glacial action, etc. Any mass of disintegrated material; debris. ⟨to be churned into the *detritus* of a defunct industry to provide a growing medium for the thousands of trees and plants that will green the valley.⟩—*Time*, May 3, 1999.

de trop *(deu TROH)* [French] Too many; too much; not wanted; superfluous.

deus ex machina *(DAY-us eks MAH-kee-nah)* [Latin, from Greek: god from a machine] In classical Greek and Roman theater, (the character of) a benevolent god lowered mechanically into the scene to resolve a difficult situation in the drama. By extension, any improbable event or device used to untangle a situation at the last moment. ⟨In western films, the *deus ex machina* often took the form of cavalry arriving just in time to prevent a massacre.⟩

dharma *(DAHR-mah)* [Sanskrit] Buddha's teaching; law; ultimate truth.

dharna *(DAHR-nah)* [Hindi: placing; the act of sitting in restraint] In India, a way of exacting payment or compliance with a demand by sitting at the oppressor's doorstep and fasting until death or until justice is done.

dhoti *(DOH-tee)* [Hindi] In India, a long cotton loincloth worn by Hindu men. ⟨"I am a blind supporter of Atal Behari," said Tyagi, 52, who was dressed in a dingy white *dhoti*.⟩—*The New York Times,* April 30, 1999.

dhow *(dow)* [Arabic] An Arabian sailing vessel with slanted, triangular sails on one or two masts.

dhurrie *(DUH-ree)* [Hindi] A heavy, woven cotton rug of India.

diaspora *(dye-AH-spoh-rah)* [Greek: scattering] The dispersion of the Jewish peoples after Roman times, or those peoples themselves living outside their traditional homeland, or the countries to which they have fled. By extension, the scattering of a religious group, or the members of a religious minority who live among people of a dominant religious group. ⟨Many refugees from Kosovo's *diaspora* have fled to the United States.⟩

dictum *(DIK-tum)* [Latin] A formal pronouncement; an authoritative statement or assertion. A maxim or saying. See also OBITER DICTUM. ⟨adding that the same *dictum* holds for young actors⟩—*Time,* April 12, 1999.

digestif *(dee-zhehs-TEEF)* [French: digestive] An after-dinner drink of liqueur or brandy, taken to help the digestion. See also APERITIF.

diktat *(DIK-taht)* [German: something dictated] A sternly worded decree or settlement handed down by those in power; often, a severe punishment inflicted on a defeated political group or nation.

dilettante *(DIH-leh-tahnt)* [Italian, from Latin] A person who engages in an activity or pursues knowledge simply for his or her own amusement. A dabbler, an amateur. Also, one who loves the fine arts.

dim sum *(dim sum)* [Chinese: touch the heart] In Chinese cooking, fried, baked, or steamed dumplings filled with pork, seafood, etc., served as a snack or appetizer.

dinero *(dee-NEH-roh)* [Spanish, from Latin] Money; currency.

dirigiste *(dih-rih-ZHEEST)* [French] One who subscribes to the principle of *dirigisme,* a political system in which the government has the power to make decisions or determine policy on economic matters.

dirndl *(DERN-dl)* [German] A woman's dress patterned after Tyrolean peasant wear, with a full skirt gathered to a tight bodice. Any full skirt gathered to a yoke or waistband.

discotheque, discothèque *(dis-koh-TEHK)* [French] A nightclub or dance hall where music for dancing is provided from recordings, accompanied often by intricate lighting effects.

diseuse *(dee-ZEUZ)* [French: a speaker] A monologuist; a female professional entertainer who performs monologues or dramatic impersonations.

distingué *(dis-stenh-GAY)* [French] Distinguished; having an air of distinction; dignified and well-bred.

distrait *(dih-STRAY)* [French] Distracted; absentminded; inattentive.

diva *(DEE-vah)* [Italian, from Latin: divine] A renowned woman singer with a superb voice; an opera star; a PRIMA DONNA. ⟨A host of other Hispanic performers, including vocalist Marc Anthony and actress turned pop *diva* Jennifer Lopez⟩—*Time,* May 24, 1999.

divan *(dih-VAN, DYE-van)* [Turkish, from Persian] A low couch or sofa without arms or a raised back, which may serve as a bed.

divertimento *(dih-vehr-tih-MEN-toh)* [Italian] An entertaining, graceful piece of music in several movements for a small orchestra or ensemble. See also DIVERTISSEMENT.

divertissement *(dee-vehr-teess-MANH)* [French] A diversion, amusement, or entertainment; a DIVERTIMENTO. A short entertainment played in front of the curtain between acts of a play or opera. ⟨A few thousand might offer a mild *divertissement.*⟩—*The Guardian,* May 9, 1999.

djellaba *(jeh-LAH-bah)* [Arabic] A long, loose robe or gown with a hood, worn by men in North African countries.

djinn See JINN.

doctrinaire *(dok-trih-NAIR)* [French] Applying principles or theories without regard for practical considerations. An impractical or dogmatic theorist; pertaining to such a person. ⟨They were careful to avoid anything too life-altering or too *doctrinaire.*⟩

dojo *(DOH-joh)* [Japanese] A place dedicated to teaching Japanese martial arts; a training hall.

dolce far niente *(DOHL-cheh fahr NYEHN-teh)* [Italian: (it is) sweet to do nothing] Pleasant inactivity or idleness.

dolce vita, la *(lah DOHL-cheh VEE-tah)* [Italian] The sweet life; a life of sensual pleasure and self-indulgence.

dolma *(DAWL-mah)* [Turkish: something filled] In Near Eastern cooking, a dish of eggplant or grape leaves or peppers, stuffed with a combination of meat, rice, and seasonings.

dolmen *(DOHL-men)* [French, from Breton] A prehistoric structure made of two or more large, rough, upright stones with a space between them, topped by a single horizontal slab of stone. Sometimes called a *cromlech*.

doloroso *(doh-loh-ROH-soh)* [Italian] In music, sorrowful; to be played in a sad or plaintive manner.

Dominus vobiscum *(DOH-mee-noos voh-BISS-koom)* [Latin] The Lord be with you.

dona *(DOH-nah)* [Portuguese, from Latin] In Portuguese-speaking countries, a title of respect or address that precedes the given name of a woman of rank. The equivalent of madam or lady.

doña *(DOH-nyah)* [Spanish, from Latin] A Spanish lady or noblewoman; a woman's title put before her Christian name.

donnée *(doh-NAY)* [French: a given; an established fact] A set of literary or artistic fundamentals or premises.

doppelgänger *(DOP-pl-geng-er)* [German: double walker] A wraith, apparition, or ghostly counterpart of someone not yet dead. Also called a *doubleganger*. ⟨Fax from Los Angeles; *In the kitchen with Ken Starr's West Coast doppelgänger*⟩—*The New Yorker,* March 8, 1999.

dossier *(DOSS-yay, doh-SYAY)* [French: bundle of papers] A file or collection of documents that relate to a particular person or topic. ⟨Some *dossiers* on covert operations will be declassified and made available to the public.⟩

douane *(doo-AHN)* [French] Customs: duties imposed on imported goods. A customhouse.

douanier *(doo-ahn-YAY)* [French] A customs official.

double entendre *(doo-bl anh-TANH-dreu)* [French] A double meaning; a phrase or word that can be understood in two ways, especially when one sense is improper or RISQUÉ. ⟨So there he is, naked, reading a newspaper and muttering feeble *double entendres,* as he first meets Mrs. Peel.⟩—*Time,* August 24, 1998.

doyen (m), **doyenne** (f) *(DOY-en, dwah-YEN)* [French] The eldest or senior member of a group; the most experienced or highest-ranking person. ⟨Dizzy Gillespie, the great *doyen* of jazz trumpet, received an honorary degree from Columbia University.⟩

dragée *(drah-ZHAY)* [French, from Greek] A sugarcoated almond or piece of candy; a sugarcoated pill.

dramatis personae *(DRAM-ah-tiss pehr-SOH-nay)* [Latin] The characters of a stage play, or a cast of characters as printed in a theater program or before the text of a drama. ⟨She was brought into the show as a versatile and dynamic addition to the *dramatis personae.*⟩

dreck *(drek)* [Yiddish, from German] A slang term for human excrement; filth; junk. By extension, inferior goods; insincere talk. ⟨Muldoon is in love with the mortal *dreck* and drainage of culture.⟩—*The New Criterion,* December 1998.

dreidel, dreidl *(DRAY-dl)* [Yiddish] A four-sided top used in a child's game often played on Hanukkah, the Jewish festival of lights.

dressage *(dreh-SAHZH)* [French, from *dresser:* to hold oneself upright; to tame] The art of training a horse to obey commands and execute the precise, formal movements required at a horse show or riding exhibition. See also MANÈGE. ⟨Jerry Diaz, who surrounds himself and his palomino with a spinning lariat as well as a balletic *dressage* demonstration⟩—*The New York Times,* November 6, 1998.

droshky *(DROSH-kee)* [Russian: wagon] In Russia, a light, open, four-wheeled carriage, especially one with a narrow bench for passengers.

duce *(DOO-cheh)* [Italian, from Latin] The leader; the title given to Benito Mussolini as premier of the Italian Fascist state from 1922 to 1943.

duenna, dueña *(doo-EHN-nah)* [Spanish, from Latin] In Spain and Portugal, an older woman who acts as a chaperon, escort, or companion to a young lady; a governess. ⟨As a young woman of good family, she could not receive a suitor without the presence of a *duenna*.⟩

du jour *(dü ZHOOR)* [French] Of the day; of the kind being prepared or served today. ⟨Indeed, the realities of the new media machine's dynamics dictate what will be the highs and lows of any story that becomes the machine's subject *du jour*.⟩—*Brill's Content,* July/August 1999.

duma, douma *(DOO-mah)* [Russian] In Russia, an assembly or a representative council. When capitalized: the name currently given to the lower house of the Russian parliament. ⟨the chairman of the *Duma* Foreign Relations Committee and an ally of the liberal opposition leader Grigory Yavlinsky⟩—*The Atlantic Monthly,* January 1996.

dumka *(DOOM-kah)* [Czech, from Ukrainian] In music, a dance-like instrumental piece based on Slavonic folk songs, characterized by abrupt changes of mood and pace.

dungarees *(dung-gah-REEZ)* [Hindi] Trousers or work clothing made of blue denim. In the singular *(dungaree)*, a coarse Indian calico.

dur *(do-er)* [German] In music, composed in a major key; major, as in"*A-dur*" (A major).

duvet *(dü-VAY)* [French: down] A comforter or quilt filled with goose down, eiderdown, etc.

dybbuk *(DIH-buk)* [Yiddish, from Hebrew] In Jewish folklore, the soul of a dead person that takes possession of a living person, or an evil spirit that acts similarly through a living being. ⟨He becomes acquainted with her "homicidal hooded stare," her "*dybbuk* fury" at his alleged failures as husband and father.⟩— *Time*, February 16, 1998.

eau de cologne *(oh deu koh-LOHN)* [French: water from Cologne] A lightly perfumed toilet water made in Cologne, Germany, since the 1700s. A generic term for any similar product.

eau de vie *(oh deu VEE)* [French: water of life] A clear, distilled spirit or brandy made from fermented fruit.

ecce homo *(EH-cheh HOH-moh)* [Latin] Behold the man: the words spoken by Pontius Pilate as he presented Christ to his accusers.

echelon *(EH-sheh-lon)* [French: transverse rung of a ladder] A level of authority or rank, as in "the upper *echelons* of government." In military parlance, a staggered formation of troops, vehicles, boats, or aircraft that creates the appearance of steps. Geese and cranes frequently fly in *echelon* formation.

echt *(ekht)* [German] Authentic; real.

éclair *(ay-KLAIR)* [French, from Latin: lightning flash] A small, oblong pastry shell made from cream puff paste, filled with custard or whipped cream and often topped with chocolate icing.

éclaircissement *(ay-klair-seess-MANH)* [French] A clarification of something obscure; a complete explanation.

éclat *(ay-KLAH)* [French: flash; burst; splinter of glass] Brilliance or splendor of action or reputation; conspicuous success; renown. General acclaim or applause. A showy display. ⟨The comedy arises from the hero's adversity, illustrated by his boiling and eating of his shoe with the *éclat* of a gourmet.⟩—*The New York Times,* December 26, 1977.

effleurage *(eh-fleu-RAHZH)* [French: a gentle stroking] In massage, a light stroking motion made with the tips of the fingers.

effluvium *(eh-FLOO-vee-um)* [Latin: a flowing out] A foul-smelling or noxious vapor; an invisible emanation, as from putrid matter; a MIASMA.

eidolon *(eye-DOH-lon)* [Greek: image; idol] An imaginary image; an apparition or phantom.

ejecta *(eh-JEK-tah)* [Latin] Matter or waste material ejected, as from the body or from an erupting volcano.

élan *(ay-LANH)* [French] Ardor; vivacity; an impetuous rush; dash.

élan vital *(ay-LANH vee-TAHL)* [French: vital energy] In the philosophy of Henri Bergson, the life force in nature as expressed through the processes of evolution.

El Niño *(ehl NEEN-yoh)* [Spanish: the boy; the Christ-child] A warm, slow, clockwise current in the northern Pacific Ocean that develops in January and February, often encompassing most of the equatorial Pacific, and causing frequently devastating disturbances in the weather of the Americas because of its abnormal temperature. See also LA NIÑA. ⟨the growing debate over global warming, as well as the phenomenon of *El Niño* and the intense smog over Southeast Asia, has pushed environmental issues to the forefront of the news.⟩—*The New York Times,* October 27, 1997.

embarcadero *(ehm-bahr-kah-DAY-roh)* [Spanish] A landing place, pier, or wharf.

embarras de richesses *(ahm-bah-RAH deu ree-SHEHSS)* [French] An embarrassment of riches: a bewildering overabundance.

embonpoint *(ahm-bonh-PWENH)* [French: in good condition] Plumpness of body; stoutness. See also ZAFTIG. ⟨but with political experience in place of *embonpoint*⟩—*The Guardian,* May 8, 1999.

embouchure *(AHM-boo-shoor, ahm-boo-SHÜR)* [French, from Latin] The mouthpiece of a woodwind or brass instrument, excepting those with double reeds; the position of the player's lips while blowing into the instrument. Also, the mouth of a river, or the opening out of a valley into flatland.

emeritus *(eh-MEH-rih-tus)* [Latin] From merit; said of a retired person who retains an honorary title, such as professor, because of past merit in that position. ⟨As pastor *emeritus,* he organized a series of seminars on matters of local community interest.⟩

émigré *(EM-ih-gray, ay-mee-GRAY)* [French] A person who emigrates, who leaves his or her homeland, frequently to escape a dangerous political situation. Applied especially to those who escaped during the French Revolution of 1789 or the Russian Revolution of 1917. ⟨Some *émigré* novelists and poets have used English, their second language, with astounding skill and originality.⟩

éminence grise *(ay-mee-nahns GREEZ)* [French: gray eminence] The power behind the throne; a person able to influence or manipulate those in high places, often in an unofficial capacity or in secret. ⟨Cardinal Richelieu was the *éminence grise* during the reign of Louis XIII of France.⟩

emir *(eh-MEER)* [Arabic: ruler] A commander, chieftain, prince, or head of state in some Muslim countries. A title of honor given to the descendants of Muhammad.

emirate *(EH-mee-rate)* [Arabic] An administration headed by an EMIR. ⟨Resentful of their Muslim leader, the indigenous people demanded the abolition of the *emirate* and the establishment of their own chiefdom.⟩

empanada *(ehm-pah-NAH-dah)* [American Spanish] A Spanish or Mexican turnover filled with meat or shellfish and vegetables, usually baked or deep-fried.

enceinte *(anh-SENHT)* [French, from Latin] Said of a woman: with child; pregnant. In military architecture, the circle of works or the wall around a fortified place, or the place so enclosed.

enchilada *(ehn-chee-LAH-dah)* [American Spanish: spiced with chili] In Mexican cooking, a TORTILLA filled with meat or cheese and baked in a spicy sauce. In slang, "the big *enchilada*" is someone seen as the most important or powerful person in an organization or group; "the whole *enchilada*" refers to the entirety of something, as in the full range of benefits or advantages. ⟨The public's hunger for shares has led Austin Grill to offer diners a helping of its new public offering along with their *enchiladas*.⟩— *Time*, March 3, 1997.

encomium *(ehn-KOH-mee-um)* [Latin, from Greek: a revelry] An oral or written expression of praise; a eulogy. ⟨The designation of "master" is an *encomium* rarely given to artists of that generation.⟩

encore *(ON-kor, anh-KAWR)* [French] Again; once more; what the audience shouts at the end of a concert to request that a performer repeat part of the program or play another piece. The piece performed in response to such a request. By extension, an additional appearance; a rerun or rematch.

en famille *(anh fah-MEE)* [French] At home; within the family; informally.

enfant terrible *(anh-fanh teh-REE-bleu)* [French: terrible child] An unmanageable child; a brat. A person whose outrageous conduct causes embarrassment; one whose work or lifestyle is aggressively unconventional or shocking.

enfilade *(anh-fee-LAHD)* [French, from *enfiler:* to thread] Gunfire that sweeps a trench or column of soldiers from one end to the other. Also, an architectural arrangement of rooms following one after the other, with doorways that allow a view from one end of the series to the other. ⟨James Stirling's much-visited Stuttgart Staatsgalerie features a traditional *enfilade* of exhibition galleries.⟩—*The New York Review of Books,* April 22, 1999.

enfin *(anh-FENH)* [French] In the end; finally; in conclusion.

engagé *(anh-gah-ZHAY)* [French] Engaged; involved; committed. ⟨Some clients found him inattentive and insufficiently *engagé.*⟩

en garde *(anh GAHRD)* [French] On guard: a fencing position assumed before beginning the action. Used by the director of a fencing match as a call to participants to prepare for action.

en masse *(anh MAHSS)* [French] In a mass or as a group; all together. ⟨Still and all, Polke's smaller drawings get fairly monotonous *en masse.*⟩—*Time,* May 31, 1999.

ennead *(EHN-ee-ad)* [Greek] Any system or group that contains nine things or individuals.

ennui *(anh-NWEE)* [French] A feeling of listlessness and boredom; weariness and vague discontent; lassitude or lack of interest due to overindulgence. ⟨Then a certain *ennui* takes over.⟩— *The Guardian,* May 2, 1999.

en papillote *(anh pah-pee-YUHT)* [French] Anything cooked in a wrapping of oiled paper or foil that may be served in its wrapping.

en passant *(anh pah-SANH)* [French] In passing; by the way.

en plein air *(anh plehn ayr)* [French] In the open air; out of doors. For example, a discussion may be held *en plein air* so that all the people may take part. See also ALFRESCO; PLEIN AIR.

en rapport *(anh rah-POHR)* [French] In agreement; in accord; in sympathetic relation.

en route *(anh ROOT)* [French] On the way; on the road.

entente *(anh-TANHT)* [French] A mutual agreement or understanding between nations, regarding matters of international importance. Also, the parties that enter into such an accord. ⟨The first Secretary of the Treasury believed that an Anglo-American *entente* was indispensable to our vital commercial interests.⟩—*The New Criterion,* May 1999.

entente cordiale *(anh-tant kor-DYAHL)* [French] A friendly agreement; a cordial understanding, as between governments. ⟨Conservatives . . . would not stand idly by while the G.O.P. drifted into an *entente cordiale* with Democrats.⟩—*Time,* August 19, 1996.

entourage *(anh-too-RAHZH)* [French] A group of attendants or followers, as those who surround an important person; a RETINUE; an escort. Also, the environment or surroundings. ⟨Trainers and other members of the heavyweight's *entourage* gathered in an adjacent suite.⟩

entr'acte *(anh-TRAHKT)* [French] An interval between acts of a play, ballet, or opera. A short piece of music or dance, or a skit performed during such an interval.

entrechat *(anh-treu-SHAH)* [French: caper] In ballet, a vertical leap in which the dancer crosses the feet several times in the air.

entrecôte *(anh-treu-KOHT)* [French: between the ribs] A French cut of meat equivalent to a rib steak or sirloin. ⟨frog's legs sautéed with butter, garlic, herbs and white wine; and *entrecôte* bearnaise.⟩—*The New York Times,* December 20, 1998.

entrée *(ON-tray, ahn-TRAY)* [French: entrance; admission] The act or privilege of admission to a place, or favored access to a person or group; the ability to approach a person, group, or place that normally would be inaccessible. Also, the main course of a meal; formerly, a dish served between the fish and meat courses at a formal dinner.

entre nous *(anh-treu NOO)* [French] Between us; confidentially.

entrepôt *(anh-treu-POH)* [French, from Latin] A warehouse or depot for commercial merchandise.

entrepreneur *(anh-treu-preh-NEUR)* [French: one who undertakes] A person who initiates and manages a business or other enterprise, often having full control and assuming responsibility for any accompanying risk; in current usage, a "business adventurer." ⟨Financial *entrepreneurs* may find it more difficult to take over voting control of large corporations.⟩

épée *(ay-PAY)* [French] A light, narrow dueling sword with a sharp point but without cutting edges. The sport of fencing with an *épée.*

epicure *(EH-pih-kyoor)* [Latin, from the name of the Greek philosopher Epicurus] A person of discriminating taste in fine foods and wines; a CONNOISSEUR.

epitome *(eh-PIT-oh-mee)* [Latin, from Greek: abridgement] A person or thing that possesses the qualities of an entire class; the personification or embodiment of such qualities. Also, an abstract or summary; a condensed account. ⟨Glyndebourne, so long regarded as the *epitome* of the British operatic establishment⟩—*The Guardian,* May 18, 1999.

Eretz Israel *(EH-retz IZ-rah-el)* [Hebrew] The land of Israel.

ergo *(EHR-goh)* [Latin] Therefore; hence. ⟨*Ergo,* one may conclude, it has also paid attention to the details that do matter.⟩—*The New York Times,* August 10, 1997.

Erin go bragh *(EH-rin goh BRAKH)* [Gaelic] Ireland forever.

errata (plural)**; erratum** (singular) *(ehr-RAH-tah, ehr-RAH-tum)* [Latin] Errors; mistakes. Although *errata* is plural, it is often used as a singular noun to indicate a list of errors and their corrections in a text. These usually appear on a separate page. See also CORRIGENDUM.

ersatz *(EHR-zahts)* [German: substitute] Describing anything artificial or synthetic; usually associated with the substitutes for coffee and other natural substances that were in short supply in Germany during both world wars. ⟨old people queueing for the tiny rations of *ersatz* coffee and boiled potatoes or scavenging for scraps in the kitchen refuse⟩—*Time,* December 14, 1998.

escadrille *(ess-kah-DRIL)* [French, from Spanish] A squadron of military aircraft, as in the *Lafayette Escadrille,* a small group of American volunteer aviators in World War I. Formerly, a small squadron of ships.

espadrille *(es-pah-DRIL)* [French, from Portuguese] A flat sandal with a rope sole and canvas uppers, and laces that tie around the ankle.

espalier *(ess-pahl-YAY)* [French, from Italian] A framework, trellis, or flat surface on which fruit trees or shrubs are trained to grow flattened out. A tree or planting so trained.

espionage *(es-pee-oh-NAHZH)* [French] Spying; gathering secret information within enemy territory. ⟨After British atomic scientist Klaus Fuchs was arrested for *espionage*, the FBI found his courier in Philadelphia.⟩

espressivo *(es-preh-SEE-voh)* [Italian] In music, with expression; expressively.

espresso *(es-PREH-soh)* [Italian: pressed] Strong, dark coffee made from specially dark-roasted beans and brewed by steam pressure.

esprit de corps *(ess-PREE deu KOHR)* [French] In a group of people sharing common goals, interests, or responsibilities: a spirit of solidarity, supportiveness, and enthusiasm; CAMARADERIE; fellowship. ⟨That *esprit de corps* has had a calming effect on Guerin.⟩— *The New York Times,* November 27, 1997.

esse *(EH-seh)* [Latin: to be; being] In philosophy, the self; existence.

estancia *(eh-STAHN-syah)* [American Spanish: dwelling] A farm or cattle ranch; a landed estate. ⟨In the high desert region of Patagonia, we visited the huge *estancia* of the local cattle baron.⟩

étagère *(ay-tah-ZHAIR)* [French] A stand, often tall, with open shelves for displaying small objects or BIBELOTS; a whatnot.

et alibi *(eht AH-lee-bee)* [Latin] And elsewhere. Abbreviated *et al.*

et alii (m), **et alia** (f) *(eht AH-lee-eye, eht AH-lee-ah)* [Latin] And others. Abbreviated *et al.*

et cetera *(eht SEH-teh-rah)* [Latin] And other things; and so forth; and the rest. Abbreviated *etc.*

etiquette *(EH-tih-keht)* [French: a label] The conventionally established rules of correct conduct in polite society, or the code of ethical behavior among the members of a profession; propriety. ⟨There was a time when the rules of *etiquette* barred children from their parents' subsequent weddings.⟩

étoile *(ay-TWAHL)* [French] A star, or something resembling a star. In ballet, a term used to designate the highest-ranking dancers of the Paris Opera.

étouffée *(ay-too-FAY)* [Louisiana French: smothered] A stew made of crayfish, vegetables, and seasonings, cooked in a tightly closed pot with a minimum of liquid.

etsi kai etsi *(eht-see KET-see)* [Greek] So-so; half and half; fifty-fifty.

étude *(AY-tood)* [French: study] A musical composition based upon a special problem of instrumental technique and designed to give the student practice in its solution.

etui *(eh-TWEE)* [French] A small case for carrying needles, toilet articles, etc.

eureka *(yoo-REE-kah)* [Greek] I have found (something): an exclamation of jubilation or triumph at a discovery.

Ewigkeit *(EH-vig-kite)* [German] Eternity; forever; always.

ex cathedra *(eks kah-THEE-drah)* [Latin: from the chair] Coming directly from the seat of power or authority, especially from the pope, as in "*ex cathedra* judgments or decisions that are considered infallible."

exempli gratia *(ek-SEM-plee GRAHT-see-ya)* [Latin] By way of example. Abbreviated *e.g.*

ex gratia *(eks GRAHT-see-yah)* [Latin] As a favor; out of a spirit of goodwill.

ex officio *(eks oh-FISH-ee-oh)* [Latin] Because of or by virtue of office or official position.

exotica *(ek-ZAH-tih-kah)* [Latin] Strange, glamorous, or strikingly unusual objects; works of art or styles from a foreign country. ⟨Among the *exotica* displayed were some museum-quality pieces of Indian beadwork.⟩

expertise *(ex-per-TEEZ)* [French: an expert's report] Expert knowledge, skill, or ability. A written assessment or evaluation by an expert.

exposé *(eks-poh-ZAY)* [French] A public revelation, especially the exposure to the public of something disgraceful or scandalous. ⟨Why write a personal account that goes far beyond the usual boundaries of a memoir to become an *exposé* as intimate as a diary?⟩—*The Guardian,* May 15, 1999.

ex tempore *(eks TEM-poh-reh)* [Latin: out of the time] At the spur of the moment; without preparation.

facade, façade *(fah-SAHD)* [French, from Italian] The main face or front of a building; the side visible to the public. An outward appearance, especially one designed to make a good impression; a false front. ⟨the *façade* of whose 18th-century house, Marchmont, concealed the tensions of a Brideshead⟩—*The Guardian,* April 10, 1999.

façon *(fah-SONH)* [French] The manner in which something is done; style; workmanship.

factotum *(fak-TOH-tum)* [Latin: do everything] A handyman or man of all work. Within an organization, a person with many different tasks and responsibilities. ⟨She became chief curator and house *factotum* for the Museum of Decorative Arts.⟩

fado *(FAH-doh)* [Portuguese, from Latin] Dating from the mid-1800s, the melancholy popular songs and ballads of the CAFÉS and CABARETS of Portugal, usually accompanied by a guitar or small instrumental groups.

fagioli (plural); **fagiolo** (singular) *(fah-JOH-lee, fah-JOH-loh)* [Italian] A kidney bean.

faience *(fah-YANHS)* [French: pottery from Faenza] A type of tin-glazed earthenware with richly colored designs, produced in Italy from the late 1300s. The term is also applied to ceramic figurines and ornaments of ancient Egypt.

fainéant *(fay-nay-ANH)* [French: a do-nothing] An idler; a shirker; a lazybones. Lazy or useless.

fait accompli *(feht ah-kom-PLEE)* [French: accomplished fact] Something that has been done and cannot be reversed. ⟨the transfer of power will soon be a *fait accompli.*⟩

faites vos jeux *(feht voh ZHEU)* [French] In the game of roulette, an instruction from the CROUPIER: Place your bets.

fakir *(fah-KEER)* [Arabic: poor] A monk of the Hindu or Muslim faith, especially a mendicant monk.

falafel, felafel *(fah-LAH-fel)* [Arabic] In Middle Eastern cooking, an Egyptian dish made of ground chickpeas or fava bean flour, garlic, onions, and spices, sometimes leavened, and deep-fried.

falsetto *(fall-SEHT-toh)* [Italian, from Latin] In music, an artificial method of singing in a range higher than one's natural range, by deliberately restricting the tone-producing apparatus; a technique sometimes used by male singers.

fandango *(fan-DANG-goh)* [Spanish] An old Spanish dance in triple time performed by a couple playing CASTANETS, beginning slowly and gradually increasing in speed and intensity.

fanfaron *(FAN-fah-ron)* [French, from Spanish] A braggart; a blusterer. Also, a fanfare.

farci, farcie *(fahr-SEE)* [French] In cooking, a term meaning stuffed or filled with something.

farouche *(fah-ROOSH)* [French] Fierce; untamed. Unsociable or sullen. Painfully shy.

farrago *(fah-RAH-goh)* [Latin: mixed fodder] A hodgepodge; a confused mixture.

fatwa, fatwah *(FAHT-wah)* [Arabic] A Muslim religious edict, intended to be obeyed by all followers of Islam. The most famous *fatwa* in modern times was issued by the Ayatollah Khomeini of Iran, who called for the assassination of the author Salman Rushdie because of what was considered his blasphemous portrayal of Islam in a novel. ⟨This is not a *fatwa* which died with the death of the religious leader who issued it.⟩— *Harper's Magazine,* March 1999.

faubourg *(foh-BOOR)* [French] A section or quarter on the outskirts of a French city; a suburb. Also, a district within the city. See also BANLIEUE. ⟨In Paris guidebooks, the seventh arrondissement has the title *Faubourg*-Saint-Germain, Invalides, École Militaire.⟩

faute de mieux *(foht deu MYEU)* [French] For lack of anything better.

fauteuil *(foh-TEUY)* [French] An upholstered armchair.

Fauves *(fohv)* [French: wild beasts] The name given to a group of early 20th-century artists, mainly French, who reacted against what they perceived as the limitations of impressionism; their works are notable for the juxtaposition of pure, vivid colors and the outlining in black of the contours of objects. ⟨critics in turn-of-the-century Paris tried to belittle the innovators by giving them nicknames like Impressionists (incapable of painting a realistic picture) and *Fauves* (wild beasts).⟩—*Time,* September 7, 1998.

faux *(foh)* [French] False; imitation; artificial. Often used in combination with another word, such as *faux-bois* (artificial wood), or *faux-marbre* (synthetic marble). ⟨while *faux* philosophers may call out their doctrines from street corners⟩—*The Christian Science Monitor,* June 11, 1999.

faux pas *(foh PAH)* [French: false step] An embarrassing social blunder; a breach of ETIQUETTE; a mistake.

fedayee (singular); **fedayeen** (plural) *(feh-dah-YEE, feh-dah-YEEN)* [Arabic: one who sacrifices himself] A Palestinian GUERRILLA or COMMANDO acting especially against Israel; usually used in the plural. ⟨That led to the second great crisis of his reign, the rise of Yasser Arafat's *fedayeen*⟩—*The Guardian,* February 8, 1999.

feijoada *(fay-ZHWAH-dah)* [Brazilian Portuguese] A Brazilian dish made with black beans, fresh and smoked meats, onions, garlic, chili, etc., sprinkled with cassava meal and served with rice.

feinschmecker *(FINE-shmeh-ker)* [German] A GOURMET; a GASTRONOME.

fellah (singular); **fellahin, fellaheen** (plural) *(FEHL-lah, feh-lah-HEEN)* [Arabic] In Egypt, a peasant or laborer.

femme du monde *(fam dü MOHND)* [French: woman of the world] A sophisticated, experienced, or worldly-wise woman. See also HOMME DU MONDE.

femme fatale *(fam fah-TAHL)* [French: fatal woman] An unusually attractive or seductive woman, especially one who leads men into disastrous situations or intrigues. ⟨Barbara Stanwyck played the cold-blooded, intriguing *femme fatale* to perfection.⟩

feng shui *(feng shway, fung shooay)* [Chinese: wind and water] The ancient Chinese art of placement and rearrangement that enables people to find the most favorable location for a home, a workplace, or for structural elements and objects within those surroundings. Based on theories derived from the I-Ching, *feng shui* teaches that buildings and landscapes have invisible zones of energy that must flow freely to allow inhabitants to achieve success and prosperity.

fermata *(fehr-MAH-tah)* [Italian: a stop; a pause] In music notation, a symbol indicating that the note or chord below it is to be held longer than its normal duration.

festina lente *(FEHS-tee-nah LEHN-teh)* [Latin] Make haste slowly.

feta *(FEH-tah)* [Modern Greek] A white, semisoft Greek cheese made with goat's milk or sheep's milk, cured in brine.

fete, fête *(fayt, feht)* [French] A celebration or festival, especially one held outdoors. To honor someone with such a celebration. See also GALA.

fête champêtre *(feht shawm-PEH-treu)* [French] A party or celebration held outdoors. In 18th-century painting, the depiction of a rural open-air feast or entertainment.

fête galante *(feht gah-LAHNT)* [French] In 18th-century painting, a depiction of leisurely dalliance in a pastoral setting, in which the figures are more graceful, aristocratic, and richly dressed than those of a FÊTE CHAMPÊTRE.

fettucine *(feh-too-CHEE-neh)* [Italian: little ribbon] PASTA that has been cut in long, flat, narrow strips.

feuilleton *(feuy-TONH)* [French: little leaf] In a European newspaper, the cultural and entertainment section devoted to light fiction, criticism, satire, and articles in a conversational or witty style.

fiancé (m), **fiancée** (f) *(fee-anh-SAY)* [French] A person who is engaged to be married.

fiasco *(fee-AS-koh)* [Italian: flask] A spectacular failure. The term derived from the example of a glassblower trying to blow a very large flask, which usually broke before it could be used. ⟨After the *fiasco* in the Senate, House Republicans are fully aware that they need to pass a full-fledged measure on gun control.⟩—*Time,* May 26, 1999.

fiat *(FEE-aht)* [Latin: let it be done] An authoritative order or decree; an authorization.

Fidelista *(fee-deh-LEES-tah)* [Spanish] A follower of Fidel (Castro). ⟨His mother, a policewoman and a staunch *Fidelista* who refused to accept gifts from a visitor, proudly pointed out photos of her cousins' suburban home and Nissan in Miami.⟩—*The New York Times,* August 31, 1994.

fiesta *(fee-EHSS-tah)* [Spanish, from Latin] A festive occasion, holiday, or celebration; a religious festival in Spanish-speaking countries.

filé, file *(fee-LAY)* [Louisiana French: ropy; stringy] A powder made from dried sassafras leaves, used as a flavoring and thickener in soups and GUMBOS.

fille de joie *(fee deu ZHWAH)* [French: girl of joy] A prostitute.

filo See PHYLLO.

finale *(fee-NAH-leh)* [Italian, from Latin] The concluding part or movement of a piece of music, or the last scene of a play; the final section of any performance or activity. ⟨The high point of the meal, a chocolate SOUFFLÉ, was also its *finale*.⟩

finca *(FING-kah)* [Spanish: property] Real estate; a country house. In Spanish-speaking countries, a large farm, ranch, or plantation.

fin de siècle *(fenh deu see-EHK-leu)* [French] The end of a century, particularly the end of the 19th century, seen as a time of change in moral and social values. Sometimes written *fin-de-siècle:* an adjective meaning decadent.

fine *(FEE-neh)* [Italian] The end.

fine *(feen)* [French, short for *fine champagne de la maison:* the house brandy] A good-quality brandy.

fines herbes *(feenz EHRB)* [French: fine herbs] A mixture of finely chopped fresh herbs used to flavor or garnish a variety of foods.

fjord *(fyord)* [Norwegian] A long, narrow indentation in a seacoast, bordered by high, rocky cliffs. Also written *fiord*.

flageolet *(flahzh-yoh-LAY)* [French] An ancient end-blown musical instrument similar to the recorder. Also, a delicately flavored bean, pale green in color, prized by the French and often served with lamb.

flagrante delicto, in flagrante delicto *(flah-GRAHN-teh deh-LIK-toh, ihn flah-GRAHN-teh deh-LIK-toh)* [Latin] In the very act of committing a crime or offense. ⟨after (her) husband and for-

mer bodyguard was photographed *in flagrante delicto* at a Riviera villa⟩—*Time,* January 20, 1997.

flak, flack *(flak)* [German acronym, from *Fliegerabwehrkanonen:*
antiaircraft gun] In North American usage, antiaircraft fire, particularly in the form of explosions that spread fragments of
steel in front of an airplane in combat. By extension, verbal
abuse or hostile criticism. ⟨Such a decision by management was
bound to produce some *flak* and fallout.⟩

flambé *(flahm-BAY)* [French: flamed] Used to describe food served
in flaming liquor, especially brandy or rum.

flamenco *(flah-MENG-koh)* [Spanish: Flemish] Pertaining to an
Andalusian Gypsy. Describing the informal Spanish songs and
dance associated with Gypsies; a vigorous, rhythmic style of
performance that involves stamping the feet and clapping the
hands.

flânerie *(flah-neh-REE)* [French] Leisurely strolling without a fixed
destination, stopping now and then to enjoy the sights. Also,
dawdling; idleness.

flâneur *(flah-NEUR)* [French] A person engaged in FLÂNERIE. ⟨Time
and again we find him in small rooms, a catatonic *flâneur,* short
of cash and poorly washed.⟩—*The Guardian,* May 8, 1999.

flic *(fleek)* [French] In French slang: a cop; a police officer.

floe *(floh)* [Norwegian: layer] A large, relatively level sheet of float-
ing ice, usually on the surface of the sea, or a detached section
of such a sheet.

flokati *(floh-KAH-tee)* [Modern Greek] A heavy woollen rug, once
handmade in Greece, with a long, shaggy pile.

flotilla *(floh-TILL-ah)* [Spanish, from French] A fleet of small naval
vessels, or a naval unit of two or more squadrons. By extension,

a group of people or things moving together. 〈Cousteau revealed a *flotilla* of wondrous creatures to an audience that was instantly entranced.〉—*Time*, March 29, 1999.

flügelhorn, fluegelhorn *(FLOO-gl-horn)* [German] A brass instrument similar to the trumpet, with the same range but a less brilliant tone that sounds best in its lower register.

foie gras *(fwah GRAH)* [French: fat liver] Liver from a specially fattened goose or duck, often rendered into PÂTÉ and considered a great delicacy.

folie à deux *(foh-LEE ah DEU)* [French] In psychiatry, a form of psychosis in which two people who are intimately associated come to share the same delusions.

fonda *(FON-dah)* [Spanish] An inn or restaurant.

force majeure *(forss mah-ZHEUR)* [French] An irresistible, superior force; an event over which one has no control or for which one is not responsible. In the law, an unforeseen and disruptive occurrence that may serve to release a party from a contract. 〈Miss Graham was a *force majeure* in the world of modern dance.〉

formaggio *(for-MAHJ-yoh)* [Italian] Cheese.

forte *(FOR-tay)* [French, from *fort:* strong] A person's particular skill, knack, or specialty; a strong point, as in "her real *forte* is musicology."

fou *(foo)* [French] Crazy; demented; foolish.

foulard *(foo-LAHR)* [French] A lightweight silk, cotton, or rayon fabric with a printed design, used for dresses, scarves, and neckties. Also a silk head scarf or necktie made from such fabric.

foyer *(fwah-YAY)* [French, from Latin: hearth] A public lobby in a hotel, apartment house, or theater; an entrance hall in a house or apartment; a vestibule. ⟨then walks through the *foyer,* knocking over a vase that smashes on the floor as he passes.⟩—*Time,* March 15, 1999.

fraises des bois *(frehz day BWAH)* [French] Wild strawberries.

framboise *(frahm-BWAHZ)* [French] Raspberry.

frappé, frappe *(frah-PAY)* [French: iced; struck] A fruit juice or PURÉE frozen to a mush; a liqueur or cordial poured over shaved ice. As an adjective: iced; frozen; chilled.

fräulein *(FROY-line)* [German] A young, unmarried woman. ⟨Steffi Graff . . . *Fräulein* Forehand had her best year⟩—*Time,* January 3, 1994.

fresco *(FREHS-koh)* [Italian: fresh] A painting executed on a wall or an exterior surface, usually on stucco or plaster, while it is still damp. See also ALFRESCO. ⟨it was evident that Opera Theater of St. Louis had adopted another approach to updating— more like the restoration of a famous *fresco.*⟩—*The St. Louis Post-Dispatch,* May 30, 1998.

fricassee, fricassée *(frih-kah-SEE)* [French] A dish of meat or chicken cut into small pieces and cooked in its own juice.

frijole *(free-HOH-le)* [Spanish] A dried bean, especially the kidney and pinto bean, used in Mexican and southwestern U.S. cooking.

frisson *(free-SONH)* [French: shudder] A shiver that may precede a fever. More generally, a sudden, small quiver of fear or emotional excitement; a thrill. ⟨You can see the pleasure in their small faces and sense the *frisson* the moment holds.⟩

frites *(freet)* [French] The informal short form of *pommes de terre frites:* French-fried potatoes.

frittata *(free-TAH-tah)* [Italian: fried] In Italian cooking, a large unfolded omelet containing vegetables, grated cheese, and seasonings.

froideur *(frwah-DEUR)* [French: coldness] An attitude of indifference, aloofness, lack of ardor, or cold superiority.

fromage *(froh-MAHZH)* [French] Cheese.

frottage *(froh-TAHZH)* [French: rubbing] In the visual arts, a technique of producing an impression of surface texture by holding a piece of paper on the surface and rubbing it with a crayon or soft pencil. A work produced by this technique. ⟨The artist used *frottage* in combination with pen and ink for some of the images.⟩

froufrou, frou-frou *(FROO-froo)* [French] Ruffles, frills, and other furbelows used to decorate women's clothing. Also, a soft rustling or swishing sound, as that made by a silk dress. Informally, fanciness; affected elegance. ⟨There is no more *frou-frou* spectacle in Paris than a Christian Lacroix haute couture show.⟩— *The Guardian,* January 20, 1999.

fugue *(fyoog)* [French, from Latin: flight] In music, a contrapuntal composition that begins with a theme stated in one part, then repeated in other parts and developed. In psychiatry, a form of amnesia during which a person assumes a new identity and, after recovery, has no memory of the episode.

führer, fuehrer *(FYOOR-er)* [German] Leader. Adolph Hitler was referred to as *Der Führer:* the leader.

fusillade *(FYOO-ze-lahd, fü-zee-AHD)* [French] A continuous or simultaneous firing of guns; a massive outburst or outpouring.

⟨Another day, another *fusillade* of TNT falls on Iraq.⟩—*Time,* March 8, 1999.

fusuma *(foo-soo-mah)* [Japanese] In a Japanese house, a sliding door that serves as a partition or a thin wall between rooms.

futbol *(FÜT-bohl)* [French slang, from English] Football, known in the United States as soccer. ⟨So what if *futbol* is the rest of the world's most popular game?⟩—*The New York Times,* November 23, 1997.

futon *(FOO-ton)* [Japanese, from Chinese] A traditional Japanese mattress, made of heavy cotton and stuffed with layers of batting, that can be folded and put away when not in use; usually placed on the floor for sleeping.

gabinetto *(gah-bee-NEH-toh)* [Italian] A cabinet or closet; by extension, a toilet.

gadje *(GAH-zhay)* [Romany] The Gypsy's word for any non-Gypsy. ⟨With that kind of sorrow-laden past, it is little wonder that these "quintessential strangers," as author Isabel Fonseca calls them, remain wary of all *gadje*.⟩—*Time,* November 20, 1995.

gaffe *(gahf)* [French] A social mistake; a blunder. See also FAUX PAS. ⟨Oddly enough, two surgical *gaffes* occurred during a routine procedure.⟩

gaga *(GAH-gah)* [French] A slang adjective meaning childish, silly, or nutty, often applied to older people in their dotage. To be *gaga* over something or someone is to be infatuated with or crazy about the object of attention. ⟨Everyone in California's capital, it seems, is *gaga* over the league's most entertaining team.⟩—*The New York Times*, May 16, 1999.

gagaku *(GAH-gah-koo)* [Japanese: music entertainment] The stately music of the Japanese court during the Middle Ages, characterized by a high-pitched drone and slowly changing clusters of tones, together with individual loud and soft drumbeats.

gaijin *(GYE-jin)* [Japanese] A foreigner; an outsider.

gala *(GAH-lah)* [French, from Italian] A occasion marked by festivity; a joyous celebration; a FETE.

galantine *(gah-lanh-TEEN)* [French] In French cooking, a cold dish consisting of boned, stuffed chicken or veal, poached and served in aspic or in its own jelly.

galimatias *(gah-lee-MAHT-yahs)* [French, from Greek] Meaningless talk; gibberish.

galleria *(gah-leh-REE-ah)* [Italian] An indoor mall; a court or passageway lined with shops.

gallimaufry *(gah-lee-MOH-free)* [French: a stew] A jumble; a hodgepodge. ⟨obliges dictionary editors to acknowledge such a *gallimaufry* of new words and phrases that even the most casual browser wants to cry havoc⟩—*Time*, July 8, 1996.

galosh (singular); **galoshes** (plural) *(gah-LAHSH, gah-LAH-shez)* [French, from Greek] A high, waterproof overshoe.

gamelan *(GAH-meh-lahn)* [Javanese] An Indonesian or Malaysian orchestra consisting of large and small gongs, bronze bars, wooden xylophones, drums, end-blown flutes, and a two-stringed violin. Traditionally, the *gamelan* plays for ceremonial occasions and for funerals.

gamin (m), **gamine** (f) *(gah-MENH, gah-MEEN)* [French] A child of the streets; a homeless child; a street urchin. As an adjective, *gamine* is used to describe a small, slender, impudent girl. ⟨It was an attempt to capture the *gamine* allure of Jean Seberg in "Breathless."⟩

ganef See GONIF.

garbanzo *(gahr-BAHN-zoh)* [Spanish] The chickpea.

garçon *(gahr-SONH)* [French] A waiter in a restaurant. A boy or youth.

garni *(gahr-NEE)* [French] Garnished; adorned; often used in reference to food.

garniture *(GAHR-nih-cher)* [French] Something that garnishes or serves as a decoration.

gasconade *(gahss-koh-NAHD)* [French: from Gascony, a former province in France] Boastful talk; bluster.

gasthaus *(GAHST-haus)* [German] A guesthouse; an inn or a tavern.

gastronome *(GAS-troh-nohm)* [French] A GOURMET; a CONNOISSEUR of fine food and wine.

gâteau *(gah-TOH)* [French] A cake. ⟨The *gâteau de riz* is what most Americans call rice pudding.⟩

gauche *(gohsh)* [French: the left (side)] Awkward; tactless; lacking social grace; clumsy; boorish. ⟨Modern design does not have to be brassy and *gauche*.⟩

gaucherie *(gohsh-REE)* [French] An awkward, crude, or tactless act; lack of sensitivity or tact in social matters.

gaucho *(GAU-choh)* [American Spanish] On the South American PAMPAS, a cowboy of mixed Indian and Spanish descent. In the fashion industry, *gauchos* are wide, calf-length trousers that resemble those worn by such cowboys. ⟨Long coats, wide lapels and (eek!) even *gauchos* are back⟩—*Time*, April 8, 1996.

gavotte *(gah-VOT)* [French, from Provençal] Originally a French peasant dance, later a popular court dance in the time of Marie Antoinette. In music, a piece based on the rhythm of the dance.

gazette *(gah-ZEHT)* [French, from Italian] A newspaper or official government journal; now used mainly in the titles of newspapers. ⟨This is the big media event of the year, a bit like the Press *Gazette* awards held in London, except the hacks north of the border don't get so drunk.⟩—*The Guardian*, May 5, 1999.

gazpacho *(gahs-PAH-choh)* [Spanish] A cold soup consisting of raw chopped tomatoes, cucumbers, onions, garlic, olive oil, and vinegar, sometimes with the addition of diced bread.

gefilte *(geh-FILL-teh)* [Yiddish] Stuffed. In Jewish cooking, *gefilte* fish is ground, boned fish mixed with MATZO meal and eggs, then shaped into balls and poached in broth.

geisha *(GAY-shah)* [Japanese, from Chinese: arts person] A Japanese woman, trained in the arts of music, dance, and conversation, who acts as a professional hostess and companion for men. ⟨he left office under criticism not for having a *geisha* mistress but for being chintzy in paying her.⟩—*The Atlantic Monthly*, January 1996.

geländesprung *(geh-LEN-deh-shprung)* [German] In skiing, a jump made from a crouching position, in which the ski poles are planted forward and used to propel the skier over an obstacle.

gemeinschaft *(geh-MINE-shahft)* [German: community] An association of people who share the same tastes and attitudes; a group notable for its sense of common identity and devotion to tradition. See also GESELLSCHAFT.

gemütlich *(geh-MÜT-likh)* [German] Pleasant and comfortable; cozy. Cordial; easygoing. 〈This old public house is renowned for its fine ale and *gemütlich* atmosphere.〉

gemütlichkeit *(geh-MÜT-likh-kite)* [German] Cordiality; amiability; coziness.

gendarme *(zhonh-DAHRM)* [French, from *gent d'armes:* men at arms] A police officer, especially in France, or an armed soldier with authority over civilians. 〈His chief of staff and six officers of a special unit of paramilitary *gendarmes* were detained pending an investigation.〉—*Time,* May 17, 1999.

gendarmerie *(zhonh-DAHR-meh-ree)* [French] A body of police officers or GENDARMES; the building housing such a group.

genie See JINN.

genre *(ZHANH-reu)* [French: genus; sort; kind] A category of artistic or literary works that have distinct form, content, or style, as the *genre* of film noir. Also used to describe a realistic style of painting that focuses on everyday life. 〈But if library exhibitions are to flourish as a *genre*〉—*The New York Review of Books,* March 4, 1999.

genro *(jehn-ROH)* [Japanese: senior statesman] A retired Japanese statesman who acted as an unofficial adviser to the emperor between 1875 and 1940; a group of such advisers.

gesellschaft *(geh-ZEHL-shahft)* [German: companionship] A company; a firm; an organized group. See also GEMEINSCHAFT.

gesso *(JEH-soh)* [Italian, from Latin] A ground or surface for painting, made by mixing gypsum or plaster of Paris and glue, sometimes also with pigment; also used in making BAS-RELIEFS. Any plasterlike mixture used to adapt a surface for painting or gilding.

gestalt *(geh-SHTAHLT)* [German: form] A functional synthesis or pattern of separate elements of experience or emotion; a unified whole that is more than the sum of its parts. In *Gestalt* psychology, the theory that a person's process of learning, perceiving, thinking, or acting is always a working from the whole to the parts, and is not a building of parts together to make a whole.

gesundheit *(geh-ZOONT-hite)* [German: good health] An interjection spoken to someone who has just sneezed.

get (singular)**; gittin** (plural) *(geht, GIH-tin)* [Hebrew] A Jewish bill of divorce, recognized by Conservative and Orthodox Jews as the only acceptable instrument for ending a marriage.

geta *(GEH-tah)* [Japanese] In Japan, a traditional wooden clog held on the foot by a thong between the first and second toes, and raised off the ground by two supports on the bottom of the sole.

gevalt *(geh-VAHLT)* [Yiddish] A noun and expletive that expresses fear or shocked amazement; a cry for help or a strong protest, sometimes preceded by "Oy!"

ghat *(gaht)* [Hindi, from Sanskrit] A wide stairway leading down an embankment to the edge of a river, used by bathers. Also, a mountain range or pass.

ghee *(ghee)* [Hindi] In India, a type of clarified butter made from buffalo's milk or cow's milk, used in cooking.

ghetto *(GEH-toh)* [Italian: foundry] Originally the name of an island (now an integrated part of Venice) where Jews were forced to live in the early 1500s; by extension, an area of any city to which Jews were restricted. Now, any section of a city inhabited mostly by an ethnic or minority group; a slum area where residents live as a result of economic or social discrimination. ⟨Life in the Warsaw *ghetto* is the subject of this painful and fascinating memoir.⟩

giaour *(zhya-OOR)* [Turkish, from Persian] A non-Muslim, especially a Christian; a nonbeliever.

gigolo *(JIG-oh-loh)* [French] A professional male dancing partner or escort. A single man who is supported by an older woman in return for his companionship and sexual favors; a kept man. ⟨The net result is that he looks like a retired US army colonel who's taken up being a *gigolo*.⟩—*The Guardian,* May 12, 1999.

gigue *(zheeg)* [French] A lively dance of the 1700s, often in rapid 6/8 or 12/8 time. Music based on the rhythm and spirit of the dance, with which some composers ended their suites of dances. The word comes from the old word for fiddle, *gigot,* so called because it looked like a leg of lamb.

glasnost *(GLAHS-nost)* [Russian] Candor; openness. A word that appeared in English during the late 1980s when Communist Party general secretary Mikhail Gorbachev encouraged freedom of the press and the elimination of censorship in the Soviet Union. ⟨Cuba may not be on the verge of tropical *glasnost,* but 40 years of isolation are drawing to a close in Havana.⟩—*Time,* May 11, 1998.

glissade *(glee-SAHD)* [French] A well-executed slide down a snowy or icy slope, on a sled or on skis. In ballet, a sliding step used as a connection to another step.

glissando *(glee-SAHN-doh)* [Italian: sliding] In music, the playing of rapid scales, up or down, with a sliding motion. On a piano, the player runs a finger across all the white or black keys. George Gershwin's *Rhapsody in Blue* (1924) begins with a solo *glissando* on a clarinet. ⟨It is full of stops and magic, an abrupt keening, here and there *glissando,* crazy syllogisms, rogue puns.⟩—*The New York Times,* August 11, 1977.

glitch *(glitsh)* [Yiddish, from German *glitschen:* to slip] Originally, to skid on a slippery surface. More recently, an annoying problem, snag, or malfunction in a plan or in a machine, especially a computer.

glockenspiel *(GLOK-n-shpeel)* [German, from *Glocke:* bell and *spielen:* to play] A portable musical instrument carried by a player in a marching band, with an array of tuned steel bars in a lyrelike frame, played with a steel rod; it has a bell-like sound.

gnocchi *(NYOK-kee)* [Italian: knuckles] In Italian cooking, small dumplings made of potatoes or flour, served with or without a sauce.

go *(goh)* [Japanese, from Chinese] A Japanese strategy game similar to chess, played by two people on a checkered board *(goban)* with 361 intersections; players attempt to conquer territory by surrounding vacant points with boundaries made of their own "stones" or pieces.

godown *(goh-DOWN)* [Malay] In India and some Asian countries, a storage place or warehouse.

golem *(GOH-lem)* [Yiddish, from Hebrew: an embryonic or incomplete substance] In Jewish folklore, an effigy of a human being brought to life by means of a charm or magic incantation; an automaton; a robot. Also, a blockhead; a clumsy person. ⟨Academic involvement in the discipline has multiplied, as have tangential pop artifacts like the best-selling Bible Code and an X-Files episode about a *golem,* the Jewish proto-Frankenstein monster.⟩—*Time,* November 24, 1997.

gondola *(GON-doh-lah)* [Venetian Italian] A long, narrow, flat-bottomed boat with high, pointed ends, designed for use on the canals of Venice, and poled or rowed by one man at the stern.

Also, an enclosed cabin attached under an airship or balloon, or one suspended from an overhead cable to transport skiers, etc., in Alpine areas. A railroad car built like a box with no top, to carry coal or other bulk products.

gondolier *(gon-doh-LEER)* [Italian] One who poles or rows a GONDOLA.

gonfalon *(GON-fah-lon)* [Italian] A banner or flag, often with tails or streamers, that hangs from a crossbar. ⟨The banner was a huge *gonfalon* that had covered the casket of Giovanni Randoccio.⟩—*The New York Review of Books,* March 4, 1999.

gonif, goniff *(GOH-nef)* [Yiddish] A thief, or a person who acts in the world of business or ideas as a petty thief; a swindler. Also written as *ganef.*

gospodin *(goss-puh-DYEEN)* [Russian] In Russia, a title of courtesy or respect equivalent to mister.

gouache *(gwahsh)* [French, from Italian *guazzo:* a place where there is water] In painting, the use of opaque watercolors mixed with gum, or the colors themselves. A painting done in such a medium. ⟨The work makes use of torn and pasted photographs, and draws upon *gouache,* acrylic, and ballpoint pen.⟩

goulash *(GOO-lahsh)* [Hungarian: herdsman's meat] A stew made with beef or veal, vegetables, sour cream, paprika, and sometimes sauerkraut; also called *Hungarian goulash.* By extension, a mixture of diverse elements; a hodgepodge.

gourmand *(goor-MANH)* [French: glutton] A person who loves to eat, especially one who eats carelessly or to excess. Not to be confused with GOURMET.

gourmandise *(goor-manh-DEEZ)* [French] The unbridled enjoyment of food and drink. ⟨The variety of dessert offerings allowed us to extend our *gourmandise* to unreasonable lengths.⟩

gourmet *(goor-MAY)* [French] A CONNOISSEUR of good food and drink; an EPICURE; a GASTRONOME. As an adjective: characteristic of fine cooking or high-quality ingredients. ⟨Already this *gourmet* prod to the marketplace has helped revive such delicacies as Bagoss cheese.⟩—*Time*, May 17, 1999.

goy (singular); **goyim** (plural) [Yiddish, from Hebrew] An often contemptuous word for a non-Jewish person; a Gentile. ⟨Of course, the 18th-century *goyim* wouldn't know from the nudnik moms Philip Roth has come up with.⟩—*The New York Times*, May 11, 1997.

graffiti (plural); **graffito** (singular) *(grah-FEE-tee, grah-FEE-toh)* [Italian: incised design] A variety of markings (such as drawings, slogans, initials, etc.) scratched, written, or spray-painted on a wall, a sidewalk, or a rock. ⟨there is a high brick wall covered in *graffiti*.⟩—*The Guardian*, May 19, 1999.

Grand Cru *(granh KRÜ)* [French: great growth] In France, a classification given by the government to a vineyard producing high-quality wine.

grande dame *(granh DAHM)* [French] A great lady; a dignified and aristocratic older woman, or one who has achieved eminence in a specific field of endeavor. ⟨For a decade she was the reigning *grande dame* of Wagnerian opera.⟩

grand mal *(granh MAHL)* [French: great ailment] Severe epileptic seizure. See also PETIT MAL.

granita *(grah-nee-TAH)* [Italian: grainy] In Italy, a form of sherbet left unbeaten during the freezing process, which has the grainy consistency of slush.

gratiné *(grah-tee-NAY)* [French] Food prepared AU GRATIN.

gratis *(GRAH-tiss)* [Latin] Free of charge; at no cost. ⟨The band was asked to play *gratis* for the benefit of local charities.⟩

gravamen (singular)**; gravamina** (plural) *(GRAH-vah-men, grah-vah-MIH-nah)* [Latin, from *gravis:* heavy] A complaint; a grievance. The main substance of an accusation or charge. ⟨From Hamilton's commentary upon the insufficiencies of Adams's character, we can grasp the *gravamen* that engendered the hostility of the Adams family.⟩—*The New Criterion,* May 1999.

gravitas *(GRAH-vee-tahs)* [Latin] Weight; weightiness; importance; consequence. Dignity or seriousness of character. ⟨For a full thirty minutes they sustained the illusion of *gravitas* once prized by Cicero and Cato the Elder.⟩—*Harper's Magazine,* March 1999.

gravlax *(GRAHV-laks)* [Swedish, Norwegian] A Scandinavian dish of raw, boned salmon cured with salt, pepper, sugar, and dill, and served with a dill and mustard dressing.

grazioso *(graht-see-OH-zoh)* [Italian] In music, an indication that the passage is to be played in a graceful and flowing manner.

grenadine *(GREH-nah-deen)* [French] A syrup made from pomegranate or red currant juice.

grillade *(gree-YAHD)* [French] Something grilled; a serving or dish of grilled or broiled meat.

grillé *(gree-YAY)* [French] Broiled; cooked on a grill.

gringo *(GRING-goh)* [Spanish, from Greek: gibberish] In Latin America, a disparaging term for an American or other English-speaking person; a foreigner. See also HAOLE.

griot *(gree-OH)* [French] In West Africa, a person who keeps an oral history of a particular tribe or group; one who entertains with storytelling, songs, and dances.

grisaille *(gree-ZYE)* [French] A style of painting executed in different tones of gray. A work of art in this style; a monochromatic work. ⟨His thin figures and small *grisaille* portraits are prized by collectors.⟩

gris-gris, grigri *(GREE-gree)* [West African French?] An African charm, fetish, or talisman.

grosgrain *(GROH-grayn)* [French: coarse grain] A heavy, horizontally corded silk or rayon fabric or ribbon.

guacamole *(gwah-kah-MOH-leh)* [Mexican Spanish: avocado sauce] In Mexican cooking, a dip or filling made from avocado mashed with onion, tomato, lemon juice, and various seasonings.

guano *(GWAH-noh)* [Spanish: fertilizer] The accumulated dung of sea birds, harvested from rocks and islands near the Peruvian coast and used for fertilizer; any similar substance used to enrich the soil. ⟨Fresh snow is made on site, air and poolwater are scrupulously filtered, *guano* is hosed away twice daily.⟩— *Time,* May 4, 1998.

guayabera *(gwah-yah-BEH-rah)* [Spanish] A tropical pleated jacket or sport shirt with large front pockets, originally from Cuba.

gueridon *(geh-ree-DONH)* [French] A small, round table or stand with one central foot or support.

guerrilla *(geh-RILL-ah, geh-REE-yah)* [Spanish] One of a mobile band of irregular soldiers that fights or harasses the enemy with hit-and-run tactics, surprise attacks, SABOTAGE, etc. Pertaining to such fighters and their activities, as in *"guerrilla* warfare." ⟨Most of the prisoners were members of the Kosovo Liberation Army (KLA) *guerrilla* force.⟩—*The Guardian, May 21, 1999.*

guillotine *(GHEE-oh-teen)* [French] An instrument of capital punishment introduced in France in 1792 and used to excess during the French Revolution: a heavy blade that drops down between two vertical posts and beheads the victim. A similar device for trimming stacks of paper, etc.

gulag *(GOO-lahg)* [Russian acronym] The network of forced-labor camps in the former Soviet Union; by extension, any prison or camp for political prisoners. The word became known in English with the publication of Alexander Solzhenitsyn's account of prison life in *The Gulag Archipelago* in 1974. ⟨It is extremely easy to condemn *gulags*⟩—*The New York Times,* November 30, 1980.

gumbo *(GUM-boh)* [Louisiana French: okra] A thick soup or stew made with seafood or chicken, okra, vegetables, and powdered sassafras leaves (FILÉ). Also *Gumbo:* a PATOIS spoken in parts of Louisiana and the French West Indies.

gung ho *(gung-hoh)* [Chinese motto: work together] A slogan used by some U.S. Marines in World War II. Informally, as an adjective: enthusiastic; eager; zealous; impassioned.

guru *(GOO-roo)* [Hindi, from Sanskrit: venerable] A Hindu spiritual teacher or guide, or the leader of a religious sect. A personal counselor or mentor. ⟨Budapest-born *guru* of progressive graphic design⟩—*Time,* May 17, 1999.

gutta-percha *(GUT-tah-PER-chah)* [Malay] The whitish gum produced by certain Malaysian trees and used as temporary dental cement and as an electrical insulating material.

habanera *(hah-bahn-YEH-rah)* [Spanish: (dance) of Havana] A stately Cuban country dance, an ancestor of the Argentine tango; the music for the dance.

habeas corpus *(HAY-bee-us KOR-pus)* [Latin: you must have the body] A writ requiring a person who has been detained or imprisoned to be brought to court or before a judge, to establish the legality of the detention. ⟨further restrictions on federal *habeas corpus* appeals; and a prison-construction bill that would steer federal aid to states with tough sentencing laws⟩—*Time*, February 20, 1994.

habitué *(hah-BIH-choo-ay, hah-bee-tü-AY)* [French] One who inhabits a specific place or visits there frequently. ⟨This neighborhood pub owes its survival to a group of loyal *habitués.*⟩

hacienda *(hah-see-EHN-dah)* [Spanish, from Latin] In Latin America, a large estate, or the main house on such an estate. A large farm, ranch, mine, or manufacturing establishment in the country.

hackmatack *(HAK-mah-tak)* [Western Abenaki] The tamarack tree, a larch of the pine family.

hai *(hye)* [Japanese] Yes.

haiku *(hye-koo)* [Japanese] A highly refined Japanese verse form written in three lines of 5, 7, and 5 syllables respectively, in which the poet can use allusions that evoke a strong, though unspoken, emotional response. Once limited to descriptions of nature and the seasons, its range of subjects has broadened. ⟨Because *haiku* almost always involves nature, Heaney sought to incorporate that element into his poems.⟩—*The New York Times*, November 12, 1998.

hajj, hadj *(hahj)* [Arabic] The pilgrimage to Mecca, spiritual center of Islam, that every adult Muslim is required to make at least once in his or her lifetime.

hakim *(hah-KEEM)* [Arabic] A wise man; a man of learning; a physician.

halutz, chalutz (singular); **halutzim, chalutzim** (plural) *(khah-LOOTS, khah-loot-SEEM)* [Modern Hebrew: pioneer] A pioneer Jewish farmer in Israel; a person who settles in Israel to work in construction, such as clearing the land or developing some part of the country.

halvah *(HAHL-vah)* [Yiddish, from Turkish and Arabic] A sweet dessert or confection of Turkish origin, made with crushed almonds or sesame seeds and honey.

hamantasch, hamantash *(HAH-man-tahsh)* [Yiddish] A Jewish pastry, shaped like a triangular pocket, filled with poppy seeds, nuts, raisins, and honey, or with prune paste, eaten at the feast of Purim.

hametz, chametz *(khah-MEHTS)* [Hebrew: that which is leavened] Any food that contains yeast or another leavening agent, forbidden to Jews during the festival of Passover; the dishes and utensils used in preparing and serving such foods.

haole *(HAH-oh-leh)* [Hawaiian: white person; foreigner] Among the Hawaiians of Polynesian ancestry, a Caucasian or white-skinned person; the Hawaiian equivalent of GRINGO.

hara-kiri *(hah-rah-KEE-ree)* [Japanese: belly out] Ceremonial suicide by slashing across the abdomen with a dagger; disembowelment, once practiced by Japanese army officers facing dishonor or a sentence of death. Also called *seppuku*.

harem *(HAH-rem)* [Arabic: forbidden] The women in a Muslim household, including family members, concubines, and servants, or the part of the house in which the women reside. Facetiously, a group of women associated with or sharing a household with one man. ⟨There were a few young men to tote heavy equipment, and an unofficial *harem* of female groupies.⟩

haricot vert *(ah-ree-koh VEHR)* [French] A green bean.

hasenpfeffer *(HAH-sen-feh-fer)* [German: rabbit (and) pepper] A highly seasoned stew of marinated rabbit, with sour cream added toward the end of cooking.

hashish *(HASH-eesh, hah-SHEESH)* [Arabic] A narcotic and intoxicant made from the tops and leaves of Indian hemp, or from the sap exuded by the tops, that can be smoked or chewed.

hasta la vista *(HAH-stah lah VEE-stah)* [Spanish] Until I see you; until we meet; good-bye. 〈Goodbye, Washington. So long, New York. *Hasta la vista,* Atlanta.〉—*The New York Times,* March 5, 1998.

hasta luego *(HAH-stah LWEH-goh)* [Spanish] See you later; good-bye.

hatha yoga *(HAH-thah YOH-gah)* [Sanskrit] In YOGA, a system of breathing exercises and sitting postures used for therapeutic purposes and to control the body.

hausfrau *(HAUSS-frau)* [German] A housewife. 〈Her husband felt she had neglected her duties as a *hausfrau* in favor of a career in journalism.〉

haute *(oht)* [French] High-class; fancy. Elevated; upper.

haute couture *(oht koo-TÜR)* [French] High fashion; the most fashionable and trendsetting among designers and dressmakers. Leading dressmakers collectively, or their products. 〈The quality of these fabrics, albeit homespun, is worthy of a *haute couture* house.〉

haute cuisine *(oht kwee-ZEEN)* [French] The art of preparing fine food; gourmet cooking.

hauteur *(oh-TEUR)* [French] Haughtiness; arrogance.

haut monde *(oh MOHND)* [French] High society; the well-to-do and well-connected. 〈All in all, it's a shameless tearjerker with *haut monde* aspirations.〉—*Time,* March 8, 1999.

hazan, hazzan *(khah-ZAHN)* [Hebrew] The cantor of a synagogue. Also written as *chazan*.

hegira, hejira *(HEH-jih-rah)* [Latin, from Arabic *hijra*: flight; departure] Any journey taken to escape danger or to seek a more desirable place. When capitalized: the flight of Muhammad from Mecca in A.D. 622, seen as the beginning of the Muslim era. Also written *hijra*. 〈Expect to see Republicans and Democrats making *hegiras* to Houston.〉—*Time,* August 12, 1996.

hibachi *(hih-BAH-chee)* [Japanese, from Chinese] A Japanese-style brazier, covered with a grill, that holds burning charcoal for outdoor cooking or heating.

hibakusha *(hee-bah-KOO-shah)* [Japanese: bombed] A person who survived the atomic bomb attacks in 1945 on the cities of Hiroshima and Nagasaki.

hidalgo *(hee-DAHL-goh)* [Spanish] In Spain, a man of the lesser nobility. In Latin America, a man of property, or one held in high esteem.

high-muck-a-muck See MUCK-A-MUCK.

hinterland *(HIN-ter-land)* [German: land behind] The backcountry; the less-developed or remote areas of a country that are far from urban centers. Also, an inland region lying just behind a coastal area.

hogan *(HOH-gan)* [Navajo: house; home] Among the Navajo people, a circular lodge made of branches and rough timbers covered with earth or sod.

hoi polloi *(HOY pol-LOY)* [Greek: the people] Ordinary people; the masses; the lower classes; riffraff. 〈In their elegant box suites, the privileged could distance themselves from the convention *hoi polloi.*〉

holocaust *(HOH-loh-kawst)* [Latin, from Greek: wholly burnt] Destruction, or a total devastation and loss of life, particularly by fire. Also, a burnt sacrificial offering. The slaughter of the Jews during World War II is referred to as "the *Holocaust.*" ⟨Knowing that the novel's characters are living on the edge of a *holocaust*⟩—*The New York Review of Books,* March 4, 1999.

homme d'affaires *(uhm dah-FAIR)* [French] A businessman.

homme du monde *(uhm dü MOHND)* [French] A man of the world; a man of wide experience and sophistication. See also FEMME DU MONDE.

Homo sapiens *(HOH-moh SAYP-yens)* [Latin: rational man] Modern man considered as a species; humankind. ⟨The continuity theory posits that some interbreeding occurred between Neanderthals and modern *Homo sapiens,* meaning that some Neanderthal genes survive in Europeans.⟩—*The New York Times,* December 1, 1998.

honcho *(HON-choh)* [Japanese, from Chinese] In slang, a chief, boss, or assertive leader. ⟨Movie-studio *honchos* . . . went mum last week when asked to comment on any connection between violent movies and violent teen behavior.⟩—*Time,* May 3, 1999.

hooch *(hootsh)* [Tlingit: a shortening of the Alaskan place-name *Hoochinoo*] In slang, any alcoholic liquor, especially cheap whiskey. Also, liquor produced and distributed illicitly; bootleg liquor. ⟨Someone on Wall Street must have tipped off Emma Lathen that the liquor industry would soon be advertising its *hooch* on television.⟩—*The New York Times,* December 8, 1996.

hookah *(HOOK-ah)* [Arabic] A tobacco pipe of the Near East with a long, flexible tube, in which the smoke cools by passing through a vessel of water. Also called *narghile, hubble-bubble.*

hoosegow *(HOOSS-gow)* [Mexican Spanish, from *jusgado:* tribunal] In slang, a jail or prison.

hors concours *(ohr konh-KOOR)* [French: out of the competition] Indicating one who is not competing or is unqualified to compete for prizes in an exhibit or contest. Pertaining to a work submitted by such a person to a competition.

hors de combat *(ohr deu kom-BAH)* [French] Out of the fight; out of action; disabled. ⟨With Alec Stewart absent and Nadeem Shahid *hors de combat,* Surrey approached their target.⟩—*The Guardian,* May 1, 1999.

hors d'oeuvre *(ohr DEU-vreu)* [French: outside the main course] An appetizer; any of various foods served before the meal to stimulate the appetite.

hosanna, hosannah *(hoh-ZAHN-nah)* [Hebrew] Praised be the Lord. A joyous exclamation of adoration or praise; an acclamation.

howdah *(HOW-dah)* [Hindi, from Arabic] A small platform or a seat for riders on an elephant or camel, often having a canopy for protection from the sun.

huarache *(wah-RAH-cheh)* [Mexican Spanish] A Mexican sandal with the upper side made of thin, woven strips of leather.

hubris *(HYOO-briss, HOO-briss)* [Greek] Overbearing pride, wanton arrogance, or excessive self-confidence. ⟨In these street gangs, flunkies engage more in *hubris* than in heroism.⟩

hula, hula-hula *(HOO-lah, HOO-lah-HOO-lah)* [Hawaiian] A native Hawaiian dance performed with rapid hip swaying and graceful, sinuous movements of the arms and hands that tell a story in pantomime.

hummus *(HOO-mus)* [Arabic: chickpea] In Middle Eastern cooking, a dip or paste made from crushed chickpeas, garlic, lemon juice, and TAHINI.

hussar *(huh-ZAHR)* [Hungarian, from Serbo-Croatian: brigand] In the 15th century, one belonging to the Hungarian light cavalry. A member of a similar regiment in some European armies, often with an elaborate and colorful dress uniform.

hypocaust *(HYE-poh-kawst)* [Latin, from Greek] In ancient Rome, a space or channel, under the floor or in the wall, in which heated air was received and distributed through a central heating system. In the summer palace of Herod the Great (d. 4 B.C.) on Masada, an excavated area under the baths where slaves kept fires hot to create a steamy atmosphere.

ibada *(ih-BAH-dah)* [Arabic: act of worship] A Muslim religious obligation, as the five daily prayers, the recital of the creed, the feast of Ramadan, the pilgrimage to Mecca, etc.

ibidem *(IH-bih-dem)* [Latin: in the aforementioned place] In the same work, chapter, page, etc., just mentioned. Abbreviated *ibid.*

idée fixe *(ee-day FEEX)* [French: fixed idea] A dominant thought or notion; an obsessing idea, sometimes delusional, that may be a symptom of psychosis.

idem *(IH-dem)* [Latin] The same; as previously mentioned. Abbreviated *id.*

id est *(ihd est)* [Latin] That is; that is to say. Abbreviated *i.e.*

idiot savant *(eed-YOH sah-VANH)* [French: learned idiot] In psychiatry, a mentally deficient person with extraordinary skill or ability in a special field, such as musical performance or mathematics. ⟨The film stars Tom Hanks as the engaging *idiot savant* from Alabama.⟩

igloo *(IG-loo)* [Inuit: house] A dome-shaped Eskimo dwelling built of blocks of hardened snow, or any structure with a similar shape. ⟨the missing tarpaulin in soggy Miami after the 1982 season and the plastic *igloo* on the Raiders' bench at frigid Shea Stadium in 1968⟩—*The New York Times,* January 13, 1999.

ikat *(EE-kaht)* [Malay] Silk fabrics, handmade by an ancient method that involves repeated binding and dyeing of the threads before they are woven. *Ikat* refers both to the process and the fabric itself. ⟨*Ikat* fabrics from silk-route cities such as Bukhara and Samarkand . . . were made by skilled artisans.⟩—*The Baltimore Sun,* April 9, 1999.

ikebana *(ih-keh-BAH-nah)* [Japanese] The Japanese art of flower arranging.

imam *(IH-mahm)* [Arabic: leader; guide] In Islam, a priest who officiates at a mosque. Also, a title given to various Muslim religious leaders. ⟨the success that Iranian cinema had when it emerged from the shadow of the *imams* and into the glare of the world screen⟩—*Time,* March 15, 1999.

imaret *(IM-ah-reht)* [Turkish, from Arabic] In Turkey, an inn or lodging for travelers.

imbroglio *(im-BROHL-yoh)* [Italian: from *imbrogliare:* to embroil] A confused or difficult situation, usually involving differences of opinion between individuals or nations; a misunderstanding with complex and bitter overtones. In music, an *imbroglio* is an intentional mixing of different themes intended to excite confusion. ⟨That chapter is expected to clarify the ties between China and some of the figures at the center of the campaign finance *imbroglio.*⟩—*The New York Times,* February 8, 1998.

impasse *(IHM-pass, am-PAHSS)* [French] A situation in which no further progress is possible, or one from which there is no escape; a deadlock, stalemate, or dead end. See also CUL-DE-SAC. ⟨They had reached an *impasse* in the negotiations and a strike seemed imminent.⟩

impasto *(im-PAHS-toh)* [Italian] In painting, a technique in which pigment is applied thickly on a surface; the paint or pigment so used. Also, enamel or a clay solution used to form a decorative low relief on a ceramic piece.

impedimenta *(im-peh-dih-MEN-tah)* [Latin: baggage] The baggage or supplies carried by an army. The encumbrances or burdens that slow one's progress; drawbacks.

impresario *(ihm-preh-SAHR-yoh)* [Italian, from *empresa*: enterprise] A person who manages, organizes, or sponsors public performances in the form of concerts, operas, ballets, etc. ⟨Sol Hurok rose from modest beginnings to become the most famous *impresario* of his time.⟩

imprimatur *(ihm-pree-MAH-toor)* [Latin: let it be printed] An official approval or license to publish a work, especially one given by a board of censors or by the Roman Catholic Church. A sanction, authorization, or approval. ⟨before the decision was given the full municipal *imprimatur*⟩—*The Guardian*, May 5, 1999.

impromptu *(im-PROMP-too)* [French, from Latin: in readiness] Improvised; done or made on the spur of the moment; extemporaneous. Anything produced with little or no previous preparation. In music, a name given to some 19th-century compositions by Schubert, Chopin, and others; a title that suggests brevity or casualness.

in absentia *(in ahb-SENT-yah)* [Latin] In absence (of the person).

inamorata *(in-ah-moh-RAH-tah)* [Italian] A woman who is loved or in love; a female lover or sweetheart.

incognito *(in-kog-NEE-toh, ihn-KOG-nee-toh)* [Italian, from Latin: unknown] With one's identity unknown or concealed; under an assumed name to avoid recognition; in disguise. ⟨Hoping to remain *incognito,* he sported sunglasses and a ridiculous false moustache.⟩

incubus *(IN-kyoo-bus)* [Latin] A male evil spirit said to have sexual congress with women in their sleep, or one who troubles people while they sleep; a nightmare. Anything that oppresses or disturbs like a nightmare. See also SUCCUBUS.

incunabula (plural); **incunabulum** (singular) *(in-kyoo-NAHB-yoo-lah, in-kyoo-NAHB-yoo-lum)* [Latin: cradle; earliest home] Specimens of books produced before 1501, in the earliest stages of European printing from movable type; the products of famous printers, such as Gutenberg and Jenson, that show the development of typography in its formative period. The beginnings; the first traces of development.

in esse *(in EHS-seh)* [Latin] In being; in actual existence.

in extremis *(in eks-TREH-miss)* [Latin] In extremity; at the point of death. ⟨For all its descriptions of famous people *in extremis,* the book is oddly humorous.⟩

infidel *(IN-fih-del)* [Latin: faithless; treacherous] One who rejects all religious belief or that of a particular faith, such as Christianity or Islam; an unbeliever.

in flagrante delicto See FLAGRANTE DELICTO.

infra dig *(IN-frah DIG)* [Latin: a shortened form of *infra dignitatem*] Beneath one's dignity. ⟨So even if the Great Analyzer would have found a laying on of hands *infra dig,* he could at least have prescribed the new home remedy and found out if it worked.⟩—*The New York Times,* April 18, 1999.

in loco parentis *(in LOH-koh pah-REHN-tiss)* [Latin] In place of a parent; in the role of a parent.

innig *(IN-nikh)* [German: intimate] Tender; heartfelt; fervent.

innuendo *(in-yoo-EN-doh)* [Latin] A subtly unpleasant insinuation; a suggestion, usually derogatory; an aspersion; a sly or indirect comment that casts doubt upon the worth of someone or something. ⟨homophobic rhetoric and *innuendo* is the last refuge of the American bigot⟩—*The Atlantic Monthly,* October 1998.

in re *(ihn REH)* [Latin: in the thing] In the matter of; concerning.

in rem *(ihn REHM)* [Latin: against (the) thing] In law, against the property, rather than against a person; not directed at any particular person.

inshallah *(in-SHAH-lah)* [Arabic] If God is willing.

in situ *(ihn SEE-too)* [Latin: in place] In the original, natural, or present site or position; undisturbed. ⟨The discovery of an entire skeleton *in situ* was of great interest to paleontologists.⟩

insouciance *(ihn-SOO-see-ens, enh-soo-see-ANHSS)* [French: freedom from worry] The quality of being carefree, lighthearted, or jaunty. ⟨She was able to hide her distress behind a FACADE of *insouciance.*⟩

intaglio *(ihn-TAHL-yoh)* [Italian, from Latin] Incised carving, as opposed to carving in relief; a design sunk below the surface of a gem, seal, or plate; a figure, design, or impression made by this method; an engraving. Signet rings and seals are usually made with *intaglio* designs that leave an impression when pressed upon wax.

intelligentsia *(ihn-teh-lih-JENT-see-ah)* [Russian, from Latin] Intellectuals or educated people considered as a class or as an elite group, especially those who are well informed and open to new ideas.

inter alia *(ihn-ter AHL-yah)* [Latin] Among other things.

internecine *(ihn-ter-NEH-sin)* [Latin] Pertaining to a struggle within a group or nation; in a conflict, destructive to both sides. Deadly; involving great loss of life. ⟨*Internecine* BBC politics are of obsessive fascination to all who work there, but not to anyone else.⟩—*The Guardian,* May 19, 1999.

interregnum *(ihn-tehr-REG-num)* [Latin: between reign(s)] A period of time between the rule of two successive sovereigns, or a period in which a state is governed by a temporary ruler. By extension, any break or interruption in the continuity of government or management.

intifada *(ihn-tee-FAH-dah)* [Arabic] A rebellion; a planned and coordinated uprising. The *intifada* began in Israel in December 1987, led by Palestinians angered by the Israeli military administration's "iron fist" policy in the occupied West Bank and Gaza territories. ⟨They were a routine part of many days during the *intifada.*⟩—*The New York Times,* June 4, 1999.

intime *(enh-TEEM)* [French] Intimate; cozy; private.

in toto *(ihn TOH-toh)* [Latin] In the whole; completely; altogether; entirely.

in utero *(ihn YOO-teh-roh)* [Latin] In the uterus; before birth.

in vino veritas *(ihn VEE-noh VEH-rih-tahss)* [Latin] In wine there is truth.

in vitro *(ihn VEE-troh)* [Latin: in glass] Describing a biological process made to take place in a laboratory vessel, such as a petri dish, rather than in a living organism or a natural location. ⟨With *in vitro* fertilization, sperm and egg are combined in a laboratory and then implanted as embryos.⟩

iota *(eye-OH-tah)* [Latin, from Greek] A very small amount; an insignificant quantity. Also, the ninth letter of the Greek alphabet.

ipse dixit *(IP-seh DIK-sit)* [Latin] He himself said it; an unverified or dogmatic assumption.

ipso facto *(IP-soh FAK-toh)* [Latin] By the fact itself; by the very nature of the act. ⟨Those who dissent on this matter have, *ipso facto,* set themselves apart from the community.⟩

Islam *(IZ-lahm, iss-LAHM)* [Arabic: submission (to God)] The religion of the Muslims, based on the words of the prophet Muhammad and the teachings of the Koran. Also, Muslim believers collectively; the countries in which Islam is the prevailing religion.

Issei *(EE-say)* [Japanese: first generation] A Japanese immigrant, especially one who came to the United States after March 14, 1907, the date of a presidential proclamation excluding Japanese laborers from the continental United States, and was not eligible for citizenship until 1952. See also KIBEI, NISEI, SANSEI.

Jacquard *(zhah-KAHR)* [French, after the inventor J. M. Jacquard] A fabric with a complex woven pattern, such as brocade or damask, produced on a *Jacquard* loom. Exhibited in Paris in 1801, the loom was the first mechanical device to weave in patterns.

Jahrzeit *(YAHR-zite)* [German] A year; the period of one year. See also YAHRZEIT.

jai alai *(HYE ah-lye)* [Spanish, from Basque] A game similar to handball, in which the players manipulate a ball with a long, curved wicker basket (CESTA) strapped to the arm.

jalapeño *(hah-lah-PEHN-yoh)* [Mexican Spanish] A small, hot, green or orange pepper used in Mexican cookery.

jalousie *(JAH-loo-see)* [French, from Italian: jealousy] A venetian blind; a shutter or screen with overlapping horizontal opaque or transparent slats that can be tilted to keep out rain and sun while letting in air and light.

jambalaya *(jum-bah-LYE-yah)* [Louisiana French, from Provençal] A Creole or Cajun stew made with some form of cured pork, chicken, shrimp, vegetables, rice, and seasonings.

janissary, janizary *(JAN-ih-seh-ree)* [French, from Turkish *yeniçeri*: new soldiery] A member of the elite Turkish troops organized in the 14th century and later suppressed. One of a group of loyal supporters, guards, or close aides.

jardiniere *(zhahr-deen-YAIR)* [French: a (woman) gardener] A pot, stand, or planter for holding flowers or plants.

jefe *(HEH-fay)* [Spanish] Chief; leader; boss. ⟨Addressing Ms. Robles as "el *jefe* grande," he praised her leadership in well-accented Spanish.⟩—*The New York Times,* July 2, 1998.

jejune *(jeh-JOON)* [Latin: fasting] Without sufficient nutritive value. Meager, empty, dull, pointless, or devoid of interest; unsatisfying to the soul or mind; childish, uninformed, or unaware. ⟨She doesn't make the *jejune* mistake of eating in front of the camera.⟩—*The Guardian,* May 22, 1999.

je ne sais quoi *(zheu neu say KWAH)* [French: I don't know what] An elusive, indefinable quality, especially one that is attractive. ⟨The atmosphere of the place has a certain *je ne sais quoi* that makes it appealing to chamber music groups.⟩

jeu de mots *(zheu deu MOH)* [French] A play on words; a pun.

jeunesse dorée *(zheu-NEHSS doh-RAY)* [French: gilded youth] Originally, the groups of wealthy and elegant youths who protested against the excesses of the Reign of Terror in France in 1793–1794. More recently, any young people possessed of wealth, elegance, and sophistication.

jicama *(hee-KAH-mah)* [Mexican Spanish] A tropical, white-fleshed root vegetable with a mild flavor, often used raw in salads.

jihad *(jee-HAHD)* [Arabic: struggle; conflict] A Muslim holy war, waged against enemies of the faith and considered a sacred obligation by followers of Islam. During the period of confrontation between Iraq and the West, several Muslim clerics urged a *jihad* against the United States. ⟨This group didn't have a purpose except to carry out the *jihad*.⟩—*The New York Times,* April 13, 1999.

jinni, jinn (singular); **jinn, jinns** (plural) *(JIH-nee, jin, jins)* [Arabic: demon] In Islamic mythology, a supernatural spirit able to assume animal or human form, said to be responsible for many of the ills that befall humans. With the appropriate magic, a *jinni* can be exploited by people. Transliterated as *genie.* Also written as *djinni, djinn, djin, jin.*

jodhpurs *(JOD-poors)* [After the former name of the state of Rajasthan, in northwestern India] Riding breeches that fit closely between the knee and the ankle, and loosely above the knee, a style adopted by military officers during the British occupation of India in the 19th century. ⟨He loved to ride, and was often seen about the White House in riding boots and *jodhpurs*.⟩

joie de vivre *(zhwah deu VEE-vreu)* [French: joy of living] A feeling of delight in being alive; intense enjoyment of life. ⟨In spite of the seriousness of the interview, her *joi de vivre* was evident in every response.⟩

jota *(HOH-tah)* [Spanish] A lively Spanish folk dance in triple time, accompanied by CASTANETS; the music for this dance.

judo *(JOO-doh)* [Japanese, from Chinese: gentle way] A method of weaponless combat based on JUJITSU, designed to overpower an opponent without inflicting serious harm. The sport of *judo* forbids the use of dangerous moves and requires great courtesy in practice. ⟨Now Mishima has made himself a tough, virile type through the force of his own will, while all of us who were on the *judo* team at school are becoming flabby and middle-aged.⟩—*The New York Times,* August 2, 1970.

jujitsu, jiujitsu *(joo-JIT-soo)* [Japanese, from Chinese: soft technique] A system of hand-to-hand combat that developed in the 1500s, involving methods of kicking, hitting, throwing, etc., calculated to turn an opponent's weight and strength against him. JUDO, KARATE, and AIKIDO are based partly on principles of *jujitsu.* See also TAE KWON DO.

juju *(JOO-joo)* [Hausa] Among the tribal peoples of West Africa, an object believed to have magical powers; a fetish or amulet. The power ascribed to such an object; a TABOO effected by it, or the rituals that accompany its use.

junta *(HOON-tah)* [Spanish, from Latin: meeting] A council; a small group of people or officials (not elected) who assume leadership of a nation, especially in the aftermath of a COUP D'ÉTAT or revolution. ⟨The new military *junta* won the support of the civilian opposition.⟩

juste-milieu *(zhüst meel-YEU)* [French] The exact middle; the happy medium; the golden mean.

juvenilia *(joo-veh-NEE-lyah)* [Latin] Those works of art or literature produced during an artist's youth. Also, art or literature created for or considered appropriate for young people. ⟨I told him I was writing something about Auden's *juvenilia.*⟩—*The New Criterion,* May 1999.

kabloona *(kah-BLOO-nah)* [Inuit] Among the Eskimo peoples, a Caucasian; a white person. See also GRINGO, HAOLE.

kabob *(keh-BOB)* [Arabic, Hindi] Usually plural: small chunks of meat on a skewer, broiled or roasted. See also SHISH KEBAB.

kabuki *(kah-BOO-kee)* [Japanese] In Japan, a form of popular drama notable for its elaborate costumes, rhythmic dialogue, and stylized gestures, in which male actors play the roles of both men and women. Also called *Grand Kabuki.* ⟨I like sumo and I like *kabuki,* but I don't necessarily have ethnocentric ideas.⟩—*Time,* April 26, 1999.

kachina *(kah-CHEE-nah)* [Hopi] Among the Hopi Indians of the southwestern United States, one of many mythical spirit ancestors, represented in religious rites by a masked dancer. Also, a painted doll carved from cottonwood root, representing such a spirit.

Kaddish *(KAH-dish)* [Aramaic: holy] In Judaism, a liturgical prayer in praise of God, part of the regular daily service in a synagogue; a form of this prayer recited during the period of mourning for a deceased family member, or on the anniversary of a death. See also YAHRZEIT. ⟨If there are no male survivors, a stranger may act as a substitute, but Szold gently rejected a male friend's offer to say *Kaddish* in her place after her father died.⟩—*The New York Times,* October 5, 1997.

Kaffir *(KAH-fer)* [Arabic: unbeliever] In South Africa, a disparaging and offensive term for a black person, originally and especially a member of the Xhosa tribes. Not to be confused with

Kafir, also called *Nuristani,* an Indo-European inhabitant of Nuristan (Afghanistan).

kaffiyeh, keffiyeh *(keh-FEE-eh)* [Arabic] A large, folded kerchief worn as a headdress by Arab men, held in place by an AGAL.

kahuna *(kah-HOO-nah)* [Hawaiian] A native priest or medicine man of Hawaii.

kaiser *(KYE-zer)* [German, from Latin: *Caesar*] A title given to an emperor of the Holy Roman Empire and, in the 19th century, to German and Austrian emperors. By extension, an autocrat; an absolute ruler, or one who behaves in the manner of a dictator.

kakemono *(kah-keh-MOH-noh)* [Japanese] A painting or text on a vertical scroll of paper or silk, hung on a wall, that can be rolled up for storage.

kalpak, calpac *(KAL-pak)* [Turkish] A large cap worn by Turks, Armenians, etc., usually made of felt or black sheepskin.

kamikaze *(kah-mee-KAH-zee)* [Japanese: divine wind] Formerly, the typhoons that destroyed much of the fleet of Mongols, Chinese, and Koreans attempting to invade Japan on two occasions in the latter half of the 13th century. In World War II, the Japanese pilots of the air force suicide squadron that deliberately crashed their bomb- and gasoline-laden planes into enemy targets. By extension, someone whose conduct is dangerously reckless. ⟨he and other senators who had voted for a bold deficit-reduction package had flown a *kamikaze* mission.⟩—*The Atlantic Monthly,* January 1997.

kampong *(KAHM-pong)* [Malay] In parts of Southeast Asia where Malay is spoken, a small village or community. A compound or enclosed area.

Kanaka *(kah-NAH-kah)* [Hawaiian: a person] A native of Hawaii or of the South Sea Islands.

kantharos *(KAN-thah-rohs)* [Greek] An ancient Greek pottery piece in the form of a deep, footed cup with two loop-shaped handles attached at the bottom of the bowl and extending above the brim.

kanzu *(KAN-zoo)* [Swahili] In central and eastern Africa, a long, white garment worn by both men and women.

kapok *(KAY-pok)* [Javanese] A silky fiber harvested from the seeds of the kapok (silk cotton) tree found in Indonesia and elsewhere in Asia, used for stuffing life preservers, life jackets, etc.

kapote *(kah-PAWT)* [Yiddish, from French] A long jacket or over-garment worn by Orthodox or Hasidic Jews.

kaput *(kah-POOT)* [German: trickless (in the game of piquet)] A slang word meaning done for, ruined, broken down, out of order, on the fritz.

karaoke *(kah-rah-OH-kee)* [Japanese: empty orchestra] In a night-club or bar, the practice of an individual singing along with a music video or recording from which the original vocal line has been removed. ⟨We belted out the choruses together as if it was last call at the hotel *karaoke* bar.⟩

karate *(kah-RAH-teh)* [Japanese] A weaponless Japanese method of self-defense that uses the hands, feet, elbows, and knees to strike forceful blows to an opponent's body. A sport based on this method. See also JUJITSU, JUDO, TAE KWON DO.

karma *(KAHR-mah)* [Sanskrit: act; deed] In Buddhism and Hinduism, the doctrine of responsibility whereby each person shall be rewarded or punished for his or her deeds in all incarnations, i.e., the sum of one's acts in one existence will decide one's fate for a succeeding existence. Loosely, fate or destiny. ⟨a kind of Buddhist position that you can't blame anyone else for your own *karma*⟩—*Time,* March 29, 1999.

kasha *(KAH-shah)* [Russian] Buckwheat groats: roasted, dehulled buckwheat or a dish made with it.

kayak *(KYE-yak)* [Inuit] An Eskimo hunting canoe with a light framework covered in sealskins, having an opening where the paddler sits and fastens the top around him or her to keep water out. A small boat similar in design, made of synthetic or other materials, used in sports.

kazachok *(kah-zah-CHAWK)* [Russian, Ukrainian] A vigorous Cossack dance for a solo male dancer, in which the dancer bounces in a squatting position and kicks out each foot alternately.

kefir *(keh-FEER)* [Russian] In Russian and Middle Eastern cooking, a yogurtlike drink made from curdled cow's milk or goat's milk.

keiretsu *(kehr-RET-soo)* [Japanese] In Japan, a group of independent companies that have close, interlocking relationships that allow them to have better control in the marketplace than they would acting individually. ⟨Wetherell contends that he runs his portfolio of start-up firms somewhat like a Japanese *keiretsu*⟩— *The New York Times,* March 15, 1999.

keister *(KEESS-ter)* [Yiddish, from German *Kiste:* box] A slang term for buttocks, rump, or rear end.

kendo *(ken-doh)* [Japanese, from Chinese: way of the sword] A Japanese style of fencing with flexible bamboo swords, practiced largely among student, police, and military organizations. Contestants wear protective clothing and head guards. ⟨Always ready for combat, he keeps his *kendo* sword in his office.⟩

kepi *(keh-PEE)* [French, from Swiss German] A French military cap with a flat top and a visor.

khaki *(KAH-kee)* [Urdu, from Persian: dusty] A color ranging from light sand to dull greenish or yellowish brown; a strong cotton fabric of this color often used in making uniforms, or a uniform made from such a fabric or color.

khan *(kahn)* [Turkic] A title held during the Middle Ages by the supreme rulers of Turkish, Tatar, and Mongol tribes, and the emperors of China. A title of respect given to officials and rulers in central Asia, Afghanistan, Iran, etc.

kibbutz (singular); **kibbutzim** (plural) *(kih-BOOTS, kih-boot-SEEM)* [Modern Hebrew: gathering] A collective farm or communal settlement in Israel. ⟨One of the great achievements of early Zionist action was the collective or *kibbutz,* which went forth to redeem the wilderness.⟩—*The Atlantic Monthly,* November 1957.

kibbutznik *(kih-BOOTS-nik)* [Yiddish, from Hebrew] A member of a KIBBUTZ. ⟨"The young don't want everything in common," said Zaks, who at 53 is the classic icon of a *kibbutznik* with his trim figure, tan, and dusty sandals.⟩—*The New York Times,* April 18, 1998.

Kibei *(kee-bay)* [Japanese] A person born in the United States of Japanese parents, but educated in Japan. See also ISSEI, NISEI, SANSEI.

kibitz *(KIH-bitz)* [Yiddish] To act as a KIBITZER.

kibitzer *(KIH-bit-ser)* [Yiddish and German: busybody] A person who looks over the shoulders of card players and offers unwanted advice or a meddlesome running commentary. Also, one who teases or cracks jokes while others are trying to concentrate on their work or on a serious conversation. The word is derived from *Kiebitz,* the German word for the lapwing, or plover. ⟨Ellis, a prominent Raleigh lawyer who has described himself as an "unofficial *kibitzer*" with the Forbes campaign⟩—*Time,* December 4, 1995.

kibosh *(KYE-bosh)* [poss. Yiddish] Originally and informally, nonsense. To put the *kibosh* on: to put an end to something; to squelch; to spoil; to veto. ⟨Our manager is trying to put the *kibosh* on a staff member who spends most of the day logged on to a chat page.⟩

kilim *(KIL-im)* [Turkish, from Persian] A handwoven, pileless spread or rug made in Turkey, the Balkans, and parts of Iran, using tapestry weave techniques.

kilo- *(KIL-oh)* [French, from Greek] In the metric system, a prefix meaning thousand, as in *kilometer:* a unit of 1,000 meters.

kimchi, kimchee *(KIM-chee)* [Korean, from Chinese] A Korean relish or side dish made with pickled or fermented cabbage, hot red peppers, and a variety of seasonings. ⟨A small dish of fiery *kimchi* is brought to the table while you read the menu.⟩

kimono *(kih-MOH-noh)* [Japanese] In Japan, a loose, buttonless robe with long, wide sleeves and a vee neck, worn by men and women as an outer garment since the 7th century; it is lapped left over right across the chest and held at the waist by a sash, or OBI.

kindergarten *(KIN-der-gahr-ten)* [German: children's garden] A school or class for young children aged four to six years.

kiosk *(KEE-osk)* [French, from Turkish] Originally, an open pavilion or summerhouse in Turkey. A similar structure that serves as a refreshment stand, newsstand, booth, etc. Also, a wide, hollow column for the posting of advertisements or notices.

kipa See YARMULKE.

kishkes, kishka *(KISH-keh)* [Yiddish, from Polish: sausage] In Jewish cooking, a gut casing filled with fat, onion, flour, seasonings, etc., and roasted. By extension, a slang term meaning guts; the innermost parts. Also called stuffed *derma.*

kismet *(KIZ-meht)* [Turkish, from Persian and Arabic] Destiny; fate.

kitsch *(kitsh)* [German: thrown together] Anything of garish appearance or content, designed to appeal to popular or undiscriminating tastes; art or literature characterized by cheap sentimentality or tawdriness. ⟨His grossly overdecorated house is a monument to *kitsch*.⟩

kiva *(KEE-vah)* [Hopi] An underground ceremonial chamber with a single entrance through a hole in its roof, symbolic of the Hopi belief that they arrived in this world by rising from another. ⟨The *kiva* is off limits to tourists and outsiders.⟩

klavier See CLAVIER.

klezmer *(KLEHZ-mer)* [Yiddish] Originally, a professional Jewish folk musician in Poland, now a player in a small band providing music for services in synagogues and entertainment at weddings and social occasions. Also, the folk music played by *klezmer* bands. ⟨After the ceremony, guests were treated to two hours of cheerful, rousing *klezmer* music.⟩

klutz *(kluts)* [Yiddish, from German *Klotz*: wooden beam] A slang term for an awkward, clumsy, or blundering person. Also, a simpleton; a blockhead.

knaidel (singular)**; knaidlach** (plural) *(KNAY-dl, KNAY-dlakh)* [Yiddish, from German *Knödel*] A dumpling made with MATZO meal and eggs, poached in chicken soup.

Knesset *(KNEH-set)* [Hebrew: gathering] The Israeli parliament, consisting of a single house or chamber of representatives, with 120 members elected under a system of proportional representation. ⟨Leading politicians have ceded power to the Orthodox rabbinate in order to obtain the support of small religious parties in the Knesset.⟩

knish *(knish)* [Yiddish, from Polish] In Jewish cooking, a roll or turnover of bread dough stuffed with meat, potato, or buckwheat, baked or fried.

knockwurst, knackwurst *(NOK-woorst)* [German] A highly seasoned sausage made from pork and beef.

koan *(KOH-ahn)* [Japanese, from Chinese: public notice] In Japanese Zen Buddhism, a meditation discipline for students consisting of paradoxical statements or questions that pose mental dilemmas for which an answer is demanded. ⟨Jackson pleasantly chuckles a no, probably holds back on offering a *koan* about one-year contracts.⟩—*Time,* January 25, 1999.

kohl *(kohl)* [Arabic] A cosmetic powder used to darken the eyelids, some form of which has been used since ancient Egyptian times.

kolkhoz (singular); **kolkhozy** (plural) *(kol-KHAWZ, kol-KHAWZ-ee)* [Russian] In the former Soviet Union, a collective farm. See also SOVKHOZ. ⟨In the dingy, four-room headquarters of the Suvorov *kolkhoz,* or collective farm⟩—*The New York Times,* April 23, 1993.

kona *(KOH-nah)* [Hawaiian] In Hawaii, a strong southwesterly winter wind that often brings rain.

kopje *(KOP-ee)* [Afrikaans] In South Africa, a small hill or mound.

kosher *(KOH-sher)* [Hebrew] Conforming to or permitted by the rules of Jewish dietary or ceremonial laws. Informally, legitimate; proper; authentic. ⟨We discovered a restaurant that specializes in *kosher* Chinese food prepared by a Chinese chef.⟩

koto *(KOH-toh)* [Japanese] A Japanese stringed instrument with a long, hollow, wooden body, an arched top surface, and six to thirteen silk strings stretched lengthwise that are tuned by placing little bridges under each one; used in GAGAKU and in nontheatrical music as a solo instrument.

koumiss, kumiss *(KOO-miss)* [Russian, from Turkic] A drink made of fermented camel's milk or mare's milk, used by the nomadic peoples of central Asia. A similar drink made from cow's milk. Scc also KEFIR.

kowtow *(kau-tau)* [Chinese] To act in a slavish, servile, or obsequious manner. The former Chinese custom of kneeling and lowering one's forehead to the ground as a sign of reverence or apology. The act of kowtowing. ⟨South Africa . . . does not owe the World Bank a dime—and is unwilling to *kowtow* to a superpower.⟩—*The New York Times,* March 26, 1998.

kraal *(krahl)* [Afrikaans, from Portuguese] In South Africa, a native village of huts within a stockade; a fenced community as a social unit. An enclosure for cattle or sheep in southern Africa.

krait *(krite)* [Hindi] In parts of Asia, a large and highly venomous snake of the cobra family.

Kremlin *(KREHM-lin)* [Russian: citadel] The Kremlin: the walled citadel of Moscow that houses the offices of the Russian government. The government of the former Soviet Union and now of Russia, especially with regard to foreign relations. ⟨Opposition deputies claimed, without offering evidence, that the *Kremlin* had offered members $30,000 each to stay away.⟩—*Time,* May 24, 1999.

kreplach *(KREHP-lahkh)* [Yiddish, from German] A Jewish dish of noodle dough stuffed with KASHA, chopped liver, cottage cheese, etc., and cooked in chicken stock. Similar to RAVIOLI.

krill *(krihl)* [Norwegian] A small, shrimplike crustacean that gathers in vast swarms in the open seas, an important food source for birds and some whales.

kudos *(KOO-dohss)* [Greek] Glory; high praise; acclaim. ⟨Recently, with the *kudos* earned by his last film, he applied again and was accepted.⟩

kulak *(KOO-lahk)* [Russian: fist (tight-fisted man)] In Russia, a prosperous peasant using hired labor and working for his own profit, in opposition to the Soviet drive to collectivize farming.

kulich *(koo-LEECH)* [Russian, from Greek] In Russian cooking, a sweet, rich yeast bread in the shape of a tall dome, served with PASKHA at Eastertide.

kung fu *(kung foo)* [Chinese: skill] An ancient Chinese form of weaponless combat, similar to KARATE.

kvell *(kvehl)* [Yiddish, from German: to gush] To be delighted; to be bursting with pride, as over some accomplishment by a family member or a friend.

kvetch *(kvehtch)* [Yiddish, from German] To complain, grumble, or whine, especially habitually. One who *kvetches* is a *kvetcher*. ⟨The majority joined the group to gossip and *kvetch* about their employers.⟩

Kwanza *(KWAHN-zah)* [Swahili: first] A harvest festival occurring between December 26 and January 1, celebrated in the United States by some African Americans.

kyogen *(kee-OH-ghen)* [Japanese, from Chinese] In Japanese theater, a short comic interlude performed between the plays of a NO cycle, to ease the tension of the drama. *Kyogen* are very broad in their humor, last about twenty minutes, and do not use music.

lachs See LOX.

lacuna *(lah-KYOO-nah, lah-KOO-nah)* [Latin: pit; hole] A gap; a section missing from a manuscript, a series, or an argument; a hiatus. ⟨There is one immense *lacuna:* an entire section on the lions of the Serengeti is missing.⟩

lagniappe *(lahn-YAHP)* [Louisiana French, from Spanish: that which is added] Something given as a bonus, a gratuity, or for good measure, as a "baker's dozen." A tip; an extra.

laisser-aller *(lay-say-ah-LAY)* [French: to allow to go] Unrestrained freedom or ease; looseness; comfortable negligence in dress or manners. ⟨His devotion to the principle of *laisser-aller* was more irritating than attractive.⟩

laissez-faire *(lay-say-FAIR)* [French: allow to act] The theory or practice of noninterference in the affairs of others; the policy of government noninterference in economic or business matters; a willingness to allow individual freedom of action. ⟨But the presidential adviser's more lasting legacy may prove to be the administration's *laissez-faire* policy on Internet commerce: no taxes, no government regulations.⟩—*The New York Times,* November 30, 1998.

laissez-passer *(lay-say-pah-SAY)* [French: allow to pass] A pass or permit used in place of a passport, often issued to members of international organizations, that may exempt the holder from certain travel restrictions.

lama *(LAH-mah)* [Tibetan: superior one] A priest or monk in Lamaism, the form of Buddhism practiced in Tibet and Mongolia. See also DALAI LAMA.

lamé *(lah-MAY)* [French] A fabric consisting of flat silver or gold metallic threads interwoven with silk, cotton, etc. ⟨Found in Paris—a preworn Nina Ricci gold *lamé* gown at a bargain price.⟩

lanai *(lah-NYE)* [Hawaiian] In Hawaii, a porch or VERANDA, sometimes furnished and used as a sitting room.

langlauf *(LAHNG-lauf)* [German: long run] A cross-country ski run, or the sport of cross-country skiing.

langouste *(lahn-GOOST)* [French] The spiny lobster; crayfish.

langoustine *(lahn-goo-STEEN)* [French] The Norway lobster: a large shrimp or prawn, also called Dublin Bay prawn. ⟨We devoured a memorable *gratin de langoustines* at Lapérouse.⟩

langsam *(LAHNG-zahm)* [German] In music, slow; slowly. See also LARGO.

La Niña *(lah NEEN-yah)* [Spanish: the girl] A cool, slow, counterclockwise current in the equatorial Pacific Ocean that develops in summer, often encompassing most of the northern Pacific, and causing frequently devastating disturbances in the weather of the Americas because of its abnormal temperature. See also EL NIÑO.

lapin *(lah-PENH)* [French] A rabbit. Also, rabbit fur trimmed and dyed to resemble more expensive fur.

lardon, lardoon *(lahr-DONH)* [French: piece of pork] In cooking, a thin strip of pork fat or bacon drawn through a piece of meat with a specially designed needle.

largesse *(lahr-ZHESS)* [French, from Latin] Generous or liberal giving; the gift or gifts abundantly bestowed. ⟨And for all Salmond's feisty talk of independence, no one has quite resolved the little matter of Westminster's *largesse.*⟩—*Time,* May 10, 1999.

largo *(LAHR-goh)* [Italian] In music, slow; broad; to be played in a slow and stately manner. See also LANGSAM. ⟨The overall pace of the narrative is *largo,* with brief interjections of staccato speech.⟩

lascar *(LAHSS-kahr)* [Urdu, from Persian] An East Indian sailor.

lavalava *(LAH-vah-LAH-vah)* [Samoan: clothing] In Samoa and other Pacific islands, a length of printed cloth wrapped around the body as a garment, worn by men and women. In Tahiti, it is called the *pareu* or *pareo.*

lavaliere *(lah-vah-LEER, lah-vahl-YAIR)* [French, after the duchess of La Vallière] An ornamental pendant, often jeweled, worn on a thin chain around the neck. Also, a small microphone that can be worn on a necklace for purposes of concealment.

layette *(lay-EHT)* [French] The supply of bedding, clothing, etc., necessary for a newborn baby.

lazaretto *(lah-zah-REHT-oh)* [Venetian Italian] First organized in Venice in 1423, a hospital for the treatment of people with infectious diseases such as plague or leprosy. A building or ship used as a place of quarantine.

l'chaim, l'chayim *(leh-KHAH-yeem)* [Hebrew: to life!] A toast, like the Spanish SALUD or the Swedish SKOAL, spoken when drinking to someone's good health or success.

lebensraum *(LAY-bens-raum)* [German: living space] A need for lands or territory claimed by a nation as necessary for economic growth or national survival; a concept used by Hitler to support Nazi expansionism in the 1930s.

lederhosen *(LAY-der-hoh-zen)* [German] Leather shorts, often with suspenders, worn by men in upper Bavaria and other Alpine regions. ⟨They sell teddy bears, including some dressed in *lederhosen* and traditional Alpine hats.⟩

legato *(leh-GAH-toh)* [Italian] In music, smoothly connected from one tone to the next without any break between.

legerdemain *(leh-jer-de-MAIN, lay-zhay-deu-MENH)* [French] Sleight of hand; hocus-pocus; trickery; artful deception. ⟨Yugoslavs themselves express wonder at how Milosevic manages this feat of financial *legerdemain*.⟩—*Time,* April 26, 1999.

legume *(LEG-yoom)* [French: vegetable] Any plant or table vegetable of the legume family, i.e., with a pod that splits along both sides, including beans, peas, alfalfa, lentils, peanuts, etc.

lei *(LAY-ee)* [Hawaiian] In Hawaii, a wreath or garland of flowers, leaves, feathers, etc., worn around the neck or as a chaplet for the head.

leitmotif, leitmotiv *(LITE-moh-teef)* [German: leading motive] A recurring theme in a musical or literary work, especially one in the operas of Richard Wagner, that is associated with a specific character, situation, or feeling. ⟨The search for acceptance became a *leitmotiv* of Albright's life, much as it had been a *leitmotiv* in the lives of her ancestors.⟩—*The New Yorker,* March 29, 1999.

lekvar *(LEHK-vahr)* [Hungarian] In Hungarian cooking, a soft, sweet paste or spread made from cooked prunes or apricots.

lèse-majesté *(lez mah-zhehs-TAY)* [French: injured majesty] A crime against a sovereign or a sovereign authority; high treason. A violation of or attack on institutions or customs cherished by a group of people. Informally, any presumptive behavior.

lettre de cachet *(leh-treu deu kah-SHAY)* [French] A letter under seal of the sovereign. Formerly, a royal order for the arbitrary imprisonment of someone. See also CACHET.

levee (1) *(LEH-vee)* [French, from Latin: raised] An embankment built along the shore of a river to prevent flooding. Formerly, a wharf or landing place. ⟨So the corps wants to raise the *levee* not only in Mayersville, the most vulnerable spot along the river, but also along 263 more miles of river running through five states.⟩—*The New York Times*, December 8, 1998.

levee, levée (2) *(leu-VAY)* [French, from *se lever:* to arise] A formal gathering or reception of visitors, held early in the day; an official reception held by or in honor of the president of the United States. Formerly, an audience given by a monarch or important person on rising from bed.

liaison *(lee-AY-zon, lee-ay-ZONH)* [French: a binding] An agency or means of maintaining or promoting communications between units of an organization; the person responsible for establishing and maintaining such a connection. Also, a secret or adulterous relationship.

lieu *(lyoo, lyeu)* [French, from Latin] Place; stead. *In lieu of:* in place of.

lingerie *(lenh-zheh-REE)* [French: linens] Women's underwear, nightgowns, stockings, etc.

lingua franca *(LING-gwah FRAHN-kah)* [Italian: Frankish tongue] Any language used in common among peoples of a region where several languages are spoken; a jargon or pidgin used to facilitate trade or commerce. ⟨that has come to be the *lingua franca* of the Web⟩—*Time*, March 29, 1999.

liqueur *(lee-KEUR)* [French] A strong, sweet alcoholic drink or cordial, such as Grand Marnier or Benedictine, often served after dinner as a DIGESTIF; usually made by mixing brandy with flavoring and sugar syrup.

litchi, lichee *(LEE-chee)* [Chinese] An edible fruit with a single seed and a sweet, firm, jellylike pulp, native to China. Also written *leechee.*

literati *(lit-er-RAH-tee)* [Latin] Those who are highly literate, scholarly, or noted for their literary achievements; intellectuals. ⟨These *literati* were asked to choose the most notable writers of the last two decades.⟩

llano *(LYAH-noh)* [Spanish] A large, grassy, treeless plain of the southwestern United States and northern Latin America. See also PAMPAS.

loess *(leuss)* [German, from Swiss German: loose; slack] A yellowish calcareous clay or silt; a windblown dust that forms fertile deposits along river valleys in Europe, Asia, and North America.

loge *(lohzh)* [French, from *loger:* to inhabit] In a theater or opera house, a box, or the front section of the lowest balcony.

loggia *(LOJ-yah)* [Italian] A roofed gallery, arcade, or portico that forms part of a building, supported by columns and open to the air on one or more sides.

Logos *(LOH-gohs)* [Greek: word] In philosophy, the principle that governs all things. Not to be confused with the plural of *logo* (short for *logotype*), a trademark or graphic symbol of a company name.

loofah *(LOO-fah)* [Arabic] A large fruit of the gourd family, also known as the dishcloth gourd; the dried, fibrous interior of the fruit is used in industrial filters and as a rough sponge for bathing and dishwashing.

lorgnette *(lorn-YEHT)* [French, from *lorgner:* to eye surreptitiously] Elegant eyeglasses or opera glasses held to the eyes by means of a long handle, popular among upper-class ladies of the 19th century. Some used the opera-glass version, which had low-power binoculars instead of simple lenses, to observe plays, concerts, and other members of the audience.

lothario *(loh-THAH-ree-oh)* [Italian, after a character in the play *The Fair Penitent,* by Nicholas Rowe (1703)] A charming man who makes a practice of seducing women. ⟨Casanova enjoyed a reputation as one of the most renowned *lotharios* of his time.⟩

louche *(loosh)* [French: cross-eyed; squinting; lacking in clarity] Used as an adjective to mean disreputable; shady; dishonorable. ⟨He was considered too *louche* to be allowed access to confidential material.⟩

loupe *(loop)* [French] A small magnifying glass that can be attached to eyeglasses or fitted into the eye socket, used mainly by watchmakers and jewelers.

loup-garou *(loo-gah-ROO)* [French] In old French folklore, a werewolf; a wolfman.

lox, lachs *(loks)* [Yiddish: salmon] Salmon that has been cured in brine and cold smoked, often eaten with cream cheese and BAGELS.

luau *(loo-AU, LOO-au)* [Hawaiian] In Hawaii, a gala outdoor feast with entertainment. Also, a cooked dish of taro leaves with octopus or chicken, usually flavored with coconut cream.

luge *(lüzh)* [French: small sled] A sled ridden by one or two people in sitting position, steered with a handheld rope and the feet, often in a chute built for the purpose. In the competitive sport, which was introduced into the winter Olympic games in 1964, the contestant lies on his or her back and steers with the feet.

lumpenproletariat *(LOOM-pen-proh-loh-TAH-ree-aht)* [from German, coined by Karl Marx in 1850: rabble proletariat] The poorest and least skilled of the industrial working classes, including vagrants, criminals, and those at the very bottom of the social heap who are too dispirited to try to better their lot. The word *proletariat* comes from a Latin term indicating a citizen of no worth to society except as a progenitor of children. ⟨all under the commanding baton of Richard Buckley, brought Berg's acerbic, atonal ode to the *lumpenproletariat* to vivid, expressionistic life⟩—*Time,* February 7, 1994.

lutefisk *(LOO-teh-fisk)* [Norwegian, Swedish] In Scandinavian cooking, dried cod soaked in a solution of water and lye, then soaked again in freshwater before cooking.

lycée *(lee-SAY)* [French, from Latin *Lyceum*] A French secondary school financed by the government.

M

macabre *(mah-KAH-breu)* [French] Ghastly; gruesome; suggestive of death. In the allegorical DANSES MACABRES of medieval times, death was represented by a dancer disguised as a skeleton leading people to the grave. The term may have been derived from medieval reenactments of the battles of the Maccabees in the 2nd century B.C. ⟨A frail and half-blind 68-year-old Florida grandmother was facing a *macabre* murder charge last night⟩—*The Guardian,* May 20, 1999.

macédoine *(mah-say-DWAHN)* [French: from Macedonia] A mixture of chopped or cut vegetables or fruits, raw or cooked, sometimes served as a salad. By extension, a medley or collection of disparate things, as in "her costume was a *macédoine* of fabrics and textures."

mâche *(mahsh)* [French, from *mâcher:* to chew] A European salad green with a small, delicate leaf and mild flavor. Also called corn salad, lamb's lettuce, or field salad.

mâché See PAPIER-MACHÉ.

machete *(mah-SHEH-teh)* [Spanish: a mallet] A broad knife with a heavy, two-foot-long blade used in Latin American countries and the West Indies to cut sugarcane and remove underbrush. The *machete* also serves as a weapon.

machismo *(mah-CHEES-moh)* [American Spanish] The expression of a need to prove one's manliness by demonstrating strength and courage; the display of MACHO qualities. ⟨This is not because Somali society is free of *machismo.*⟩—*The New York Review of Books,* March 4, 1999.

macho *(MAH-choh)* [American Spanish: male] An adjective meaning manly, assertive, virile, courageous, dominating, or having a strong sense of one's own power. ⟨she doesn't quite fit in to the *macho* boys' club of Los Angeles television.⟩—*The St. Louis Post-Dispatch,* January 24, 1999.

madrigal *(MAD-rih-gahl)* [Italian] An unaccompanied part-song for three to six voices, frequently in counterpoint, using nonreligious texts of an occasionally bawdy nature, popular in the 16th and 17th centuries. Also, a short lyric love poem of the 16th century and later, often designed to be set to music.

maelstrom *(MAYL-strom)* [Dutch: grinding stream] A whirlpool of great strength and size, such as the legendary Moskentraumen whirlpool off the northwest coast of Norway, vividly described in Edgar Allan Poe's "Descent into the *Maelstrom.*" By extension, a violently agitated state of affairs; a tumult or pandemonium. ⟨she attracted, wherever she went, a *maelstrom* of publicity.⟩—*Time,* March 22, 1999.

maestro *(mah-ESS-troh)* [Italian: master] An eminent person in any of the arts, especially a respected composer, conductor, performer, or teacher in music. Used as an honorary title. ⟨Even in his eighties, the *maestro* continued to conduct major works from memory.⟩

Mafia *(MAH-fee-ah)* [Sicilian dialect, of obscure origin, possibly meaning courage, BRAVURA, or "my faith"] A name applied indiscriminately in the 19th century to groups of Sicilians who shared a common hostility to legal authority and who believed that true justice could only be achieved directly, i.e., through the VENDETTA. The word is now applied to any secret society engaged in criminal activities such as racketeering, drug trafficking, smuggling, prostitution, etc., and which provides protection for its members.

mafioso *(mah-fee-OH-soh)* [Italian] A person belonging to a MAFIA organization. ⟨Two brothers and a triad again, this time with a view as cynical as that of a retired *mafioso.*⟩—*Time,* June 7, 1999.

mafiozy *(mah-FYOH-zee)* [Russian, a transliteration of the Italian *mafiosi*] Members of any Mafia-like group engaged in organized crime; racketeers.

magna cum laude *(MAG-nah koom LAU-deh)* [Latin: with great praise] A phrase used on a diploma to indicate one of three honors for high academic achievement. The others are CUM LAUDE and SUMMA CUM LAUDE. ⟨She graduated *magna cum laude* and earned a master's degree one year later.⟩

magnum opus *(MAG-num OH-puss)* [Latin: great work] A masterpiece, especially the best single work, or the body of work of a composer, artist, or writer. ⟨Dante's *magnum opus* is the "Divine Comedy."⟩

maharaja, majarajah *(mah-hah-RAH-jah)* [Hindi, from Sanskrit: great king] The former title of a prince of India, especially of one ruling an important Indian state. ⟨Kashmır's *maharaju* at partition was Hindu and chose to be part of India⟩—*The New York Times,* June 9, 1999.

maharani, maharanee *(mah-hah-RAH-nee)* [Hindi: great queen] The former title of the wife or widow of a MAHARAJA, or of a sovereign Indian princess.

maharishi *(mah-hah-REE-shee)* [Sanskrit: great saint] A Hindu man of great wisdom and spiritual knowledge; an honorary title given to a religious sage. ⟨This *maharishi* claimed to hold the secret of physical levitation.⟩

mahatma *(mah-HAHT-mah)* [Sanskrit: great soul] In theosophy and some Asian religions, a title of respect for a holy man or a man revered for saintliness and wisdom. ⟨Today we invoke Gandhi as the *Mahatma,* the Father of the Nation.⟩

Mahdi *(MAH-dee)* [Arabic: he who is guided] In Sunni Islam, the restorer of the faith; the messiah who will establish justice, impartiality, and religious purity on earth.

mahimahi *(MAH-hee-MAH-hee)* [Hawaiian] A warm-water food fish also known as dorado, prized for its firm-textured and flavorful meat. Although sometimes called the dolphinfish, it is not a mammal, as are the true dolphins.

mahout *(mah-HOOT)* [Hindi] In India and the East Indies, an elephant driver or keeper.

maidan *(my-DAHN)* [Hindi] In India, an open space used for parades, sports, or as a market area, usually located in or just outside a town. ⟨In Calcutta we watched a procession from the entrance to the *Maidan,* the city's Central Park.⟩

maillot *(my-YOH)* [French: bathing suit; tights; a flexible covering] A simply styled one-piece swimsuit, or the tights worn by acrobats and dancers. Also, a knitted shirt or pullover such as the *maillot jaune,* the yellow jersey worn by the lead cyclist in the Tour de France.

maisonette *(may-soh-NET)* [French] A small house, often attached to a larger building. Also, a duplex apartment. ⟨Adrian had this *maisonette* in Hampstead where he had torn out the roof and put these shelves in like a couchette.⟩—*The Guardian,* April 3, 1999.

maître d'hôtel *(MEH-treu doh-TEL)* [French: master of the hotel] Currently, a headwaiter; also, a steward, butler, or the manager or owner of a hotel. In cooking, *sauce maître d'hôtel* consists of melted butter, lemon juice, or vinegar and parsley. ⟨who before enrolling had been a waiter, head waiter and *maître d'hôtel*⟩—*The New York Times,* December 8, 1996.

majordomo *(MAY-jor-DOH-moh, MAH-yor DOH-moh)* [Spanish, from Latin: head of the house] The chief steward or man in charge of a royal household or princely residence; a palace official. Also, a butler, or one whose profession is making arrangements for others.

maksoorah *(mahk-SOO-rah)* [Arabic] In a mosque, the ornamental screen, partition, or wooden box that encloses a space set apart for prayer or for a tomb. Also written *maqsurah.*

maladroit *(mal-ah-DROYT, mahl-ah-DRWAH)* [French] Lacking adroitness or skill; clumsy; awkward; blundering.

mala fide *(MAH-lah fied)* [Latin] In bad faith. Fraudulent; not genuine. See also BONA FIDE.

mala fides *(MAH-lah fiedz)* [Latin] Bad faith; the intent to deceive or defraud. See also BONA FIDES.

malaise *(mah-LEHZ)* [French, possibly a contraction of *mal à l'aise:* ill at ease] A state of physical discomfort or weakness that may signal the onset of sickness; a vague sensation of dread or mental lethargy. Also, a collective uneasiness, as in "the general *malaise* caused by an increase in terrorism." ⟨Adding to the *malaise* is a sinking feeling that the country's glory days as a global pacesetter are over.⟩—*Time,* April 26, 1999.

malapropos *(mahl-ah-proh-POH)* [French] Inappropriate; untimely; out of place; as in "a *malapropos* comment."

malchik *(MAHL-chik)* [Russian] Boy.

mal de mer *(mahl de mehr)* [French] Seasickness; nausea caused by the motion of a boat.

mal du pays *(mahl dü pay-EE)* [French] Homesickness; unhappiness springing from a longing for home or for one's native land.

malentendu *(mahl-anh-tanh-DÜ)* [French: badly heard] A misunderstanding or misconception; a mistake, as in "The relationship was based, unfortunately, on a series of *malentendus.*"

malihini *(mah-lee-HEE-nee)* [Hawaiian] A person newly arrived in Hawaii; a newcomer to the islands.

mañana *(mahn-YAH-na)* [Spanish: morning] Tomorrow, or (less specifically) in the near future; at some other time.

manège *(mah-NEZH)* [French, from Italian] The art of schooling and riding horses, or a school where horses are trained and riders are taught horsemanship. Also, the formal paces or movements of a trained horse. See also DRESSAGE.

manicotti *(mah-nee-KOT-tee)* [Italian: sleevelets] In cooking, a baked dish consisting of tubular pasta stuffed with cheese and covered in tomato sauce.

manitou *(MAH-nee-too)* [Algonquian: he is god] A good or evil spirit, one among many in the Algonquian religion, who governs nature and life; a spirit or object with supernatural powers, or the personification of such a spirit.

mannequin *(MAN-ih-kin)* [French, from Dutch] A life-size wooden model of the human figure used for fitting or making clothes; a dressmaker's or tailor's dummy, sometimes representing the body only from neck and shoulders to the thighs. Also, a woman who models clothing. ⟨The display included four *mannequins,* each bearing the likeness of a Beatle.⟩

mano a mano *(MAH-noh ah MAH-noh)* [Spanish: hand to hand] On an equal footing. A face-to-face competition or duel; a direct confrontation or rivalry, as in "a *mano a mano* struggle between two members of the school board." In direct opposition. ⟨She goes *"mano a mano"* with drug lords.⟩—*The Christian Science Monitor,* June 1, 1999.

manqué *(manh-KAY)* [French, from *manquer:* to lack] Unfulfilled; unsuccessful; having fallen short of a desired goal or standard, as in a "Mozart *manqué,* an unsuccessful musician." ⟨FDR forging the vital Anglo-American alliance to win World War II, manifestly a "Hamiltonian Alliance" *manqué*⟩—*The New Criterion,* May 1999.

mansard *(manh-SAHR)* [French, after the 17th-century French architect François Mansart] An angled roof design in which the slope from ridge to eaves has two distinct surfaces or sections: the upper section is nearly flat, with a low pitch, while the lower section is almost vertical, of steep pitch, thus providing more interior space under the roof. ⟨the *mansard* roofs of Second Empire architecture, cafés in the square⟩—*The Guardian,* February 20, 1999.

mantilla *(mahn-TEE-yah)* [Spanish: saddlecloth] In Spain and Latin America, a light scarf or veil, often of lace or silk, arranged over a woman's head and shoulders. It is sometimes draped over a high comb. ⟨She was wearing a black *mantilla,* what she'd worn each of her two times in the presence of a Pope.⟩—*The Atlantic Monthly,* April 1996.

mantra *(MAHN-trah)* [Sanskrit] A Buddhist or Hindu incantation or prayer; words or sounds, often repeated, that are thought to have spiritual or mystical power. ⟨That has become a kind of *mantra* to those who would deny the existence of corruption.⟩

maquette *(mah-KET)* [French, from Italian: small sketch] A small, three-dimensional model or study for a sculpture or an architectural design. Not to be confused with *moquette,* a fabric used for carpeting. ⟨Sachiko Cho, who leads the artist's crew, works out the design directly on the wall, at a scale 15 times larger than the *maquette.*⟩—*The New York Times,* April 22, 1999.

maquillage *(mah-kee-YAHZH)* [French] Makeup; cosmetics used on the face or body to cover blemishes or alter one's appearance. Also, the makeup, wigs, etc., used in stage performance.

Maquis *(mah-KEE)* [French: dense brushland] The French resistance movement against the Nazis, organized during World War II; a member of the movement.

maquisard *(mah-kee-SAHR)* [French] A member of the MAQUIS.

maraca *(mah-RAH-kah)* [Portuguese] A percussion instrument: a hollow gourd with a wooden handle, filled with seeds or beans that rattle when shaken. *Maracas* are often played in pairs, one in each hand, to enhance the rhythm of Latin American dance music. ⟨We rushed off to attend a mariachi-and-*maraca* picnic at the local park.⟩

marais *(mah-RAY)* [French] A swamp, wetland, or BAYOU.

marc *(mahr)* [French] The residue (skins, pips, stems) that remains after grapes or other fruit have been pressed to extract their juice. Also, a French brandy made by distilling the residue.

marginalia *(mahr-jin-AYL-yah)* [Latin] Marginal notes; comments written into the margins of a text. 〈An academic who's been editing the *marginalia* of Coleridge thinks we should be encouraged to do so〉—*The Guardian,* February 15, 1999.

mariachi *(mah-ree-AH-chee)* [Mexican Spanish] A small Mexican street band, usually two or three players who perform for tips, or the music performed by such a band. 〈Where else in hockey do they feature a Night of Dueling *Mariachi* Bands〉—*The New York Times,* April 26, 1998.

marijuana *(mah-ree-WAH-nah)* [Mexican Spanish] The hemp plant; the dried flowers and leaves of the hemp plant smoked in cigarettes as a narcotic.

marimba *(mah-RIM-bah)* [Bantu] A musical instrument similar to the xylophone, with graduated, tuned hardwood bars; beneath each bar is a resonator designed to enhance the sound. The *marimba* is played with mallets.

marinade *(mah-ree-NAYD, mah-ree-NAHD)* [French, from Portuguese: to cure in brine] A liquid mixture in which meat, fish, or vegetables can be soaked before cooking, to intensify the flavor; usually made of wine or vinegar, oil, salt, spices, herbs, etc.

marinara *(mah-ree-NAH-rah)* [Italian: sailor's style] In Italian cooking, a meatless sauce made from tomatoes, garlic, onions, and oregano.

marionette *(mah-ree-oh-NET)* [French: little Marion] A puppet with articulated limbs, animated from above by means of strings attached to the limbs; some complex 19th-century *marionettes* have as many as twenty strings; a skillful manipulator can imitate almost all human gestures.

marmite *(mahr-MEET)* [French] A large, covered cooking pot made of earthenware, porcelain, or metal, used for making soups, stews, and stock. Well-flavored CONSOMMÉ is often referred to as *petite marmite.*

marque *(mark)* [French, short for *marque de fabrique:* trademark] A product style or model, especially one for a racing or luxury vehicle. A symbol associated with a particular business or artisan. ⟨But this year, as Packard lovers celebrate the company's 100th anniversary, the *marque* will be featured at the Pebble Beach Concours in August.⟩—*The New York Times,* June 18, 1999.

marquisette *(mahr-kee-ZET)* [French: little marquise] A lightweight net fabric of silk, rayon, cotton, or nylon, used for curtains and clothing.

marron *(mah-RONH)* [French] A large European chestnut, often used in stuffings or preserved in sugar syrup. The candied chestnuts are called *marrons glacés.*

martinet *(MAHR-tih-net, mahr-tee-NAY)* [French: after the 17th-century drillmaster, General Jean Martinet] One who demands that rules and regulations be obeyed to the letter; a strict disciplinarian, especially among the military. ⟨A renowned technician and *martinet* of the baton, he shaped the orchestra in his own perfectionist image.⟩

masa *(MAH-sah)* [Spanish: dough] A specially treated Mexican corn flour or dough used to make TORTILLAS. *Masa harina* is the dehydrated version.

mascara *(mah-SKAH-rah)* [Spanish, from Arabic: mask] A cosmetic mixture applied to eyebrows and eyelashes to darken or color them.

massif *(mah-SEEF)* [French: massive] Heights or peaks that form a compact group, or the central grouping of summits in a mountainous area, as in France's *Massif Central.* ⟨where the tents are outlined against the snow-capped Suva Gora *massif*⟩—*The Guardian,* April 11, 1999.

matador *(MAH-tah-dor)* [Spanish: killer] A bullfighter, one responsible for killing the bull with a sword. Also, the name given to an American surface-to-air missile. See also TOREADOR, TORERO. ⟨the world's premier female *matador*, retired, saying she was no longer willing or able to battle the machismo of her male colleagues⟩—*Time,* May 31, 1999.

maté *(MAH-tay)* [American Spanish: small teapot] Tea made from the dried leaves of a South American holly tree, also called Paraguay tea, or *yerba maté.*

matelot *(maht-LOH)* [French] A sailor or seaman.

matelote *(maht-LOHT)* [French] In France, a rich stew containing freshwater fish and/or eel, cooked in wine and butter.

matériel *(mah-teh-ree-EL)* [French] All the supplies, arms, etc., needed to equip a military force, as distinct from personnel. Similarly, all the materials required by an organization or business. ⟨Soviet war *matériel* included surface-to-air missiles, patrol boats with missiles, and MiG-21 fighters.⟩

matinee, matinée *(mah-tih-NAY)* [French: morning] A stage performance, concert, or movie that takes place in the daytime, usually in the afternoon.

matzo, matzoh *(MAHT-zoh)* [Hebrew] The unleavened bread made of wheat flour and water, eaten by Jews during the festival of Passover, usually in the form of large, square crackers. ⟨Yesterday I took him to the Second Avenue Deli, and he gulped down *matzoh*-ball soup and a turkey sandwich.⟩—*Time,* July 21, 1997.

mauvais goût *(moh-vay GOO)* [French] Bad taste in social and cultural matters; the inability to sense what is fitting, harmonious, beautiful, tactful, or polite.

mauve *(mohv)* [French: mallow plant] A pale purple mixed with bluc, gray, or rose; originally a purple aniline dye. The 1890s, a period of prosperity and contentment for some, are often referred to as the *Mauve Decade.*

maven, mavin *(MAY-ven)* [Yiddish, from Hebrew] A CONNOISSEUR or expert; a specialist. ⟨But in the twelfth of his thirteen chapters, "The Language *Mavens,"* Pinker takes a little holiday from science.⟩—*The Atlantic Monthly,* March 1997.

mazel tov *(MAH-zl toff)* [Yiddish, from Hebrew: good luck] Best wishes; congratulations; an expression used by Jews to mark happy occasions or a successful outcome. ⟨*"Mazel tov,"* the Prime Minister reportedly replied. "Good work."⟩—*The New York Times,* September 5, 1993.

mazuma *(mah-ZOO-mah)* [Yiddish, from Hebrew] A slang term for money; ready cash. ⟨losing a few customers to the competition is well worth the 40,000 *mazuma* the site earns in exchange⟩—*Time,* December 17, 1996.

mazurka *(mah-ZOOR-kah)* [Polish: from Mazovia, a district in northern Poland] A vigorous Polish folk dance in 3/4 time, usually danced by couples, or the music for such a dance.

mea culpa *(MAY-ah KOOL-pah)* [Latin] My fault; my blame; a phrase used to acknowledge personal responsibility. ⟨Version Three was NATO's partial *mea culpa*—the admission by one pilot that he had dropped a single bomb on a single column⟩—*The Guardian,* April 18, 1999.

meerschaum *(MEER-shawm)* [German: sea foam] A light, heat-resistant mineral, also called sepiolite, that is used to make tobacco-pipe bowls that gradually take on a delicate brownish tint with use. The pipe itself is referred to as a *meerschaum.* ⟨Would he make an appearance, leaping across the living room to land at his piano without spilling a drop of bourbon, *meerschaum* pipe still clenched in his teeth?⟩—*The New York Times,* July 19, 1998.

mega- *(MEH-gah)* [Greek] A prefix meaning large, as in *megadose* or *megastructure.* In the metric system, it indicates one million times, as in *megabytes, megahertz, megavolts,* etc.

megillah *(meh-GIL-lah)* [Yiddish: scroll; Hebrew: the Book of Esther] An overly detailed account or narrative; an unnecessarily lengthy explanation. ⟨The President and First Lady wanted it to be less of a *megillah*⟩—*Time,* January 20, 1997.

mélange *(may-LANHZH)* [French] A mixture; a medley.

melee *(MAY-lay, may-LAY)* [French] A confused hand-to-hand struggle involving several people; a brawl, free-for-all, or donnybrook. By extension, tumult or utter confusion.

memento mori *(meh-MEN-toh MOH-ree)* [Latin: remember that you die] A reminder or emblem of death or mortality, such as a skull or a hangman's noose. ⟨He said that memory, especially *memento mori,* is of particular significance now in Hong Kong, where people await the retrocession to China.⟩

memorabilia *(meh-moh-rah-BEE-lyah)* [Latin] Souvenirs; mementos; things or events that merit remembering and recording. ⟨In Minneapolis, a *memorabilia* store called Startifacts is asking $15,000 for a toupee once worn by Frank Sinatra⟩—*The St. Louis Post-Dispatch,* March 2, 1999.

ménage *(may-NAHZH)* [French] A household or domestic establishment; the people who make up a household. Also, housekeeping or cleaning. See also MÉNAGE À TROIS.

ménage à trois *(may-NAHZH ah TRWAH)* [French: a household of three] A home in which three people live in a shared physical relationship, most commonly a husband and wife with the man's mistress or with the wife's lover. ⟨The three lovers set-tled into an anguished *ménage à trois* held together by their common devotion to the child.⟩

menagerie *(meh-NAJ-er-ee, meh-NAH-zher-ee)* [French] A group of wild or unusual animals housed for exhibition to the visiting public, or the place where they are kept in captivity. By exten-sion, a group of people with unusual qualities or diverse back-grounds; a motley crowd.

menhir *(MEN-heer)* [Breton: long stone] A tall, upright stone mon-ument or megalith with a rough surface, dating from prehis-toric times. Found chiefly in Brittany and Cornwall, *menhirs* are sometimes arranged in lines or circles. ⟨It's best to travel by bicycle, which allows one to spot stone crucifixes or the lonely *menhir* looming in a cow pasture.⟩

menorah *(meh-NOH-rah)* [Hebrew: lamp stand] In Jewish wor-ship, a ceremonial candelabrum with seven or more branches.

mensch *(mehnsh)* [Yiddish: man; human being] A man who is decent and reliable; an honest, morally correct person. ⟨He was hailed as a great jurist, a great speaker, and an all-around *mensch.*⟩

menudo *(meh-NOO-doh)* [Spanish: small; Mexican Spanish: giblets] A highly spiced Mexican soup or stew made from calves' feet, tripe, hominy, and vegetables, often served on New Year's Day.

mercado *(mehr-KAH-doh)* [Spanish] A market or trading center.

merengue *(meh-REN-gay)* [American Spanish] A ballroom dance from the Dominican Republic and Haiti, in rapid ²/₄ time, that became popular in the United States.

meringue *(meh-RANG)* [French] A delicate pastry, pastry shell, or topping, made from egg whites beaten with sugar or syrup and usually baked.

merino *(meh-REE-noh)* [Spanish, from Arabic] A breed of sheep, originally from Spain; the fine, silky wool for which the breed is famous, or the high-quality fabric or yarn made from that wool.

mesa *(MAY-sah)* [Spanish, from Latin: table] A high, flat tableland or plateau with steep rocky slopes, common in the plains and deserts of the southwestern United States and Mexico.

mésalliance *(mayz-ah-lee-ANHS)* [French] Marriage with a person of inferior social position, or with someone lacking financial resources; a misalliance.

mescal *(mehs-KAHL)* [Mexican Spanish] A Mexican cactus (agave), also called *peyote;* an intoxicating drink made from fermented and distilled agave juice, with hallucinogenic properties. ⟨Seeking visionary insights, he guzzled *mescal* and whiskey.⟩

meshuga, meshugge *(meh-SHOO-geh)* [Yiddish, from Hebrew] A slang term meaning crazy, nuts, insane. Also written as *meshugah, meshuggah.*

meshuggener, meshugana *(meh-SHOO-geh-nah)* [Yiddish, from Hebrew] A slang term for a crazy or excessively foolish person. Also written as *meshuggana.*

mesquite *(meh-SKEET, MEHS-keet)* [Mexican Spanish] A thorny shrub or small tree found in the southwestern United States, Mexico, and parts of South America; its pods are used for cattle fodder, and the aromatic wood is a popular fuel for outdoor grilling or barbecuing.

mestiza (f), **mestizo** (m) *(meh-STEE-zah, meh-STEE-zoh)* [Spanish, from Latin: mixed] A person of mixed racial descent, especially one of mixed Central or South American Indian and Spanish blood. See also MÉTIS/MÉTISSE. ⟨Mexico is to a significant extent a homogeneous society: 90 percent of the population is *mestizo.*⟩—*The Atlantic Monthly,* February 1997.

métier *(may-TYAY)* [French] A person's trade, occupation, or profession; an area of work or activity for which one has special talent or training. See also FORTE. ⟨He . . . found his high-school *métier* in producing cartoons and magazines.⟩—*The Guardian,* May 16, 1999.

métis (m), **métisse** (f) *(may-TEES)* [French, from Latin: of mixed blood] A person of mixed racial descent, especially one of North American Indian and French Canadian, or white, ancestry. See also MESTIZA/MESTIZO.

meunière *(meun-YAIR)* [French, from *à la meunière:* in the manner of the miller's wife] In French cooking, fish that has been dipped in flour, SAUTÉED quickly in butter and lemon juice, and garnished with parsley. ⟨diners enjoy green-bean salad laced with foie gras, preserved duck and excellent sole *meunière.*⟩— *The New York Times,* June 7, 1998.

mezzanine *(MEZ-ah-neen)* [French, from Italian; Latin] In a theater, the lowest balcony or the front rows of the balcony. A partial floor between the main floors, often between the ground floor and the one above it.

mezzo *(MET-zoh)* [Italian] In the arts: half, medium, or middle, usually combined with another word, e.g., MEZZOTINT, *mezzo*-soprano, or *mezza* voce (with half the power of the voice). ⟨No less direct was the Carmen of *mezzo*-soprano Suzanna Guzman, a fire-eating singing actress.⟩—*Time,* June 22, 1998.

mezzo e mezzo *(MET-zoh ay MET-zoh)* [Italian] A slang expression for "half and half"; "fifty-fifty."

Mezzogiorno *(MET-zoh JYOR-noh)* [Italian: midday] Southern Italy. Similar to the French term MIDI. ⟨sociologist Raffaele Romanelli on development in the *Mezzogiorno*⟩—Italian edition of *The New York Review of Books,* March 4, 1999.

mezzotint *(MET-zoh-tint)* [Italian, contraction of *mezza tinta:* half dyed] A method of engraving on a roughened metal plate by scraping or polishing certain areas to produce subtle gradations of tone.

miasma *(mee-AZ-mah)* [Latin, from Greek: pollution] Harmful or foul-smelling air caused by rotting organic matter. By extension, an unwholesome or morbid atmosphere or influence.

Midi *(mee-DEE)* [French: noon] Southern France. Similar to the Italian term MEZZOGIORNO.

mignon *(meen-YONH)* [French] Small, cute, dainty, or delicate and pretty, as in *filet mignon,* a small and delicate-flavored cut of meat.

mikado *(mih-KAH-doh)* [Japanese: exalted gate] Formerly, a title given to the emperor of Japan, used mostly in English. Also, the title of an operetta by Gilbert and Sullivan, first performed in March 1885.

mikvah *(MEEK-vah, MIK-vah)* [Hebrew] In Orthodox Judaism, the cleansing and purifying ritual bath required on some occasions, as before the Sabbath.

milieu *(mee-LYEU)* [French, from Latin: middle] The setting, sphere, surroundings, or environment, often of a social or cultural nature, as in "the artistic *milieu.*" ⟨In *milieus* like these . . . it seems no more than reasonable for the Church's rulers to adopt the language of imperial Rome.⟩—*The New York Review of Books,* March 4, 1999.

minaudière *(mee-noh-DYAIR)* [French: an affected person] A small case, carried like a handbag, made to hold a woman's personal items or cosmetics; often elaborately embroidered or jeweled. See also ETUI.

minestrone *(mih-nes-TROH-neh)* [Italian: rich soup] A thick Italian soup typically containing dried beans, pasta, and vegetables, often served with grated cheese. There is no single recipe; rather, it is based on whatever materials are at hand, including leftovers.

minutiae (plural); **minutia** (singular) *(mih-NOOSH-yah)* [Latin: smallness] Trifles; small or unimportant matters; precise details, as in "the *minutiae* of the law." ⟨The study focused on the *minutiae* of describing fossil species.⟩

mir *(meer)* [Russian: peace] The world; peace. In prerevolutionary Russia, a peasant commune or village of farmers, later replaced by the collective farm. Also, the name of the Soviet-built space station launched in 1987. ⟨Russian space officials announced Tuesday that unless private funding . . . comes to the rescue, the space station *Mir* will be abandoned to die a fiery death in the Earth's atmosphere sometime in spring 2000.⟩—*Time*, June 1, 1999.

mirabile dictu *(mee-RAH-bee-leh DIK-too)* [Latin] Wonderful to relate; strange to say. ⟨But then—*mirabile dictu*—through the hubbub of the marketplace, there was a tiny whisper of sanity.⟩—*The Guardian*, April 25, 1999.

mirador *(mih-rah-DOR)* [Spanish, from Latin: to look or wonder at] An enclosed balcony affording an extensive view; a watchtower or lookout site.

mise en bouteille *(meez anh boo-TAY)* [French: put in a bottle] On a wine bottle (or its cork), a statement that identifies the bottler and the place where the wine was bottled, as in *"mise en bouteille au château"*: bottled at the winery.

mise en page *(MEEZ anh PAHZH)* [French] The placement of text or illustration on the printed page.

mise-en-scène *(meez ahn SEN)* [French] In theater or filmmaking, the placement of scenery, props, actors, etc.; the stage or studio setting itself. By extension, the general environment or physical surroundings. 〈As director, she was responsible for every aspect of the *mise-en-scène.*〉

miso *(MEE-soh)* [Japanese] In Japanese cooking, a paste made with fermented soybeans, salt, and a cereal grain, used to flavor sauces and soups.

mistral *(mee-STRAHL)* [French, from Provençal: master wind] A cold, dry, violent wind that blows down from the north along the lower Rhône Valley through southern France and nearby areas.

mitzvah *(MITZ-vah)* [Hebrew] In Judaism, a commandment, precept, or rule of conduct taken from the Bible or issued by a rabbi; any commendable or praiseworthy deed. See also BAR MITZVAH, BAT MITZVAH.

moccasin *(MOK-kah-sin)* [Algonquian] A light, heelless shoe with sides and bottom made of a single piece of soft leather. By extension, any comfortable shoe made of soft leather and without a prominent heel.

moderato *(moh-deh-RAH-toh)* [Italian] A musical term meaning in moderate time, or moderately. A musical passage or movement to be played at moderate speed.

modus operandi *(MOH-dus oh-peh-RAHN-dee)* [Latin] A manner of proceeding; a way of working or operating. Abreviated as *m.o.* or MO, especially in contemporary detective fiction. 〈Over the years, we've developed a *modus operandi* for family vacations.〉

modus vivendi *(MOH-dus vee-VEHN-dee)* [Latin] A way of living; lifestyle. A temporary agreement between disputing parties that enables them to continue debate until a final settlement is reached. ⟨shows no understanding at all of Alf Ramsey's *modus vivendi*⟩—*The Guardian,* February 15, 1999.

mogul *(MOH-gul)* [Persian: Mongol] A person of great power, as were the Muslim invaders of India in the 16th century. The heads of the great Hollywood motion picture studios of the 1930s were referred to as *moguls.* ⟨Alfred Hugenberg, the press *mogul* and Krupp chairman.⟩—*The New York Review of Books,* March 4, 1999.

mole *(MOH-lay)* [Mexican Spanish] In Mexican cooking, a smooth, pungent sauce based on chili peppers, vegetables, spices, and (often) a small amount of unsweetened chocolate.

molto *(MOHL-toh)* [Italian] In music, a term meaning very, or much, as in "*molto* vivace": very lively, or "*molto* semplice": very simple and unaffected.

momzer, mamzer *(MOM-zer)* [Yiddish, from Hebrew] An illegitimate child; a bastard; a detestable person. An untrustworthy, difficult, or impudent person. Sometimes used affectionately to describe a clever child or someone who is unusually resourceful. Also written as *momser.*

monde *(monhd)* [French] People; society; the world; everything that exists. See also FEMME DU MONDE, HOMME DU MONDE, TOUT LE MONDE.

monsieur *(meu-SYEU)* [French: my lord] The French title of courtesy or term of address for a man, equivalent to mister or sir. The more formal title of *monseigneur* is conferred upon princes, bishops, cardinals of the church, etc.

monsignor *(mohn-seen-YOR)* [Italian] In the Roman Catholic Church, a title given to certain priests and officials; a person holding this title.

monsoon *(mon-SOON)* [Dutch, from Portugese, from Arabic: season] A seasonal wind of southern Asia and the Indian Ocean that changes direction with the seasons; in India, the summer winds that bring heavy rains; the rainy season that results from the *monsoon.* ⟨[They] will be forced to leave the mountain in two weeks when the climbing season gives way to the annual *monsoons.*⟩—*The Guardian,* May 17, 1999.

montage *(monh-TAHZH)* [French, from *monter:* to mount] The technique of creating a composite picture by combining pieces from other pictorial elements or designs. In motion pictures, the technique of combining several short, disconnected shots to suggest a change of place or the passage of time; the partial superimposition of a number of shots to form a single image. A work produced by any of these methods.

Montagnard *(monh-tahn-YAHR)* [French: mountaineer] In the Vietnamese highlands, one of a group of dark-complected people of mixed ethnic origin. ⟨This officer and a sergeant said they were told by their *Montagnard* mercenaries there were a dozen to 20 Caucasian bodies found.⟩—*Time,* June 29, 1998.

moraine *(moh-RAYN)* [French, from Savoyard dialect] Debris in the form of boulders, gravel, sand, and dirt, torn from mountain slopes by glacial movement and deposited at the sides or base of the glacier; a mound or ridge formed by such deposits. Long Island, New York, consists entirely of terminal *moraine* from the glaciers of the last Ice Age. ⟨The *moraine* pens up the vast field of icebergs that keeps ships away from the front of the glacier.⟩

morceau (singular); **morceaux** (plural) *(mohr-SOH)* [French] A fragment; a piece; a small part separated from the whole; a short passage of music or poetry.

morgue *(morg)* [French, from the building in Paris that housed unidentified bodies] A mortuary; a place where dead victims

of accidents or other violence are kept until they can be identi-
fied or buried. Also, in a newspaper office, the reference file of
old clippings and records maintained in case of need, or the
place where such material is kept. ⟨They had to pick up the
body from the city *morgue.*⟩

moshav (singular)**; moshavim** (plural) *(moh-shahv, mo-shah-VEEM)*
[Hebrew: dwelling] In Israel, a cooperative settlement that consists of small farm units. See also KIBBUTZ.

mosque *(mosk)* [French, from Italian and Arabic] A Muslim place
of public worship; a temple.

mot *(moh)* [French, from Latin: word; utterance] A witty remark
or saying. See also BON MOT.

motif *(moh-TEEF)* [French] A distinctive, recurring theme, idea,
or subject in an artistic or literary work or piece of design; in
music, a theme or melody that is repeated and sometimes
developed. Also, a prevailing idea or dominant feature. See also
LEITMOTIF. ⟨According to reports in the trade press, Luper's *motif*
is the number 92⟩—*The Guardian,* May 7, 1999.

mot juste *(moh JÜST)* [French] The most precise or appropriate
word; the perfect expression. ⟨This author found the *mot juste*
to describe the social life of her celebrated neighbor.⟩

moue *(moo)* [French] A facial expression of displeasure; a grim-
ace of petulance or disdain, made by pushing out the lips; a
pout. ⟨She registered her opinion with a *moue* of distaste.⟩

moussaka *(moo-SAH-kah)* [Greek, Turkish] A dish of Balkan origin, made with ground meat, eggplant, and tomato sauce,
topped with a rich white sauce containing cheese and spices.

mousse *(mooss)* [French: foam; froth] A rich dessert, frozen or
served very cold, based on whipped cream or beaten eggs, or

both; a molded, SOUFFLÉ-like dish of PUREED fish, meat, or vegetables. A frothy preparation used to hold the hair in place.

moyen-âge *(mwah-yen AHZH)* [French] The Middle Ages.

mozzarella *(moht-zah-REH-lah)* [Italian] A soft, bland Italian cheese that melts easily, often used as a topping on PIZZA or other dishes; it is made from buffalo's milk or cow's milk.

muck-a-muck *(MUK-ah-muk)* [Chinook jargon: plenty to eat] In slang, when preceded by the word "high-," an important or high-ranking person with an arrogant or officious manner.

muezzin *(moo-EZ-zin)* [Turkish, from Arabic] A crier who summons the Muslim faithful to prayer several times each day, chanting the AZAN from a minaret or a high place on a MOSQUE. ⟨As the *muezzin's* call to prayer echoes down the marble corridors of Southeast Asia's largest MOSQUE⟩—*Time,* November 30, 1998.

mufti *(MUFF-tee)* [Arabic] Plain clothes; civilian dress, especially when worn by someone usually seen in uniform. In ISLAM, an expert in religious law; a legal adviser. ⟨The vast majority of Muslims observe the fast, which in Egypt begins after the crescent of the new moon is spotted from the desert by lookouts for the Grand *Mufti,* the nation's highest religious authority.⟩—*Time,* January 27, 1997.

mujahedin, mujahideen *(moo-jah-heh-DEEN)* [Arabic or Persian: one who fights in a JIHAD] In Afghanistan and Iran, the Muslim rebels or GUERRILLA fighters. Also written *mujaheddin, mujahidin.*

mukluk *(MUK-luk)* [Alaskan Eskimo: bearded seal] A soft, furlined Eskimo boot made of reindeer skin or sealskin; a similar boot or lounge footwear made in the United States from less exotic materials.

mullah *(MULL-ah)* [Turkish, Persian, Urdu, from Arabic: master] A Muslim title of respect for a religious leader or teacher of sacred law. Also, a Turkish provincial judge. ⟨The *mullah*, a cleric, is not known to be related to the current President.⟩—*The New York Times*, September 28, 1996.

mumbo jumbo *(MUM-boh JUM-boh)* [West African, possibly Mandingo] Meaningless ritual; senseless observance; needlessly complicated incantation or language; gibberish; gobbledygook. A fetish, or object of superstitious reverence or fear. ⟨with enough visual panache and sub-spiritual *mumbo jumbo* to appeal to adults as well.⟩—*The Guardian*, April 24, 1999.

musique concrète *(mu-ZEEK konh-KREHT)* [French: concrete music] Music based on tape-recorded sounds generated by hardware or machines, or recorded natural or musical sounds, often electronically distorted, and arranged in patterns, combinations, sequences, etc.

mutatis mutandis *(moo-TAH-tiss moo-TAHN-diss)* [Latin] Changes having been made. ⟨*Mutatis mutandis* . . . we can hope for a peaceful settlement.⟩

muumuu *(moo-moo)* [Hawaiian] In Hawaii, a long, loose, flowing woman's garment, gathered at the neckline, usually made of bright-colored cotton; a housedress in similar style. ⟨She celebrated her 85th birthday in a brilliant *muumuu* with matching turban.⟩

muzhik, mujik *(moo-ZHEEK)* [Russian: man; husband] In czarist Russia, a peasant. More recently, a colloquial term for "a man's man." Also written *moujik, muzjhik.* ⟨Mr. Stepashin is a former fireman with no known interests outside work and a reputation as a *muzhik,* or macho man.⟩—*The Guardian*, May 13, 1999.

N

nabob, nawab *(NAY-bob, nah-BOB, nah-WAHB)* [Hindi] Under the old MOGUL empire, a viceroy, or governor. More recently, a European whose wealth was acquired in India, or any powerful or immensely wealthy person. ⟨In 2003, go the national-security *nabobs,* China will have a new and improved generation of nuclear weapons.⟩—*Time,* May 27, 1999.

nacelle *(nah-SELL)* [French: small boat] On an aircraft, balloon, or motorcycle, an enclosure that houses the engine, or one in which passengers or cargo are carried. ⟨Engines and fuel tanks, carried outside the fuselage of a plane, are enclosed in *nacelles* to reduce air drag.⟩

nacho *(NAH-choh)* [Mexican Spanish] A popular snack made from TORTILLA chips topped with melted cheese and chopped chili peppers.

nacre *(NAH-ker)* [French, from Italian, Arabic] Mother-of-pearl.

nada *(NAH-dah)* [Spanish] Nothing; not at all. See also DE NADA.

nadir *(NAY-der, NAY-deer)* [Arabic: opposite (the zenith)] On the celestial sphere, the point exactly beneath the position of the observer and diametrically opposite the ZENITH; the lowest point. By extension, the time of greatest personal or societal distress or adversity. ⟨He feels that the Thatcher government represents the antithesis of that sentiment and the *nadir* of the post-war selfishness that his story excoriates.⟩—*The New York Times,* October 19, 1986.

naïf, naif *(nah-EEF)* [French, from the masculine form of *naive*] Usually used as a noun: a person who lacks worldly experience or informed judgment; one who is unaffected, artless, or uncritical.

nainsook *(NAYN-sook)* [Urdu, Hindi: pleasure of the eye] A fine, soft, lightweight cotton cloth similar to BATISTE.

naissance *(nay-SANHS)* [French] A birth; a beginning; the creation of a being, an idea, an organization, a movement, or a trend. See also RENAISSANCE.

naïveté *(nah-eev-TAY)* [French] The state or quality of being naive. See NAIF. ⟨Juve's passing and movement and their ability to retain possession highlighted United's *naïveté* at this level.⟩—*The Guardian,* March 19, 1999.

nano- *(NAH-noh)* [Greek, from *nanos:* dwarf] A combining form meaning minute, or abnormally small. In the metric system, one-billionth of a particular unit, as in *nanosecond.*

napoleon *(nah-POH-lee-en)* [French, after Napoléon Bonaparte] A light pastry with custard or cream filling between each of three layers, usually topped with a light frosting or with powdered sugar.

narghile See HOOKAH.

narwhal *(NAHR-wahl)* [Norwegian, Swedish, Danish] A small whale that inhabits arctic waters, having a long, straight tusk (grooved in a spiral) extending from the upper lip.

nature *See* AU NATUREL.

nautch *(nawch)* [Hindi: dance] In India, an entertainment or exhibition of dances performed by professional dancing girls, called *nautch* girls.

navarin *(nah-vah-RENH)* [French, from the (Greek) Bay of Navarin, or the battle of Navarino (1827)] A French stew made from lamb *(navarin d'agneau)* or mutton *(navarin de mouton)* and vegetables.

nawab See NABOB.

nebbish *(NEH-bish)* [Yiddish, from Czech] An unfortunate; a weak, luckless, and ineffectual person; a wimp; a loser; a pitiful specimen.

née *(nay)* [French: born] Born with the name of. Used to indicate the maiden name of a married woman, as in "Mrs. Abigail Adams, *née* Smith."

negligee *(NEH-glih-zhay)* [French: neglected] A woman's loose robe or dressing gown, often made of light, sheer fabric; any informal, comfortable garment. Used as an adjective: carelessly dressed.

nemesis *(NEM-eh-sis)* [Greek, from *némein:* to dispense justice] In classical myth, the goddess of retribution. A person who represents the destruction of a plan or project; something that cannot be overcome or conquered. ⟨It seems that 10 straight judicial defeats before his old *nemesis,* Judge Bullingham (Bill Fraser), convinced Rumpole that it was time to try being an orange in the Florida sun.⟩—*The New York Times,* October 11, 1984.

nene *(nay-nay)* [Hawaiian] The state bird of Hawaii; a wild, brownish gray goose.

nepenthe *(neh-PEN-thee)* [Greek: no sorrow] As described in the *Odyssey,* a drug or drink with sedative properties that induces forgetfulness of trouble or sorrow; anything that causes a pleasant sensation of oblivion.

ne plus ultra *(neh ploos ool-trah)* [Latin: no more beyond] The utmost point; the acme; perfection; the highest degree of a state or quality. ⟨the holocaust remain(s) the 20th century baseline for the discussion of evil, the *ne plus ultra.*⟩—*Time,* July 20, 1998.

n'est-ce pas? *(ness PAH)* [French] Isn't that so? Don't you agree? The equivalent in German is NICHT WAHR?

netsuke *(NET-soo-keh)* [Japanese] A decorative figure carved in wood or ivory or cast in ceramic or metal, once worn on a man's sash as a toggle, often with small items suspended from it. *Netsuke* are prized by many collectors.

névé *(nay-VAY)* [Franco-Provençal] The granular snow that accumulates on high mountain slopes and is eventually compressed into glacial ice; skiers refer to it as "corn snow" or "spring snow."

nexus *(NEK-sus)* [Latin: a joining] A link between members of a series or group; a connected group or series. By extension, the essence or core of something or of a situation. ⟨with only a marginal impact on Scotland's own political *nexus.*⟩—*The Guardian,* April 18, 1999.

niche *(neesh)* [French, from Latin] A shallow nook or recessed space in a wall, often arched, in which a statue or art object is displayed. Figuratively, a location or position in life that is appropriate for someone or something, as in "She found her *niche* as a photographer of babies." ⟨She was given another chance, as cohost of a morning talk show, and instantly found her *niche.*⟩—*Time,* August 8, 1988.

nichevo *(nee-cheh-VOH)* [Russian] Nothing. It doesn't matter. Don't mention it.

nicht wahr? *(nikht VAHR)* [German] Isn't that so? See also N'EST-CE PAS?

nimbus *(NIM-bus)* [Latin: cloud] In art, a luminous aura surrounding a person or thing, especially a deity or holy person; a halo; the atmosphere around a person of unusual fame or glamour. Also, a dense, low cloud mass that yields continuous rain or snow. ⟨A reputation for quiet and effective mediation is beginning to glow like a *nimbus* about his head.⟩

niña (f), **niño** (m) *(NEEN-yah, NEEN-yoh)* [Spanish] A child. See also LA NIÑA, EL NIÑO.

ninja *(NIN-jah)* [Japanese, from Chinese: he who endures] In feudal Japan, a mercenary skilled in the martial arts and in covert operations such as ESPIONAGE, SABOTAGE, and assassination. ⟨In densely populated East Java, a mysterious spate of gruesome *"ninja*-style" murders has gone on for more than six months.⟩—*Time,* February 8, 1999.

nirvana *(nir-VAH-nah)* [Sanskrit: extinction] In Buddhist and Hindu teaching, a liberation of the self from passion, desire, pain, and worldly cares; a state of bliss or absolute inner harmony. ⟨According to tradition, after the Buddha attained *Nirvana* his body was cremated and a number of teeth were found in the ashes.⟩—*The Guardian,* May 22, 1999.

Nisei *(nee-say)* [Japanese: second generation] A person born in the United States of immigrant Japanese parents, especially those who were forced into isolated camps, in a misguided attempt to increase security during World War II. See also ISSEI, KIBEI, SANSEI. ⟨Although her parents were *Nisei,* they continued to speak Japanese at home.⟩

No, Noh *(noh)* [Japanese, from Chinese: ability] An aristocratic and highly stylized form of drama, developed in Japan in the 14th century, using poetry, prose, chorus, and dance. *No* plays are short, tragic, and have little plot. See also KYOGEN.

noblesse oblige *(noh-BLESS oh-BLEEZH)* [French: nobility requires] The understanding that the privileged existence of those in high places entails a moral responsibility to act honorably and generously toward others. ⟨Gillespie, exercising a monarch's *noblesse oblige,* also appeared, unbilled, at "Bebop, Forty and Under," a JVC program that I missed.⟩—*The Atlantic Monthly*, March 1992.

noisette *(nwah-ZEHT)* [French: little nut; kernel] A hazelnut, or the light-brown color of hazelnut. Also, a small, round cut of meat, such as a tenderloin of beef.

nolo contendere *(NOH-loh con-TEN-deh-reh)* [Latin: I do not wish to contend] In criminal law, a defendant's plea that acknowledges the validity of conviction but denies guilt; the plea has the same effect as an admission of guilt, but allows the defendant to plead not guilty to charges in other proceedings.

nom de guerre *(nonh deu GAIR)* [French: war name] A pseudonym or assumed name, chosen to conceal one's identity during a particular action. Men who joined the French Foreign Legion frequently took a *nom de guerre*. See also NOM DE PLUME.

nom de plume *(nonh deu PLÜM)* [French] A pen name; a false name used to conceal an author's identity. The 19th-century English novelist Mary Ann Evans had her work published under the *nom de plume* of George Eliot. ⟨he chose the name of his favorite restaurant as a *nom de plume*.⟩—*The New Yorker*, March 8, 1999.

non compos mentis *(non com-pohs MEN-tiss)* [Latin] Not of sound mind; mentally unstable; incapable of normal mental function. ⟨At least one elderly relative is *non compos mentis* and unable to care for himself.⟩

nonpareil *(non-pah-RYE)* [French] Without equal; peerless; a paragon. Also, a small chocolate candy decorated with tiny grains of white sugar.

non sequitur *(non SEH-kwih-toor)* [Latin: it does not follow] An illogical or irrelevant conclusion, or an inference that does not follow from the premise. Any statement that has no connection or relevance to what has preceded it. ⟨George's indulgent prodding of Gracie's flighty *non sequiturs* and malapropisms helped make them the most popular male-female comedy act of the century.⟩—*Time,* March 18, 1996.

nosh *(nawsh)* [Yiddish: to nibble; gnaw] A slang term meaning to snack or eat between meals; the snack itself.

nostrum *(NOH-strum)* [Latin: ours] A homemade medicine; a quack medicine or remedy that has no proven benefit, especially one falsely advertised. By extension, a favorite plan, theory, or remedy for political or social problems; a PANACEA.

nota bene *(NOH-tah BEH-neh)* [Latin: note well] Take notice. Often abbreviated in a text as *N.B.*

note verbale *(noht vehr-BAHL)* [French] A written, unsigned communication delivered by a diplomat to a foreign government.

nougat *(NOO-get, noo-GAH)* [French] A chewy candy made from roasted nuts and honey or sugar syrup, sometimes with the addition of egg whites.

nouveau riche (singular)**; nouveaux riches** (plural) *(noo-voh REESH)* [French] A person who has recently become rich; one who flaunts his or her new wealth. ⟨Here, the *nouveaux riches* have spirited immense sums of money out of the country in recent years, adding to the economic debacle.⟩

nouveauté *(noo-voh-TAY)* [French: newness] A novelty; a new thing.

nouvelle cuisine *(noo-VEL kwee-ZEEN)* [French: new cooking] A French style of cooking, introduced in the 1970s, that replaces butter, cream, lard, and other traditional elements with reduced stocks, herbal flavorings, and lighter, fresher ingredients. ⟨In New York City, *nouvelle cuisine* is already old hat.⟩

nouvelle vague *(noo-vel VAHG)* [French: new wave] The young generation of the artistic AVANT-GARDE. The group of young

French and Italian directors of the late 1950s who experimented with a looser, more spontaneous and intimate style of film-making. ⟨The films of the '60s were informed by the example of the *Nouvelle Vague*, a French political movement inspired by the polemics of the great director Jean-Luc Godard.⟩—*Time*, April 28, 1997.

novella *(noh-VEL-lah)* [Italian] A short novel, short narrative, or morality tale such as those in Giovanni Boccaccio's *Decameron* (1351–1353). Prose fiction that is longer and more developed than a short story; a novelette. ⟨Henry James's brilliant *novella* of moral humiliation, "The Spoils of Poynton."⟩

novena *(noh-VEH-nah, noh-VEE-nah)* [Latin, from *novem:* nine] In the Roman Catholic Church, a series of special public or private prayers held on nine successive days, often the nine days before a feast, in honor of the Virgin Mary or a saint.

novia (f), **novio** (m) *(NOH-vee-yah, NOH-vee-yoh)* [Spanish] In the feminine: a FIANCÉE or bride; a sweetheart or girlfriend. In the masculine: a FIANCÉ or bridegroom; a sweetheart or boyfriend.

nu *(noo)* [Yiddish, from Russian] Well? So? What's new? How goes it? How about it? So what?

nuance *(nü-ANHS)* [French: shade; hue] A fine or subtle shade of meaning; a subtle difference in expression. A delicate variation in tone or color. ⟨The companies distinguish their products with *nuances* of wording which acknowledge Elsener's initiative.⟩—*The Guardian*, May 22, 1999.

nudj, nudje *(noodj)* [Yiddish] A slang term for a pest; a badgerer; a nag; a bore. To pester; to be tedious or tiresome. Also written *nudzh, noodge.*

nudnik *(NOOD-nik)* [Yiddish] A slang term for an annoying, tiresome, dull person; a pest. ⟨Jane Austen masterfully portrayed one hen-pecking, match-making, officious *nudnik* of a mother after another.⟩—*The New York Times*, May 11, 1997.

nuée ardente *(nü-ay ahr-DONHT)* [French: fiery cloud] In a volcanic eruption, a destructive, incandescent cloud of gas-enveloped volcanic particles that flows rapidly down the slightest incline. Sometimes called a *glowing avalanche.*

numen *(NOO-men)* [Latin: divine nod] A divine power or presiding spirit said to inhabit a person or an object that is regarded with awe. An inner quality or force that guides and animates.

nunchaku *(nun-CHAH-koo)* [Okinawan Japanese, from Taiwanese dialect] A defensive hand weapon used in parts of Asia: two short hardwood sticks connected by a heavy rope or chain that extends the width of the body.

nuncio *(NOON-see-oh)* [Italian, from Latin: messenger] A representative of the pope, accredited to a foreign court or civil government; an envoy with the status of ambassador. ⟨The Colombian bosses allegedly employ Carillo as a kind of *nuncio* for communicating information to the Mexican federation.⟩—*Time,* May 29, 1995.

nyet *(nyeht)* [Russian] No. ⟨the nonnegotiable *nyet* delivered by Nikita Khrushchev at the United Nations⟩

obeah, obi *(OH-bee-ah)* [Gullah, etc.: magic; charm] A form of belief that involves the practice of sorcery, exercised in parts of Africa, the southeastern United States, the West Indies, and South America; a charm or fetish used by its practitioners.

obento See BENTO.

obi *(oh-bee)* [Japanese: girdle] In Japan, a long, broad sash wrapped around a woman's waist over a KIMONO, with a loop or bow in the back.

obiter dictum *(OH-bih-tehr DIK-tum)* [Latin: said by the way; said in passing] A judge's opinion on a point that is not essential to his decision on a case, and therefore has no binding authority. By extension, a passing comment or observation; an incidental remark. ⟨In this unheroic age, when we all try to reduce our comments to what lawyers call *obiter dictum* (things said in passing), it's tempting to lump the spread of disclaimers with other cultural phenomena.⟩—*The New York Times,* January 3, 1999.

objet d'art *(ob-zhay DAHR)* [French] Any object or item of artistic value; a term generally applied to small objects.

objet trouvé *(ob-zhay troo-VAY)* [French: found object] Something natural or machine-made that is considered beautiful or aesthetically pleasing, displayed alone or incorporated into a work of art. Old machine parts, for example, or bits of found metal are sometimes used in modern sculpture.

oblast *(OH-blahst)* [Russian, from Old Slavonic: on authority] A province or region. In the former Soviet Union, an administrative or territorial division that was sometimes autonomous. ⟨The most prominent candidate . . . was running for the upper chamber in Kaluga *Oblast,* or province.⟩—*The New York Times,* December 8, 1993.

ocarina *(ok-ah-REE-nah)* [Italian] A simple musical instrument made of clay, shaped like an elongated egg, with a hole to blow into and six finger holes to control the pitch; its sound is similar to that of a flute. Also called "sweet potato."

octavo *(ok-TAH-voh)* [Latin: in an eighth] A printer's full-size sheet folded into eight leaves, or sixteen pages, forming a book of about 6 × 9 inches; usually reserved for printing choral music.

oda, odah *(OH-dah)* [Turkish] A room inside a HAREM.

odalisque *(oh-dah-LEESK)* [French, from Turkish] A female concubine or slave in a HAREM; a painting or representation of such a person. ⟨William painted her in the languorous pose of an *odalisque.*⟩

odeum *(OH-deh-um)* [Latin, from Greek *odeon:* song hall] A theater or hall designed for dramatic or musical performances. In ancient Greece and Rome, a roofed structure for such entertainment.

odium *(OH-dee-um)* [Latin] The disgrace or reproach attached to something hateful. The state of being hateful or the quality of hatefulness. Loathing; hatred; extreme dislike or aversion. ⟨After he was found to be a paid informer, an aura of *odium* surrounded him.⟩

oeil-de-boeuf *(EUY-deu-BEUF)* [French: eye of an ox] In architecture, a small circular or oval window, sometimes called a *bull's-eye window;* often seen in 17th-century English manor houses.

oeillade *(eu-ee-YAHD)* [French] An amorous glance; a furtive or impertinent glance or stare.

oeuvre *(EU-vreu)* [French: a work] The works of an author, composer, painter, etc., seen as a whole, or any single work of such a person. ⟨An American Picasso, maybe? No: the *oeuvre* lacks that vast span.⟩—*Time,* November 9, 1998.

oficina *(oh-fee-SEE-nah)* [Spanish] An office or shop.

ogre *(OH-ger)* [French, from Latin Orcus: god of the underworld] In fairy tales, a voracious giant who devours small children; a hideous monster; a cruel or barbarous person.

ojo *(OH-hoh)* [Spanish] Eye.

olio *(OH-lee-oh)* [Spanish, from *olla:* pot; stew] A miscellaneous collection; a hodgepodge, medley, or POTPOURRI of musical or literary pieces; a dish containing many ingredients. Not the same as the Italian word *òlio:* oil.

olla *(OH-LAH, OY-ah)* [Spanish] A pot or kettle, particularly a traditional Spanish earthenware cooking pot.

olla podrida *(OH-lah poh-DREE-dah)* [Spanish: rotten pot] A Spanish stew made with meat and/or chicken, chickpeas, CHORIZO, and vegetables. Also, an OLIO.

ombudsman *(ahm-BUDZ-men)* [Swedish: legal representative] An official appointed to investigate individuals' grievances against public authorities, companies, universities, etc. ⟨As *ombudsman* for the magazine, it was his job to hold editors and writers to a high standard of performance.⟩

omen *(OH-men)* [Latin] An event or phenomenon regarded as a prophetic sign; an augury or portent.

omertà *(oh-mehr-TAH)* [Italian] The code of silence; an oath of secrecy. An important element in the MAFIA's system of private justice, which forbade its people to seek help from or cooperate with legal authorities. Failure to keep *omertà* would result in reprisals from the Mafia. ⟨The culture of *omertà* still prevails in the Tuscan countryside.⟩—*The Guardian,* March 27, 1999.

omnia vincit amor   See AMOR VINCIT OMNIA.

ongepotchket *(AWN-geh-potch-kit)* [Yiddish, from German *Patsch:* a blow] Put together in a sloppy or senseless manner: excessively decorated in tasteless fashion; overly BAROQUE in style.

onomatopoeia *(on-oh-mah-toh-PEH-yah)* [Greek: word making] The formation of words that imitate what they represent, or that imitate natural sounds associated with the word, e.g., "crack," "sizzle," or "cuckoo."

onus *(OH-nus)* [Latin] A burden; the responsibility for doing something; a duty; an obligation. ⟨Rather than putting the *onus* solely on developing countries, however, the international community should focus on how the so-called Group of Three (Japan, the U.S. and Germany) created so much liquidity.⟩— *Time,* May 18, 1998.

onus probandi *(OH-nus proh-BAHN-dee)* [Latin] The burden of proof; the obligation to prove an allegation or charge that rests with the person making it.

op. cit. See OPERE CITATO.

opéra bouffe *(oh-peh-rah BOOF)* [French] A comic opera; a farce in the form of an opera.

opera buffa *(oh-peh-rah BOO-fah)* [Italian] A comic opera of the 18th century, often in two acts. The GENRE of such works. ⟨an *opera buffa* by Martìn y Soler, from which Mozart borrowed a theme for a scene in "Don Giovanni"⟩

opéra comique *(oh-peh-rah koh-MEEK)* [French] An opera, usually a comedy, with spoken dialogue.

opera seria *(op-eh-rah SEH-ree-ah)* [Italian] An 18th-century dramatic or serious Italian opera, usually in three acts; Mozart's *Idomeneo* is an example. ⟨The *opera seria* of the early 1600s was an attempt to revive the spirit of Greek tragedy.⟩

opere citato *(op-eh-reh see-TAH-toh)* [Latin] (In the) work(s) already cited; often abbreviated *op.cit.*

operetta *(op-er-EHT-tah)* [Italian] A popular musical play with spoken dialogue, often of a sentimental or humorous nature.

opprobrium *(oh-PROH-bree-um)* [Latin] The disgrace or humiliation brought by a shameful act; infamy. A cause of reproach, disdain, or disgrace.

opus *(OH-pus)* [Latin: a work] A musical composition; one of a list of musical works numbered in order of their creation or publication. Also, a literary work such as a novel or poem. ⟨In 1995 Bradshaw brought Davies and Winnipeg composer Randolph Peters together to create the actual *opus.*⟩—*Time,* April 26, 1999.

oratorio *(or-ah-TOH-ree-oh)* [Italian: small oratory; a place for prayer] A musical composition for chorus, orchestra, and solo voices, often dramatizing a religious story, but without scenery or action. ⟨The festival will conclude with a performance of "Golgotha," an *oratorio* by the Swiss composer Frank Martin.⟩

oregano *(oh-REH-gah-noh)* [Spanish, from Latin: wild marjoram] An aromatic, perennial herb of the mint family, used often as a seasoning in Italian and Mexican cooking.

origami *(oh-ree-GAH-mee)* [Japanese] The ancient Japanese art of folding a sheet of paper to represent an animal or flower, without recourse to scissors or glue.

ormolu *(OR-moh-loo)* [French: milled (ground) gold] Gilded brass or bronze; an alloy of copper, tin, and zinc that looks like gold, used to decorate furniture, art objects, jewelry, etc. Also, the objects made with or from *ormolu.* Sometimes called *mosaic gold.* ⟨the signs of the zodiac and the phases of the moon, all in bronze and *ormolu*⟩—*The New York Times,* November 29, 1984.

osso buco, osso bucco *(OS-soh BOO-koh)* [Italian] In Italian cooking, a dish of braised veal shanks prepared with olive oil, wine, tomatoes, etc.

ostinato *(os-tee-NAH-toh)* [Italian: obstinate; persistent] In music, a tone or figure, usually in the bass line, that repeats without change while the rest of the music continues.

ottoman *(OT-toh-men)* [French, from Italian, after the founder of the Ottoman Empire] A cushioned footrest; a low, upholstered seat or DIVAN, usually without arms or back.

oubliette *(oo-blee-EHT)* [French: from *oublier:* to forget] A secret, underground cell in a castle, with an entrance that was only a hole in the stone floor above, where individual prisoners were kept, usually until they died. ⟨In this final picture the legendary figure of the president of the First Czech Republic gazes from his homemade *oubliette* like Vodník himself peering from some South Bohemian pond.⟩—*The New Criterion,* May 1999.

oud *(ood)* [Arabic: wood] An Arabian stringed instrument similar to the lute.

outrance *(oo-TRANHS)* [French] The utmost extremity. To or unto *outrance:* to a degree beyond all limits.

outré *(oo-TRAY)* [French: exaggerated] Bizarre, outrageous, or beyond the limits of what is thought proper or tasteful. ⟨the hotbed of *outré* contemporary art⟩

ouzo *(OO-zoh)* [Greek] A clear Greek liqueur or APERITIF flavored with anise; like ABSINTHE, it turns milky when water is added.

oxymoron *(ok-see-MOH-ron)* [Greek: smart stupidity] A self-contradictory expression, such as "wise fool." ⟨The enigmatic and versatile heroine of the novel has been described as an *oxymoron* incarnate.⟩

pachinko *(pah-CHING-koh)* [Japanese: little click] A Japanese pinball game played on a vertical machine. 〈But a two-week trip through the day-to-day world of coffee shops, *pachinko* parlors, schools, bars, train stations, and living rooms reveals something very different.〉—*Time,* February 8, 1999.

pachisi, parchesi *(pah-CHEE-zee, par-CHEE-zee)* [Hindi: twenty-five] In India, a board game of ancient origin for four players, similar to backgammon; moves are made by throws of cowrie shells or dice, with the highest throw being twenty-five. Also written as *parchisi.*

pachuco *(pah-CHOO-koh)* [American Spanish, from Mexican Spanish: a worthless card hand] A Mexican American teenager who belongs to a street gang, especially a gang notable for its gaudy style.

padrone *(pah-DROH-neh)* [Italian] A master or boss; one who employs and exploits immigrant workers by failing to provide proper working conditions, housing, etc. Also, an Italian innkeeper or employer of street musicians. See also PATRÓN.

paean *(PEE-ahn)* [Latin, from Greek] A hymn of praise, triumph, or exultation. In classical Greek literature, a hymn to Apollo. 〈It was a fitting *paean* to a much loved and admired critic.〉

paella *(pah-AY-yah)* [Spanish, from Catalan: pan or pot] A popular Spanish dish of chicken, shellfish, rice, and vegetables, flavored with saffron; also, the pan in which it is cooked.

paillasse *(pye-YAHS)* [French] A mattress filled with straw; a pallet.

paillette *(pye-YET)* [French] A spangle or sequin used to decorate a dress or costume. In enameling, a bit of metal or colored foil.

paisano *(pye-ZAH-noh)* [Spanish, from French: peasant] Compatriot; fellow countryman; comrade; pal. The Italian word is *paesano.*

pajamas *(pah-JAH-mahs)* [Hindi, from Persian: leg garment] Nightclothes, or informal daytime wear that consists of loose trousers and a jacket or blouse. In the Orient, trousers worn by both men and women.

palapa *(pah-LAH-pah)* [Mexican Spanish] A small, roughly made shelter or simple house with a thatched roof, often open at the sides; a similar structure, such as a beach house, in a resort area.

palaver *(pah-LAH-ver)* [Portuguese, from Latin: speaking; story] Formerly a discussion or parley between European explorers, traders, etc., and primitive peoples. More recently, idle chatter; empty talk; cajolery; flattery. As a verb, to talk persuasively; to cajole. ⟨where a group of New York conservatives meet monthly for drinks and *palaver*⟩—*Time,* January 4, 1999.

palazzo *(pah-LAHT-zoh)* [Italian] A palace; a splendid private residence or public building. ⟨Its offices, in a crumbling *palazzo* near the Pantheon⟩—*The Guardian,* May 7, 1999.

palette *(PAL-eht)* [French, from Latin: spade; shovel] A thin tablet or board with a hole for the thumb at one end, upon which painters lay and mix their colors. The range of colors used by a particular artist or, more generally, the range of techniques of any artist. Not to be confused with *palate* or *pallet.* ⟨Her *palette* consists mostly of earth tones, with occasional outbursts of stronger color.⟩

palimpsest *(PAH-limp-sest)* [Greek: scraped again] Originally, a parchment that had one layer of writing erased so that another document could be written over it. Because ancient writing materials, such as papyrus or parchment, were costly, they were often scraped clean and reused. Said also of something painted on a canvas that has already been used for another painting.

palisade *(PAL-ih-sayd)* [French, from Latin: stake] A strongly built barrier or enclosure made of pointed stakes or pales set into the ground and lashed together. Also, a line of high cliffs; a rocky precipice.

palomino *(pah-lo-MEE-noh)* [American Spanish: like a dove] A golden brown or light tan horse with cream-colored mane and tail, bred mostly in the southwestern United States.

pampas *(PAHM-pas)* [American Spanish, from Quechua] The immense treeless, grassy plains of southern South America, particularly Argentina, that stretch from the Andes to the Atlantic Ocean. ⟨Families living in the *pampas* pay dearly for water and must store it in private cisterns.⟩

panacea *(pah-nah-SEE-yah)* [Latin, from Greek: all-healing] A cure-all; a remedy for all troubles or diseases, including social and political problems. ⟨Experts were quick to say that Orlistat is hardly a *panacea* for obesity⟩—*The New York Times,* April 27, 1999.

panache *(pah-NAHSH)* [French, from Italian and Latin] Originally, an ornamental plume or arrangement of feathers on a helmet or cap. Now used to mean verve; ÉLAN; flair; a stylish and confident manner. ⟨As an actor, he won the hearts of many with his *panache* and whimsicality.⟩

pandemonium *(pahn-deh-MOH-nee-um)* [Latin, from Greek: all demons] Total tumult; uproar; utter chaos. ⟨In a preview of the anticipated *pandemonium,* Meriwether's introduction at a recent preseason scrimmage prompted more than 1,000 students to stomp and chant.⟩—*Time,* December 14, 1998.

pandit See PUNDIT.

panettone *(pah-neh-TOH-neh)* [Italian, from Latin: a little loaf] An Italian holiday bread made with yeast, candied fruit, raisins, nuts, and brandy. Also a type of cured, air-dried sausage.

pan forte *(pahn FOR-teh)* [Italian: strong or hard bread] A hard, chewy pastry covered with powdered sugar.

paniolo *(pah-nee-OH-loh)* [Hawaiian, from Spanish] A cattle herder; a cowboy.

panzer *(PAHN-zer)* [German: armor plating] Armored, as in a *"panzer* division." An armored vehicle, especially a tank, that is part of a mechanized troop unit or division in the German army.

paparazzo (singular)**; paparazzi** (plural) *(pah-pah-RAHT-zo, pah-pah-RAHT-zee)* [Italian: originally the name of a character in George Gissing's novel *By the Ionian Sea* (1901), later the name of a photographer in Federico Fellini's film *La Dolce Vita* (1960)] A freelance photographer who takes informal, unposed pictures for publication, especially one devoted to the pursuit of celebrities.

papier-mâché *(pahp-YAY-ma-SHAY)* [French: chewed paper] A substance made of pulped paper mixed with glue, oil, resin, etc.; it is molded while wet and becomes hard as it dries, and is often used to make decorative objects in place of more expensive materials. By extension, easily ruined or discredited; false; illusory. ⟨*Papier-mâché* sculptures can be light, delicate, and surprisingly strong.⟩

papirosa *(pah-pee-ROH-sah)* [Russian] Formerly, a generic term for "cigarette"; now it refers to the old-style Russian cigarette made with a hollow cardboard tube attached to a modest amount of tobacco wrapped in thin paper.

papoose *(pah-POOS)* [Narraganset, Massachuset] Among some North American Indians, a baby or small child, particularly one wrapped tightly to a board and carried on the mother's back. ⟨they'll send it a signal causing it to open up, revealing the *papoose*-like Sojourner rover inside.⟩—*Time,* July 7, 1997.

paradigm *(PAH-rah-dyme)* [Greek, from *paradeigma:* pattern] A standard pattern against which similar patterns can be compared; something that can be used as a model or example.

paramo *(PAH-rah-moh)* [Spanish] A high, cold, barren plain, especially one in South America; in the Andes, a cold drizzle or blizzard.

parang *(PAH-rang)* [Malay] A large, heavy Malaysian sheath knife, used as a weapon or tool.

paravent *(PAH-rah-vonh)* [French: against the wind] A screen, often composed of several panels, designed to protect against drafts or to conceal something.

pareo, pareu See LAVALAVA.

pareve *(PAHR-veh)* [Yiddish] In the dietary laws of Judaism, any food that has no meat, milk, or milk product among its ingredients.

par excellence *(pahr EK-seh-lehns, pahr ek-seh-LANHS)* [French] In the highest degree; superior; beyond compare; preeminent. ⟨At the turn of the century, it was the residential street *par excellence* for affluent families.⟩

parfum *(pahr-FUNH)* [French] Perfume; scent.

pariah *(pah-RYE-ah)* [Tamil] A social outcast; a person or animal that is despised or shunned by others. In southern India and Burma, a member of a low CASTE. ⟨Some punk artists have made the transition from musical *pariahs* to mainstream acceptance.⟩

pari-mutuel *(pah-ree-MYOO-choo-el)* [French: mutual bet] A form of betting on horse races in which those with winning tickets share in the total amount wagered, less a percentage for the track and taxes. ⟨Eight states currently allow *pari-mutuel* wagering over the phone, and that industry wants the door left open to moving those operations online⟩—*The New York Times,* October 24, 1997.

pari passu *(PAH-ree PAH-soo)* [Latin] With equal speed; of the same pace. Fairly; without partiality.

parka *(PAHR-kah)* [Aleut] A hooded fur jacket or outer garment worn by Eskimos; a similar garment, lined and waterproofed for protection against extreme cold.

parlando *(pahr-LAHN-doh)* [Italian] In music, sung or played in a speaking manner, as though reciting or narrating.

parmigiana *(pahr-mee-JYAH-nah)* [Italian, from the city of Parma] In Italian cooking, a dish prepared with Parmesan cheese.

parterre *(pahr-TAIR)* [French: on (the) ground] In a theater or auditorium, the section of seats in the rear of the main floor, under the balcony. Also, the level space in a garden, with flower beds arranged in a pattern.

parti pris *(pahr-tee PREE)* [French: part taken] A foregone conclusion; a position or opinion formed in advance. ⟨Having no *parti pris* in the debate, he was able to be reasonably objective.⟩

partita *(pahr-TEE-tah)* [Italian: divided] Originally, a set of musical variations; more often an 18th-century solo or instrumental suite, or a composition with several movements.

partitur *(pahr-tee-TOOR)* [German] A musical conductor's score, with all the intrumental parts displayed.

partitura *(pahr-tee-TOO-rah)* [Italian] See PARTITUR.

parvenu *(PAHR-veh-noo)* [French, from *parvenir:* to arrive; to reach] An upstart; a person of obscure or doubtful origin who has suddenly attained wealth or position but lacks the style of behavior, dress, etc., usually associated with such a position. See also ARRIVISTE, NOUVEAU RICHE. ⟨The investment *parvenus'* belief in equities is reinforced by two key factors.⟩—*The Guardian,* May 15, 1999.

pas de deux *(pah deu DEU)* [French] A dance for two soloists. In classical ballet, a set dance that includes an ENTRÉE, an ADAGIO, separate variations for the ballerina and her partner, and a CODA performed by both, as the famous *pas de deux* in Michel Fokine's ballet *Les Sylphides* (1909).

paseo *(pah-SAY-oh)* [Spanish: a leisurely walk; a stroll] A public park or place for walking; a promenade; an avenue or boulevard lined with trees.

paskha *(PAHS-khah)* [Russian, from special use of "Easter"] In Russian cooking, a rich, molded Easter dessert made with pot cheese, butter, cream, sugar, raisins, nuts, and candied fruit; it is served with KULICH, the Easter cake.

paso doble *(PAH-soh DOH-blay)* [Spanish: double step] A Spanish dance; not a two-step as its name suggests, but rather a rapid one-step, usually in ⁶/₈ time. Also, a quick march often played at bullfights.

passacaglia *(pah-sah-CAHL-yah)* [Italian, from Spanish *pasacalle*] A slow, stately French court dance in triple time. In music, a form similar to the chaconne.

passé *(pah-SAY)* [French: past] Out-of-date; old-fashioned; no longer widely used; past his/her/its prime. ⟨There are those who would say that E. B. White is *passé*—a square, too neat and correct in his respect for the niceties of the language, the prototypal "New Yorker" writer of the era before the magazine got greened.⟩—*The New York Times,* September 19, 1977.

passe-partout *(pahs-pahr-TOO)* [French: passes everywhere] A master key; something that allows entry everywhere. Also, a decorative mat for a picture; a simple method of framing a picture, using a sheet of glass with the picture and a backing held together with strips of tape over the edges.

passim *(PAH-sim)* [Latin] Here and there: in bibliographic references, *passim* indicates where the writer has used material scattered throughout a particular source.

pasta *(PAH-stah)* [Italian, from Latin] A flour-based dough that is produced in a great variety of styles, shapes, and sizes, such as macaroni, RAVIOLI, noodles, etc.; one of the mainstays of Italian and Asian cooking.

pasticcio See PASTICHE.

pastiche *(pah-STEESH)* [French, from Italian *pasticcio*: pie; botch] An artistic work containing sections, themes, or techniques created by several different authors or composers. By extension, an incongruous mixture of elements taken from several sources; a hodgepodge. ⟨Heatherley's odd *pastiche,* which is in the Frick show, derives equally from Ingres (the nude back) and Hieronymus Bosch (the queer goblin figures).⟩—*Time,* November 23, 1998.

pastille *(pah-STEEL, pah-STEE)* [French, from Spanish] A medicated or flavored lozenge; a small sugar candy. Also, a cone-shaped compound of aromatic substances that can be burned to perfume the air.

pastorale *(pah-stoh-RAHL)* [Italian] A work of art based on a rustic theme.

pâté *(pah-TAY)* [French] A preparation of ground, seasoned liver and meat, baked in loaf form and usually served cold in slices or as a spread; also made with fish, shellfish, or mixed vegetables. *Pâté de foie gras* (goose-liver pâté) is one of its most elegant forms. ⟨The Périgord region in France is renowned for the quality of its truffles and *pâtés.*⟩

paterfamilias *(PAH-tehr fah-MEEL-yahs)* [Latin] The father of the family; the master of the household. Under the old Roman laws, an independent man. ⟨We came to pay homage to the late, great *paterfamilias* of AVANT-GARDE music.⟩

patina *(pah-TEE-nah)* [Italian, from Latin: pan; plate] A green copper rust or VERDIGRIS covering the surface of old bronze, copper, or brass that may indicate great age; a glossy surface on woodwork that is the result of aging. A surface of antique appearance. ⟨These implements bore the *patina* of long and faithful use.⟩

patio *(PAH-tee-oh)* [Spanish] An inner courtyard; an open, paved area beside a house, used for lounging or outdoor dining.

patois *(pah-TWAH)* [French: clumsy speech] A local or rustic dialect, especially in France, that differs noticeably from the standard language; a provincial form of speech; jargon. ⟨a theater troupe that performs in the original Macanese *patois,* an archaic blend of Portuguese and Cantonese⟩—*Time,* April 19, 1999.

patrón *(pah-TROHN)* [Spanish] In the southwestern United States and Mexico, an employer; a boss; a proprietor. ⟨I found myself

assisting the *patrón* of a tortilla factory.⟩—*The New Criterion,*
May 1999.

patroon *(pah-TROON)* [Dutch, from French, from Latin] Under
the old Dutch governments of New York and New Jersey, the
owner of a landed estate with some manorial privileges, i.e.,
the right to impose fees or taxes. ⟨In the 1600s, the Dutch West
India Company granted large riparian estates to company members who would become *patroons* of farm settlements.⟩

pavé *(pah-VAY)* [French: a small paving stone] A street pavement.
In jewelry making, a close setting of stones or jewels in which
no metal can be seen.

peccadillo *(peh-kah-DIL-loh, peh-kah-DEE-yoh)* A small sin; a minor
offense; a trifling fault. ⟨there are several books out in China
which deal with the President's *peccadilloes.*⟩—*Time,* July 6, 1998.

pell-mell *(pehl mehl)* [French, from *pêle-mêle*] In reckless haste; in
a confused and disorderly manner; higgledy-piggledy. A confused or jumbled crowd or mixture. ⟨Largely overlooked amid
the *pell-mell* advances and publicity about them are fundamen-
tal changes in the character of medical innovation and in society's reaction to such progress.⟩—*The New York Times,* May 10,
1998.

pelota *(peh-LOH-tah)* [Spanish: ball] A Basque and Spanish ball
game, the ancestor of JAI ALAI, or the ball used in both games.

penchant *(PEN-chant, panh-SHANH)* [French, from *pencher*: to
lean] A strong liking, inclination, or taste for something; a
strong feeling in favor of something. ⟨There are no traces of
his *penchant* for whisky and cigars.⟩—*The Guardian,* May 25,
1999.

pentimento *(pen-tee-MEN-toh)* [Italian, from Latin: repentance] In
painting, the ghostly reappearance of elements or images that
the artist tried to conceal by overpainting. See also PALIMPSEST.

pepitas *(peh-PEE-tahs)* [Spanish: seeds; pips] A Mexican snack food of pumpkin or squash seeds, usually roasted and salted.

per annum *(per AN-um)* [Latin] By the year; annually.

per capita *(per KAH-pih-tah)* [Latin: by heads] By or for each person. ⟨In a country with a *per capita* income of only $300 a year, about 36% of Cambodians live below the official poverty line.⟩— *Time,* May 17, 1999.

per diem *(per DEE-em)* [Latin] By the day; each day. An allowance for each day's incidental expenses, especially those incurred while working away from the home office. ⟨The hearings will be held before a hearing officer whose *per diem* payments may be substantial.⟩

perestroika *(peh-reh-STROY-kah)* [Russian: restructuring] A name given by Communist Party general secretary Mikhail Gorbachev to the goals of increased economic efficiency, an end to mismanagement, and the improvement of morale in the Soviet Union of the late 1980s. ⟨Shevardnadze, the former Soviet Union foreign minister best known for carrying out Mikhail Gorbachev's *perestroika* reforms, left the hospital late Tuesday.⟩

pergola *(PEHR-goh-lah)* [Italian, from Latin] An arbor with a trellised roof covered in climbing vines or flowers, supported on columns.

per se *(per SAY)* [Latin] By or in itself; intrinsically.

persiflage *(PER-sih-flahzh)* [French] Banter; a light, teasing, or flippant style of writing or conversation.

persona *(pehr-SOH-nah)* [Latin: mask; character] A character in a literary work. In Jungian psychology, the public personality; figuratively, a mask assumed by someone in response to the demands of his or her situation or environment, or for purposes of concealment, defense, etc. A public role or personal image. See also DRAMATIS PERSONAE. ⟨Much of the ANC's good-will has derived from Mandela's inspirational *persona*.⟩—*Time*, June 2, 1999.

persona grata *(pehr-SOH-nah GRAH-tah)* [Latin] A welcome or acceptable person; a diplomat whose credentials are honored by the accrediting government.

persona non grata *(pehr-SOH-nah non GRAH-tah)* [Latin] An un-welcome or unacceptable person; a diplomat whose credentials are considered unacceptable by an accrediting government. ⟨The Kaiser is *persona non grata* among them because he is be-lieved to have been a vital factor in the industrialization of Ger-many.⟩—*The Atlantic Monthly*, June 1925.

pesto *(PEHS-toh)* [Italian: crushed] In Italian cooking, a sauce made of ground basil, garlic, cheese, and olive oil; it can be added to a thick soup or served over pasta.

petard *(peh-TAHR)* [French, from *péter*: to break wind] An explo-sive device once used to break through walls or gates; a small firecracker. The expression "hoist by [or with] one's own *petard*" means to be harmed by one's own plans or actions against another. ⟨If history is any judge, this bigot, like so many others, will one day hoist himself upon his own *petard*.⟩—*Time*, March 8, 1999.

pétillant *(pay-tee-YANH)* [French] In describing wine: sparkling; bubbly; foaming, like champagne.

petit beurre *(peu-tee BEUR)* [French: little butter] In French cook-ing, a small oblong or round butter cookie, usually unadorned.

petite bourgeoisie *(peu-teet boor-zhwah-ZEE)* [French] The lower middle class; those members of the BOURGEOISIE having the least wealth and the lowest social standing. A *petit bourgeois* is a per-son who belongs to this class.

petit four *(peu-tee FOOR)* [French: small oven] A bite-size square tea cake that has been frosted and decorated.

petit mal *(peu-tee MAHL)* [French: small sickness] A relatively mild attack of epilepsy; symptoms may include momentary loss of attention, or sleepiness. See also GRAND MAL.

petits pois *(peu-tee PWAH)* [French] Small green peas.

peyote See MESCAL.

phyllo, filo *(FIH-loh)* [Modern Greek] In Middle Eastern and Greek cooking, sheets of paper-thin dough baked in layers with various fillings, used to make appetizers and desserts.

piazza *(pee-AHT-zah)* [Italian, from Latin and Greek] In Italy, an open area, marketplace, or public square in a city or town; a plaza. In the United States, a large porch or VERANDA on a house.

picador *(pih-kah-DOR)* [Spanish: pricker] A mounted bullfighter whose role is to enrage and weaken the bull by pricking its shoulders with a lance.

picante *(pih-KAHN-tay)* [Spanish, from *picar:* to sting or bite] Hot and spicy; highly seasoned; stinging. Used to describe a hot sauce or dish made with hot peppers that "bite" the tongue. See also PIQUANT.

picaresque *(pih-kah-RESK)* [Spanish, from *picaresco:* roguish] Describing a type of novel (originally Spanish) that relates the adventures of a roguish hero in a series of realistic and often humorous episodes. Also, characteristic of rogues; rascally; raffish. Not to be confused with *picturesque.*

picayune *(pih-kah-YOON)* [Provençal: small copper coin] Having little value; of little account; trifling; paltry. Also, petty or mean; carping.

piccolo *(PIH-koh-loh)* [Italian: small] A small transverse flute that sounds an octave higher than the ordinary flute.

pièce de résistance *(PYESS deu ray-zee-STANHS)* [French] The most notable or important work in a collection; the most remarkable item, feature, event, etc., of a series; a special attraction. The most important course of a meal. ⟨The *pièce de résistance* was Carbone's nerve-calming second goal.⟩—*The Guardian*, January 25, 1999.

pièce d'occasion *(PYESS doh-kahz-YONH)* [French] Something composed, prepared, or used for a special occasion.

pied-à-terre *(pyayd-ah-TAYR)* [French: foot on the ground] A temporary or secondary residence, as an apartment kept for occasional use. ⟨The agency leased a building as a dormitory-style *pied-à-terre* for its busy models.⟩

pied noir *(pyay NWAHR)* [French: black foot] Under the former French rule of Algeria, a disparaging term for anyone of French origin living there. More recently, a French person born in Algeria.

pignon *(pihn-YON)* [Spanish, from Latin] An edible, subtly aromatic seed found in the cones of some European pine trees and used in cooking; a pine nut. See also PIÑON.

pilaf, pilau *(pee-LAHF, pee-LAW)* [Turkish, from Persian] In the Middle East and parts of Asia, a dish of rice (SAUTÉED in butter) and fish, meat, or poultry, prepared with a variety of seasonings.

piñata *(pihn-YAH-tah)* [Spanish, from Italian, from Latin] In Mexico and Central America, a colorful crock or PAPIER-MÂCHÉ figure filled with sweets, party favors, toys, etc.; on a festive occasion it is suspended (from a tree branch, for example) while blindfolded children use sticks to break it open.

pince-nez *(PENHS-nay)* [French: pinches the nose] A pair of glasses without temple (side) pieces, held in place by a spring that grips the bridge of the nose. ⟨a stringy and dejected man, bald but not sufficiently so, with *pince-nez* like a dismal pair of birds on either side of his nose⟩—*The New York Times Book Review,* March 24, 1991.

piñon, pinyon *(pihn-YON)* [Spanish, from Latin] One of several pine trees of the southwestern United States and Mexico that bear edible seeds or pine nuts. See also PIGNON.

pinto *(PIN-toh)* [Spanish] Speckled; mottled; spotted, as a *pinto* bean or *pinto* horse.

piquant *(pee-KANH)* [French: prickling] Pleasantly pungent or sharp in flavor or smell; tart; spicy. Agreeably stimulating or interesting; lively; charming.

pique *(peek)* [French: sting; prick] A feeling of annoyance, resentment, irritation, or hurt pride. To stimulate or arouse, as in "to *pique* one's interest." ⟨Failure was attributed to an oversupply of childish *pique* and capriciousness on the part of the director.⟩

piqué *(pee-KAY)* [French: quilted; back-stitched] A cotton, silk, or rayon cloth woven lengthwise with raised cords, or with a raised honeycomb pattern *(waffle piqué)*.

piroshki, pirozhki *(pih-ROHSH-kee, pih-rosh-KEE)* [Russian] In Russian cooking, small, baked turnovers or pastries, filled with a seasoned mixture of meat and/or vegetables.

pirouette *(pih-roo-EHT)* [French: a whirl] In dance, a rapid, spinning movement of the entire body on one foot. To perform such a movement. By extension, an abrupt change of position or opinion. ⟨We wanted you to get our reporting on how and why Clinton made his amazing *pirouette* while the news was still fresh and timely.⟩—*Time,* August 31, 1998.

pirozhki See PIROSHKI.

piste *(peest)* [French: animal track] The track or trail made by a wild animal. Also, a track for competing cyclists; a downhill ski run.

pistolero *(pih-stoh-LEH-roh)* [Spanish] A gunman, gangster, or hired killer; a bodyguard. Formerly, one of a group of mounted bandits. ⟨The exotic Latin *pistolero,* once a Hollywood institution, is disappearing.⟩

pizza *(PEET-sah)* [Italian] A flat, oven-baked crust topped or filled with tomato sauce and cheese and garnished with sausage, peppers, mushrooms, etc.

pizzeria *(peet-seh-REE-ah)* [Italian] A place where pizza is made and sold.

pizzicato *(pit-sih-KAH-toh)* [Italian] In music, for players of stringed instruments, it means plucked with the fingers instead of stroked with a bow. A note or passage played in such fashion.

placard *(PLAH-kerd, PLAH-kahr)* [French, from Dutch: to plate] A poster; a notice or proclamation displayed in a public place, or one carried by someone picketing or demonstrating. To post a notice; to advertise or announce by means of *placards.*

placebo *(plah-SEE-boh)* [Latin: I shall please] A harmless substance given (as if it were medicinal) to humor or reassure a patient, or as a dummy in a controlled experiment on the effects of a drug. By extension, something said or done to satisfy or please. ⟨The company offered a *placebo* of extra benefits to ease the inconvenience of relocating.⟩

plage *(plahzh)* [French, from Latin: a region] The seashore; a sandy beach at a seaside resort.

planchette *(planh-SHET)* [French: little board] A small, heart-shaped board set on casters with a vertical pencil mounted at its center; it is said to trace clairvoyant messages or subconscious thoughts at spiritualist SÉANCES when the fingers are rested lightly upon it.

plangent *(PLAN-jent)* [Latin: lamenting] Resounding noisily and mournfully, like a bell; reverberating; resonant. ⟨It seemed that I was standing in the outer reaches of beyond—that Chernyshevsk was lost in it, hunkered down against *plangent* gales blowing from nowhere to nowhere.⟩—*The Atlantic Monthly*, April 1997.

plastique *(plah-STEEK)* [French] A puttylike explosive substance that can be shaped by hand, used in guerrilla warfare and by terrorists.

playa *(PLY-ah)* [Spanish, from Latin: beach; shoreline] A shallow desert basin with a flat floor that becomes a lake after a heavy rainfall.

plaza *(PLAH-zah)* [Spanish] A public square or an open market area in a town or city. Along an expressway, an area containing service stations, etc. for public use.

plein air, plein-air *(plehn-ayr)* [French: open-air] Used in reference to some French impressionist painters whose works depict scenes, people, and objects seen outdoors, especially in bright sunlight. See also ALFRESCO, EN PLEIN AIR. ⟨It made you approach Monet in a new way, not as the grand old man of *plein air* painting, but as a vigorous twentieth-century innovator.⟩—*The New Criterion*, December 1998.

pleno jure *(PLAY-noh JOO-reh)* [Latin] With full authority; with full right.

plethora *(PLEH-thoh-rah)* [Greek] An oversupply; too much. ⟨Six decades of musical history are deftly shoehorned into a show that skips lightly across times and places and drops a *plethora* of great showbiz names⟩—*The Guardian,* May 11, 1999.

plié *(plee-YAY)* [French: folded] In ballet, a movement with the feet turned out, the knees bending, and the back held straight.

plotz *(plots)* [Yiddish] In slang, to faint or collapse from surprise, emotion, or weariness.

poco *(POH-koh)* [Italian, from Latin] In music, a little; slightly; somewhat. *Poco a poco:* little by little; gradually.

podesta *(poh-deh-STAH)* [Italian] The chief magistrate of a village or town; the person of power. ⟨The Fascists appointed one of their own to be *podesta* in each village.⟩

pogrom *(POH-grom, poh-GROM)* [Russian: devastation] An organized slaughter, carried out with the unofficial support of the authorities; a mob attack against a national, racial, or religious minority, originally against the Jews in Russia. The first *pogrom* occurred after CZAR Alexander II was assassinated in 1881. ⟨When, between November of 1938 (the Kristallnacht *pogrom*) and March of 1939 (the German occupation of Prague), it became clear that Germany was seeking European hegemony⟩— *The Atlantic Monthly,* July 1991.

poilu *(pwah-LÜ)* [French, from Latin: hairy; bearded] An ordinary French soldier of World War I; an infantryman; a "grunt."

pointillism *(PWENH-tee-yizm)* [French, from *pointiller:* to mark with dots] In neo-impressionist painting, a technique for creating effects of light by crowding a surface with small spots of varying colors; these are said to be blended by the viewer's eye.

poireau (singular)**; poireaux** (plural) *(pwah-ROH)* [French] A leek.

politico *(poh-LIH-tih-koh)* [Italian, Spanish] A politician.

pollo *(POHL-yoh, POH-yoh)* [Spanish] Chicken. In Mexican slang, an illegal immigrant who has paid to be smuggled into the United States.

poltergeist *(POHL-ter-ghyst)* [German, from *polter:* to knock or rattle, and *geist:* ghost] A noisy, unseen ghost, given to loud knocking or throwing things about in the dark of night. ⟨Harry takes classes in potions, *poltergeists* patrol the halls, and Harry gets to show his true mettle.⟩—*Time,* April 12, 1999.

pompadour *(POM-pah-door)* [French, after the marquise de Pompadour] A hairstyle in which the hair is brushed up high from the forehead; a similar, older style for women, with the hair brushed up and over a roller or pad.

poncho *(PON-choh)* [American Spanish, from Araucanian] A blanketlike South American cloak, with a hole in the middle for the head; a similar waterproof cloak worn as a raincoat.

pontoon *(pon-TOON)* [French, from *ponton:* a flat-bottomed boat; a punt] A flat-bottomed boat or hollow metal cylinder used in the construction of a temporary bridge. A float for a derrick or for a seaplane. ⟨They ran the *pontoon* boat upriver and caught two whoppers.⟩

poppycock *(POP-pee-kok)* [Dutch: soft dung] Nonsense; hogwash; humbug; pretentious talk. ⟨This is just so much literary *poppycock.*⟩

porte cochere *(port koh-SHEHR)* [French: coach gate] A covered gateway leading into a courtyard; a porch that covers the door to a building and shelters people and vehicles.

portico *(POHR-tih-koh)* [Italian, from Latin] A porch; a structure attached to a building, with a roof supported by columns. Similar to a PORTE COCHERE.

portmanteau *(port-man-TOH)* [French: coat carrier] Originally a case for clothing that was designed to be used by someone on horseback. More recently, a leather suitcase or trunk that opens into two equal compartments. A *"portmanteau* word" is a blend of two words that form a single word, such as *motel,* from *motor* and *hotel.* The first to use the term may have been Lewis Carroll, in an explanation of some of the words in "Jabberwocky," a ballad that appears in *Through the Looking Glass* (1872).

posada *(poh-SAH-dah)* [Spanish] An inn or boardinghouse, especially a government-sponsored lodging that offers rooms for tourists at reasonable rates in a historic or resort area.

poseur *(poh-SEUR)* [French] A person who tries to impress others by affecting a particular (and unnatural) manner or attitude. ⟨As with any musical trend, it attracted more shabby *poseurs* than savvy innovators.⟩

posse *(PAH-see)* [Latin] An armed force; a group of men having, or presuming to have, legal authority. See also POSSE COMITATUS. ⟨The *posse* was an important institution in American frontier life.⟩

posse comitatus *(PAH-see koh-mee-TAH-tus)* [Latin: POSSE of the county] A group of men called together by a sheriff or peace officer to assist in making arrests, stopping a riot, etc.

poste restante *(pohst reh-STANHT)* [French: standing post] In France, a direction written on mail indicating it should be held at the post office until the addressee calls for it.

postiche *(poh-STEESH)* [French, from Italian: added to] A substitute or imitation. Something made and added after a work is complete, e.g., an inappropriate architectural ornament. Artificial; counterfeit.

postmeridian *(pohst-meh-RIH-dee-en)* [Latin] Pertaining to or occurring in the afternoon.

post meridiem *(pohst meh-RIH-dee-em)* [Latin] After midday; between noon and midnight. Abbreviated P.M.

postmortem *(pohst-MOHR-tem)* [Latin: after death] Taking place or performed after death; relating to the examination of a body after death. Informally, a detailed discussion of something that has ended, of an accomplished fact. ⟨Actually, in Urbinati's play, the night's earlier events aren't being widely discussed at McDonald's, although if they were it would indeed be a *post-mortem.*⟩— *The New York Times,* March 6, 1998.

postpartum *(pohst-PAHR-tum)* [Latin] In obstetrics, after childbirth; relating to the period of time after delivery. The term *"postpartum* blues" refers to the melancholia that sometimes afflicts women who have just given birth. ⟨She was treated for *postpartum* depression.⟩

postprandial *(pohst-PRAN-dee-al)* [Latin] After a meal, especially after dinner. ⟨the sort of man of whom fellow admirals in their clubs over *post-prandial* port used to say: he's a frightful old caviller⟩—*The Guardian,* May 22, 1999.

potage *(poh-TAHZH)* [French] In France, any thick soup or broth, the equivalent of the Middle English *pottage.*

potlatch *(POT-latsh)* [Chinook] A ceremonial feast of Native Americans of the Pacific Northwest at which they gather to exchange gifts and demonstrate their individual wealth. ⟨At their weekend *potlatch* . . . tribal well-wishers came from as far away as Arizona.⟩—*The Christian Science Monitor,* May 25, 1999.

potpourri *(poh-poo-REE)* [French: rotten pot] A mixture of fragrant dried flower petals and spices, kept in a jar and used to perfume a room. A miscellaneous collection of literary or musical pieces; a medley or OLIO. Any mixture of disparate elements. ⟨At a time when our country is at war, it seems bizarre that this young author should offer up such a *potpourri* of social trivia.⟩—*The Guardian,* May 16, 1999.

pourboire *(poor-BWAHR)* [French: for drinking] A tip; a gratuity. See also BAKSHEESH.

pourparler *(poor-pahr-LAY)* [French: for talking] A preliminary consultation or informal conference.

pourriture noble *(poo-ree-tür NOH-bleu)* [French] In winemaking, noble rot: a fungus cultivated in some processes that has the effect of concentrating the juice and raising the sugar content.

pousse-café *(pooss-kah-FAY)* [French: (it) pushes (the) coffee] A small glass of LIQUEUR or brandy served after coffee, especially a glass containing layers of different liqueurs poured so they remain visibly separate.

powwow *(POW-wow)* [Narraganset] Among North American Indians, a ceremony performed to heal the sick or promote success in hunting or warfare. A council held among Native Americans. Informally, any conference or meeting for discussion. ⟨Appearing at a 36-state *powwow* on pre-K in September, Education Secretary Richard Riley promised increased federal collaboration.⟩—*Time*, November 9, 1998.

précis *(PRAY-see)* [French, from Latin: cut short] A concise summary or abstract of a document, book, or article; a work that has been reduced to its essentials; an abridgment. ⟨this procedure does provide readers with a kind of *précis* of Auden's movements, activities and infatuations.⟩—*The New Criterion*, May 1999.

premiere *(preh-MEER, prem-YAIR)* [French: first] The first public performance or showing of an opera, play, film, etc. To present or perform publicly for the first time, as in "The new work was *premiered* at the Metropolitan Opera."

presidio *(preh-SIH-dee-oh)* [American Spanish, from Latin] A garrison or fortress, especially in countries formerly under the control of Spain; a Spanish prison or penal colony.

prie-dieu *(pree-DYEU)* [French: pray God] A small desk or stand for kneeling at prayer, with a small shelf above to hold a prayer book.

prima donna *(PREE-mah DOHN-nah)* [Italian: first lady] The most important female singer in an opera company. Informally, a temperamental person, or one whose feeling of self-importance makes her difficult to work with. ⟨a glamorous and difficult *prima donna*, but a fine musician nevertheless⟩

prima facie *(PREE-mah FAY-shee)* [Latin] At first sight; as it first appears. In law, a *prima facie* case is one that appears, at first view, to be valid; *prima facie* evidence is evidence that would establish the fact alleged unless rebutted. ⟨although Villa did argue a strong *prima facie* case for winning the title with an all-English team⟩—*The Guardian*, May 15, 1999.

primus inter pares *(PREE-mus in-tehr PAH-rehs)* [Latin] First among equals. ⟨As it is in international air travel, English may be *primus inter pares* on the Internet.⟩

prix fixe *(pree FEEX)* [French] A fixed price charged for any meal chosen from those listed on the menu. See also À LA CARTE, TABLE D'HÔTE.

pro bono *(proh BOH-noh)* [Latin: for the good] Anything done without charge, particularly legal services, for the good of a person or of society. *Pro bono publico*: for the public welfare; for the benefit of the public. ⟨Attorneys are expected to do *pro bono* work for those residents who cannot afford legal fees.⟩

pro rata *(proh RAH-tah)* [Latin] In proportion to the amount of work done, or to the normal rates paid; according to the calculated share. As an adjective: proportionately determined. ⟨Some sports-related income now includes, among other things, a *pro rata* share of permanent seat licenses.⟩

prosciutto *(proh-SHOO-toh)* [Italian, from Latin] In Italian cooking, a dry-cured, salted ham that is served in very thin slices.

protégé *(PROH-teh-zhay)* [French: protected] A person under the care, protection, or patronage of someone older and more powerful or influential. ⟨Coaches accompany their *protégés* to important competitions and exhibition events.⟩

pro tempore *(proh TEHM-poh-reh)* [Latin] For the time being; temporarily. Often shortened to *pro tem.*

provenance *(PRAH-veh-nens, proh-veh-NANHS)* [French] A source; a place of origin or a history of ownership, especially of a work of art or an antique. ⟨No doubt the bell's *provenance* contributed to its mythic quality.⟩—*The Atlantic Monthly,* June 1998.

proviso *(proh-VYE-zoh)* [Latin: it being provided] A clause in a contract or statute in which something is described as a condition of an agreement; a stipulation or requirement. ⟨This month, the computer will replace one of the readers—with the *proviso* that a second reader will be consulted if the computer and human-reader scores differ by more than a point.⟩—*Time,* February 15, 1999.

pueblo *(PWEH-bloh)* [American Spanish; town; people] Among the Native Americans of the southwestern United States, a communal stone or ADOBE building, often with several stories, terraces, and flat roofs. A member of a tribe living in a *pueblo* village, or the village itself. ⟨He was surrounded by Apaches, Navajos and numerous *Pueblo* tribes whose people have lived in well-ordered communities along the Rio Grande for nearly a thousand years.⟩—*The New York Times,* March 8, 1998.

pukka *(PUK-kah)* [Hindi: substantial; ripe] Among Anglo-Indians: reliable, genuine, or of good quality. ⟨The great British social experiment of the past decade: open door policy, banging dance music and *pukka* class.⟩—*The Guardian,* May 22, 1999.

pukka sahib *(PUK-kah SAH-heeb)* [Hindi: good master] A form of polite address used by a Hindu when speaking to a colonial authority during the time of British rule in India.

pulque *(PULL-kay)* [Mexican Spanish] A cloudy, sourish beer made from the fermented juice of the agave or maguey plant; a popular tonic and thirst-quencher in Mexico.

punctilio *(punk-TIH-lee-oh)* [Italian, from Spanish] A fine point of honor, ceremony, or etiquette; care in observing formalities or correctness. ⟨As a diplomat, he was noted for his honesty and *punctilio* in difficult negotiations.⟩

pundit *(PUN-dit)* [Hindi, from Sanskrit] In India, a man of great wisdom and learning; also used as a title of respect. By extension, an expert or one who comments or criticizes in an authoritative manner, such as television's Sunday morning *pundits* or "talking heads." ⟨he takes direct (and hilarious) aim at Wall Street money manager/*pundit*/provocateur (and TIME columnist) James J. Cramer⟩—*Time,* May 17, 1999.

punkah *(PUN-kah)* [Hindi, from Sanskrit] In India, a fan consisting of a light frame covered with cloth and suspended from the ceiling, moved by machinery or by a servant.

purdah *(POOR-dah)* [Hindi, Urdu: curtain] Among some Muslims and Hindus, the practice of keeping women hidden from men or from strangers by requiring them to veil their faces, or by confining them to screened or curtained areas of the house. ⟨The Taliban has no intention of easing the stern commandments that have virtually locked women away in a modern *purdah.*⟩—*Time,* October 13, 1997.

puree, purée *(pyoo-RAY)* [French: strained] Food that has been cooked and strained to produce a thick mash. To make a *puree,* usually of fruit or vegetables. ⟨whole tomatoes, cooked quickly and canned in a thick *puree*⟩

putsch *(pootsh)* [Swiss German: shock; violent blow] A planned, armed uprising or raid designed to overthrow a government; a COUP. Adolf Hitler achieved notoriety when he tried, unsuccessfully, to instigate a coup aimed at the Bavarian government in the "beer-hall *putsch*" in Munich in 1923. ⟨General Jaruzelski's martial-law *putsch* against Solidarity in 1981 was well remembered.⟩—*The Guardian*, April 11, 1999.

puttee *(puh-TEE)* [Hindi: bandage] A long strip of cloth that World War I soldiers wound around their calves from ankle to knee for protection. Later, a shaped leather gaiter worn over the calves.

putz *(puhts)* [Yiddish, from German] In slang, a jerk; a fatuous or foolish person. Also, a penis; used as the most offensive of insults. ⟨Rosten adds a cautionary note: "*Putz* is not to be used lightly or when women or children are around."⟩—*The New York Times*, October 22, 1998.

quadrille *(kwah-DRILL)* [French, from Spanish] A square dance for four couples, brought from France to the United States through New Orleans. Some of its elements have been adopted into the American square dance.

quartier *(kahr-TYAY)* [French, from Latin] In France, an administrative division of a city; a neighborhood or quarter, as in the *Quartier Latin* in Paris. Also, a district in a city or town inhabited by a particular ethnic or professional group.

quattrocento *(KWAH-troh CHEN-toh)* [Italian: four hundred] The 15th century, i.e., the years of the 1400s. ⟨Had he ever published them, his scientific musings would surely have seemed as revolutionary to his *Quattrocento* contemporaries as did his ideas on perspective and color.⟩—*Time*, December 9, 1996.

quenelle *(keh-NEHL)* [French, from German *Knödel:* dumpling] In French cooking, a dumpling of finely minced meat or fish mixed with egg, then poached and served with a cream sauce.

qué pasa? *(kay PAH-sah)* [Spanish] What's happening? What's going on?

querida (f), **querido** (m) *(keh-REE-dah, keh-REE-doh)* [Spanish] Dear one; beloved.

quesadilla *(kay-sah-DEE-yah)* [Mexican Spanish] In Mexican cooking, a folded TORTILLA filled with cheese, onions, and chilis, which is fried or broiled.

queue *(kyoo, keu)* [French, from Latin: tail] A braid of hair worn at the back of the head; a pigtail. Also, a line of people or vehicles waiting their turn. To *"queue* up" is to join or form such a line. In computer terminology, a series of documents stored temporarily, e.g., in a printer memory, waiting to be processed in turn. ⟨posted an online message to clients trading at its Internet site telling individual investors that their orders would be held in a *queue* for execution when trading resumed⟩—*The New York Times,* October 27, 1998.

quiche *(keesh)* [French, from German *Küchen:* cake] A tart filled with custard and flavored with bacon, onion, and cheese *(quiche lorraine)* or with vegetables.

quidnunc *(KWID-noonk)* [Latin: what now?] A person with a strong desire to know the latest news; a busybody or gossip.

quid pro quo *(KWID proh KWOH)* [Latin: something for something] Something given or taken in return for something else; a substitute. ⟨This is a high-stakes *quid pro quo* that the environmentalists would have been seen as churlish to have refused.⟩—*The Atlantic Monthly,* January 1997.

qui vive *(kee VEEV)* [French: who goes there?] On the *qui vive:* on the lookout; on the alert; watchful.

raconteur *(rah-konh-TEUR)* [French] A skilled storyteller; one who is adept at relating anecdotes. ⟨Our local pub attracted a number of charming and fluent *raconteurs.*⟩

raga *(RAH-gah)* [Sanskrit: color] In Indian music, a set of (usually) five to seven notes that are used without exception as a basis for elaborate improvisation. By following these traditional melodic and rhythmic formulas, players try to evoke an emotional state or mood that is unique to the particular *raga*. The term dates from the 5th century A.D.

ragout *(rah-GOO)* [French] In French cooking, a dish of stewed meat, vegetables, or fish in a spicy sauce.

raison d'être *(ray-sonh DEH-treu)* [French] Reason for being; the purpose or justification for the existence of something. ⟨Although the hotels have done a brilliant job of creating a SMORGASBORD of entertainment, the city's *raison d'être* is never to be ignored⟩—*The New York Times,* February 15, 1998.

ramie *(RAM-ee)* [Malay] An Asian plant whose fibers are used to make cordage and some textiles. A fabric made from the plant.

ranchero *(rahn-CHAY-roh)* [American Spanish] A person who owns or operates a ranch.

rapido *(RAH-pee-doh)* [Italian, Spanish] In Italy and many Spanish-speaking countries, an express train.

rappel *(rah-PEHL)* [French: recall] In mountaineering, a technique for descending a steep cliff by means of a double rope that is passed through a sheave fixed at a higher point and paid out gradually. To descend using this method.

rapport *(rah-POHR)* [French, from Latin] Connection or relation; a sympathetic or harmonious accord, as in "a close *rapport* with a family member." ⟨The talk began and *rapport* came easily to these two men, both masters of the art of banter.⟩—*The New York Times,* June 11, 1972.

rapprochement *(rah-prosh-MANH)* [French] The act of bringing together; often used to describe the reestablishment of cordial relations between nations, political groups, individuals, etc., that have been divided by ideological conflict. ⟨Mao's wife . . . who had formerly been absolutely against a *rapprochement* with the United States⟩—*The New York Review of Books,* March 4, 1999.

rara avis *(rah-rah AY-viss)* [Latin: rare bird] A rare person. Anything very rare or unique.

ratatouille *(rah-tah-TOO-ee)* [French] A vegetable stew, originally from Provence, that contains eggplant, zucchini, tomatoes, green peppers, onions, and garlic; it is served hot or cold.

rathskeller *(RAHTS-keh-ler)* [German: town hall cellar] A beer hall, especially one below street level.

ravioli *(rah-vee-OH-lee)* [Italian: little turnips] In Italian cooking, small squares of PASTA dough filled with meat, cheese, or minced vegetables, usually poached and served with a sauce.

realpolitik *(ray-AHL-po-lee-teek)* [German, a coined word] A political philosophy based on reality rather than ideals and high principles, i.e., based on power. ⟨Washington's initial *realpolitik* inclination to stay out of Iraq's civil war was prudent.⟩—*The Atlantic Monthly,* July 1991.

rebozo *(reh-BOH-zoh)* [Spanish] In Spain and Mexico, a woman's long scarf, sometimes embroidered, worn draped over the head and shoulders.

réchauffé *(ray-shoh-FAY)* [French] Reheated, as leftover food. By extension, anything dated or stale that is being put into a new form, such as a rehash of a literary work.

recherché *(reu-shair-SHAY)* [French: rare; uncommon] Carefully sought out; exotic; of rare quality, appeal, or refinement; obscure to the point of being far-fetched. Also used in a derogatory sense to mean affected, precious, or pretentious. ⟨For some of its special customers, the gallery kept a collection of *recherché* old prints.⟩

réclame *(ray-KLAHM)* [French] Publicity; advertisement. By extension, a desire for publicity or attention.

recto *(REK-toh)* [Latin] The right-hand page of an open book or manuscript, usually odd-numbered. The left-hand page is called the VERSO.

reductio ad absurdum *(reh-DUK-tee-oh ahd ahb-SOOR-dum)* [Latin] Reduction to the absurd: proof of the falsity of a statement by showing its logical consequence to be absurd; carrying a principle to unreasonable lengths. ⟨The weepy, shrieking girls who surround him reach a *reductio ad absurdum* when the star presents one grateful girl with his sweaty handkerchief.⟩—*The New York Times,* December 4, 1968.

redux *(rih-DUKS)* [Latin] An adjective meaning brought back, revived, or returning, as in "the Roaring Twenties *redux.*"

regalia *(rih-GAYL-yah)* [Latin] The equipment and attire that symbolize royalty; finery; dressy clothes; fancy trappings. ⟨Halliday is offered photographs that Molly had taken of [the foreign secretary] in transvestite *regalia.*⟩—*Time,* December 7, 1998.

regatta *(reh-GAH-tah)* [Venetian Italian] A series of boat races, organized as an event.

regime, régime *(reh-ZHEEM, ray-ZHEEM)* [French, from Latin] A system or method of administration or government; a prevailing system; the period of time during which a particular ruler or government holds power. See also ANCIEN RÉGIME.

regisseur, régisseur *(ray-zhee-SEUR)* [French: manager; agent] A stage director or stage manager for a theatrical work.

remuda *(reh-MOO-dah)* [American Spanish] A change of horses. A selection of saddle horses herded together to provide ranch hands a choice of mounts.

renaissance *(REH-neh-sahnss, reh-nay-SANHS)* [French: rebirth] Any period of great revival of creativity in the arts and knowledge. When capitalized: the period that began in Italy during the 14th century with the translation of the texts of Aristotle and others saved from the Alexandrian library; a transition from the medieval to the modern world which spread through the rest of Europe and lasted until the 1600s. The style of art, architecture, literature, etc., that developed during this period.

rendezvous *(RON-day-voo)* [French: betake yourselves] A meeting or an appointment to meet at a certain place or time; a planned meeting or joining of military forces. A place chosen for a meeting. To gather at an agreed time and place. ⟨their *rendezvous* was refreshingly spontaneous⟩—*The Guardian,* May 19, 1999.

renvoi *(ranh-VWAH)* [French: a sending back] A disciplinary or punitive measure undertaken by a government, resulting in the expulsion or deportation from the country of a foreign diplomat or an undesirable alien.

repartee *(reh-pahr-TEE)* [French] A prompt and witty reply; a clever retort; conversation characterized by such replies. The ability to make quick and witty rejoinders.

repertoire *(REH-per-twahr)* [French, from Latin: inventory; catalog] The stock of plays, roles, operas, pieces, etc., that a person or company is prepared to perform; the list of works available in a particular artistic domain. The stock of techniques, devices, or skills used in a particular occupation or field. Also called *repertory*. ⟨In some cities, the symphonic *repertoire* has only recently expanded to include modern works.⟩

reportage *(reh-pohr-TAHZH)* [French] The act of reporting the news, or reported news collectively. An investigative report prepared for publication or broadcast, based on direct observation or research, that examines a current or historical event. ⟨His dispatches from Kosovo have provided perhaps the only objective *reportage* from the war zone appearing daily in the Western press.⟩—*Time*, April 30, 1999.

res publica (singular); **res publicae** (plural) *(rehs POO-blih-kah)* [Latin: public matter] The commonwealth; the republic; the state. In the plural: things belonging to the state.

ressentiment *(reh-sanh-tee-MANH)* [French: resentment; animosity] A cynical or defeatist state of mind, resulting from the belief in a universal indifference or hostility to humanity and its aspirations; the conviction that it is useless to attempt to better one's lot in life.

résumé, resume *(REH-zoo-may)* [French] A summary; a written account of a person's educational and professional background, for use in applying for a job. Also written *resumé*. See also CURRICULUM VITAE.

retinue *(REH-tih-nyoo)* [French, from *retenir*: to retain] A body of retainers or attendants accompanying an important person; an escort. See also CORTEGE.

retroussé *(reh-troo-SAY)* [French] Turned up; usually used to describe someone's nose.

retsina *(REHT-sih-nah)* [Modern Greek] In Greece and Cyprus, a white or rosé wine flavored with resin or pine pitch.

revanche *(reu-VANHSH)* [French: revenge] The policy of a state determined to reoccupy lands or territory lost to another state through war; the political policy of revenge for a previous military defeat. Also called *revanchism (reu-VANH-shizm)*. One who supports such a policy is a *revanchist (reu-VANH-shist)*.

reveille *(REH-veh-lee)* [French, from *réveiller*: to awaken] An early morning bugle call to summon military personnel, or the hour at which it is sounded. Any signal to "rise and shine."

revenant *(reu-veh-NANH)* [French, from *revenir*: to return] One who returns. An apparition; a ghost; one who returns as a spirit after death.

ricochet *(RIK-oh-shay)* [French] The motion of rebounding or deflecting from a surface, as when an object hits a surface with a glancing blow. To move or rebound in this way. ⟨He seemed to feel his heart *ricochet* around his rib cage.⟩

rien ne va plus *(ree-ENH neu vah plü)* [French] In the game of roulette: no further bets (will be accepted).

rifacimento *(rih-fah-chee-MEN-toh)* [Italian] A remaking; an adaptation, as of a musical or literary work.

rigor mortis *(RIH-gor MOR-tiss)* [Latin] The muscular stiffening that occurs in the body after death.

rijsttafel *(RICE-tah-fel)* [Dutch: rice table] An Indonesian meal consisting of boiled rice surrounded by many spicy side dishes of meat, seafood, vegetables, sauces, etc.

rillettes *(ree-YEHT)* [French] In France, a form of potted pork or goose meat, seasoned, cooked, and pounded to the consistency of a paste or spread.

riposte *(ree-POHST)* [French, from Italian] In fencing, a quick return thrust. In speech, a rapid, clever reply or counterstroke, especially in response to a verbal attack. ⟨All attempts to question her ability were met with impressive *ripostes* from the candidate.⟩

risorgimento *(rih-sor-jee-MEN-toh)* [Italian: *resurgence*] A period of rebirth or increased activity. When capitalized: the popular uprising that began in the Italian provinces in the 1750s and grew inexorably until Giuseppe Garibaldi entered Rome with his army and proclaimed the unification of Italy in 1870. ⟨A new spirit of unity amid diversity characterizes the art of the *Risorgimento.*⟩

risotto *(rih-ZOT-toh)* [Italian: rising again] In Italian cooking, rice simmered in broth with the addition of small amounts of meat, seafood, vegetables, cheese, etc.; the finished dish has a creamy consistency.

risqué *(ree-SKAY)* [French] Slightly indecent; bordering on impropriety; off-color, as in "a *risqué* style of comedy." ⟨The pictures were considered too *risqué* for publication.⟩

rivière *(rih-VYAIR)* [French: river] A necklace of diamonds or other precious stones, usually in several strings.

rocaille *(roh-KAH-yeh)* [French: pebbles] In the architecture and decorative arts of the ROCOCO period, an extravagantly fanciful style of ornamentation based on rock, shell, and plant forms combined with scroll motifs. Also called *style rocaille (steel roh-KAH-yeh).*

rococo *(roh-KOH-koh, roh-koh-KOH)* [French] A style of decoration and architecture developed in France in the 1700s, soon adopted by other European countries, characterized by tall and slender proportions, delicate curvilinear designs, elegant and elaborate ornamentation, pastel colors, and lavish gilding. By extension, a fantastic, florid, or overelaborate style in literature, speech, music, etc.

rodomontade *(roh-doh-monh-TAHD)* [French, from Italian, after Rodomonte, the braggart king in Matteo Boiardo's poem *Orlando Innamorato* (c. 1506)] A pretentious speech; blustering, boasting, or bragging talk.

roman à clef *(roh-MANH ah KLAY)* [French: novel with a key] A fictional literary work based upon historical characters and events, or one in which well-known real people are portrayed as fictional characters. ⟨Margaret Truman, the daughter of President Harry S Truman, has written *romans à clef* set in the White House among the real people who were there when she was young.⟩

roman-fleuve *(roh-manh-FLEUV)* [French, from *roman:* novel, and *fleuve:* great river] Originating in France, a form of the novel, often in several volumes, that portrays the history of several generations of a family or a social group. Also called a *saga novel.* ⟨Her entire career . . . has flowed into this *roman fleuve.*⟩— *The New York Times,* October 26, 1980.

ronin *(ROH-nin)* [Japanese] A SAMURAI warrior who no longer has a master. ⟨choosing instead an anarchical and *ronin*-like life of ephemeral alliances that live and die within a single evening's session⟩—*Time,* April 9, 1997.

rostrum *(ROSS-trum)* [Latin: beak] A platform, stage, or pulpit for public speaking; a podium or dais. Also, a beaklike part of the prow of an ancient warship, used for ramming an enemy vessel.

rotisserie *(roh-TISS-eh-ree)* [French: roaster] A broiler with a rotating spit for broiling chicken, etc.

roué *(roo-AY)* [French] A libertine; a licentious man; a profligate; an elegant DEBAUCHEE.

rouille *(ROO-ee-yeh)* [French: rust] A hot, rust-colored sauce of southern France consisting of crushed garlic, olive oil, hot red pepper, etc., often served with BOUILLABAISSE.

roulade *(roo-LAHD)* [French] In French cooking, a slice of meat or fish rolled around a filling and braised. In music, a highly ornamental passage for the voice, sung with a single syllable. ⟨The main title music melds traditional marching-band triumphalism with Janácek-like brass *roulades,* and leads this time into a Prokofiev-like DENOUEMENT shot through with Mahlerian trumpet calls.⟩—*The Guardian,* May 14, 1999.

rucksack *(ROOK-sak)* [German] A backpack; a knapsack.

ryokan *(ree-oh-kahn)* [Japanese] A small Japanese hotel or inn in traditional style, one whose floors are covered with TATAMI.

sabot *(sah-BOH)* [French] A shoe hollowed out from a single block of wood, as those worn in Belgium, France, and the Netherlands by workers and farmers. Also, a shoe with a wooden sole.

sabotage *(SAH-boh-tahzh)* [French, from *saboter:* to botch] Willful or malicious damaging of materials or machinery, or the disruption of production (e.g., in a factory) by hostile agents or dissatisfied employees; any attempt to disable, cripple, or undermine. To inflict damage, especially in a covert manner. The word derives from *sabot,* a wooden clog that 18th-century mill workers tossed into the machines in an act of defiance. ⟨[The] power failure . . . appears to have been an act of *sabotage,* the authorities said Friday⟩—*The New York Times,* October 25, 1997.

saboteur *(sah-boh-TEUR)* [French] A person who engages in SABOTAGE.

sabra *(SAH-brah)* [Hebrew, from Arabic: prickly pear] A person born in Israel. ⟨Mr Barak is a classic example of the *Sabra* elite.⟩—*The Guardian*, May 18, 1999.

sachem *(SAH-chem)* [Narraganset] Among the Native Americans of the northeastern United States, a chief of a tribe, or one of the chiefs of a confederation of tribes. Informally, the head of a political party.

sachet *(sah-SHAY)* [French] A small cloth bag filled with an aromatic substance, such as lavender, and placed among linens and clothing to scent them. ⟨The attic had a fine aroma, a mixture of must and the sage and lavender *sachets* kept in trunks of old clothing.⟩

safari *(sah-FAH-ree)* [Swahili, from Arabic] A journey; an organized expedition in wild country, particularly in East Africa, with equipment, provisions, and professional guides, for the purpose of hunting or studying wild animals in their own habitat. Any long, venturesome journey, especially one on foot. ⟨Going on *safari* in game parks is a popular form of tourism in Kenya.⟩

sake *(SAH-keh)* [Japanese] A Japanese beverage made from fermented rice, drunk either hot or cold. Although it is sometimes called rice wine, *sake* is technically a beer, because it is made from grain.

sala *(SAH-lah)* [Spanish] A large room, parlor, or reception room in a house.

salaam *(sah-LAHM)* [Arabic: peace] In Islamic countries, a greeting, usually accompanied by a low bow; a respectful salutation.

salon *(sah-LON, sah-LONH)* [French, from Italian: hall] A spacious and elegant reception room or drawing room for receiving guests. A gathering of distinguished guests in such a room, especially in Paris in the 17th and 18th centuries. A place used for exhibiting works of art. An establishment where a hair-dresser, cosmetician, or COUTURIER receives clients.

salsa *(SAHL-sah)* [Spanish: sauce; gravy] A modern style of Latin American popular music that combines elements of jazz and rock with Cuban dance rhythms; a ballroom dance (originally Puerto Rican) similar to the mambo, performed to this music. Also, in Mexican cooking, a spicy sauce containing tomatoes, onions, and chilies.

salvo *(SAHL-voh)* [Italian, from Latin] A simultaneous firing of artillery or bombs; a volley of fire given as a salute. A round of applause. ⟨This deal was the latest *salvo* in a battle between new Internet companies and the older behemoths of the telephone industry.⟩

samadhi *(sah-MAH-dee)* [Sanskrit: establish; make firm] In many types of YOGA, a state of complete absorption in an object of meditation. In Buddhism, collectedness of the mind on a single object through the gradual lulling of mental activity. In Hinduism, the highest levels of mystical contemplation.

samba *(SAHM-bah)* [Portuguese] A Brazilian couple dance characterized by very fast steps in ²⁄₄ time, with complex rhythms.

samizdat *(SAH-meez-daht)* [Russian] In the former Soviet Union, a network of underground publishers engaged in the clandestine printing and private distribution of forbidden dissident literary works or periodicals that were considered inappropriate or seditious by the state. Also, any work made available to readers through this system. Some Russian authors, now well known, had their works published first by *samizdat,* enabling their voices to be heard outside the Soviet Union. ⟨Typewritten manuscripts of the novels have circulated widely in the Soviet Union in what is called the *samizdat,* or hand-to-hand press.⟩—*The New York Times,* December 11, 1970.

samp *(samp)* [Narraganset] Coarsely ground Indian corn, usually boiled and eaten with milk and sugar.

sampan *(SAM-pan)* [Chinese: three boards] A simple small boat of the Far East, with a roofed section for one or two passengers or baggage; it is rowed or poled by a single boatman.

samurai *(SAH-moo-rye)* [Japanese] A member of a hereditary class of professional warriors in medieval Japan, each dedicated to protect his lord from any threat. ⟨Lurching from surrealism to farce to melodrama to sentiment, Kikujiro shows that there's nothing more bizarre than a *samurai* cinéaste trying to prove he's a sweetie.⟩—*Time*, June 7, 1999.

sangfroid *(sanh-FRWAH)* [French: cold blood] Presence of mind; composure; coolness in a difficult situation; self-control. ⟨The renowned British *sangfroid* was tested severely last week by the threat of a strike.⟩

sans *(sanh)* [French] Without.

sansculotte *(sanh-kü-LOT)* [French: without knee breeches] Originally, a term of contempt applied by aristocrats to anyone belonging to the poorer class of French revolutionaries in 1789; the name comes from the fact that such people dressed in long trousers rather than the knee breeches worn by the upper classes. Later, a popular name adopted by the Jacobins. By extension, any radical or revolutionary person.

Sansei *(SAHN-say)* [Japanese: third generation] A grandchild of Japanese who emigrated to Canada or to the United States. See also ISSEI, KIBEI, NISEI.

sans souci *(sanh soo-SEE)* [French: without care] Carefree; free and easy.

sari *(SAH-ree)* [Hindi] A garment made of a single long piece of cloth, often of silk, wrapped around a woman's body, with the loose end draped over the head or the shoulder.

sarong *(sah-RONG)* [Dutch, from Malay] A simple garment made of a single piece of cloth wound around the body; the principal garment worn by both men and women on the Malay Peninsula.

sashimi *(sah-SHEE-mee)* [Japanese] In Japanese cooking, a dish of raw fish cut in small slices, often served with soy sauce and WASABI-root paste. See also SUSHI.

sati See SUTTEE.

satori *(sah-TOH-ree)* [Japanese, from the verb "to awaken"] In Zen Buddhism, the abrupt or spontaneous inner experience of enlightenment that is the principal goal of Zen followers; a state of mind similar to spiritual rebirth, which cannot be explained by logic or reason and which may be prompted by a trivial event. ⟨In Zen, it is described as *satori* and in Buddhism the experience of the void, or "suchness." In Chinese Taoism, it is oneness with the Way⟩—*The Guardian,* January 23, 1999.

satrap *(SAH-trap)* [Persian] A governor of a province of Persia in the time of Alexander the Great, appointed by the emperor. A subordinate ruler, often a tyrannical one. ⟨One reason is that he lacks an independent political base, and thus must remain dependent on the whims of powerful *satraps* in the United Front and Congress⟩—*Time,* May 5, 1997.

sauerbraten *(SAU-er-brah-tn)* [German: sour roast] A German dish of braised beef, previously marinated in vinegar, sugar, and seasonings.

sauerkraut *(SAU-er-kraut)* [German: sour greens] Cabbage that has been shredded, salted, and fermented in its own juice.

sault *(soo)* [Canadian French, from French *saut*: a leap] A waterfall or rapids.

sauna *(SAW-nah)* [Finnish] A room or bathhouse fitted with a means of producing thick steam in which a person sits and sweats, sometimes striking his or her skin with light birch rods, then moving into a cold environment to close the pores. ⟨Spa facilities may include a pool, whirlpools, and a Finnish *sauna.*⟩

sauté, saute *(soh-TAY, saw-TAY)* [French, from *sauter:* to jump] To cook quickly in a pan or skillet, using a small amount of fat. A dish prepared in this manner.

savanna, savannah *(sah-VAH-nah)* [Spanish] A flat plain with grasses and a scattering of trees, often at the edge of forested areas in the tropics.

savant *(sah-VANH)* [French, from Latin] A person of exceptional or profound learning; a scholar of great erudition. See also IDIOT SAVANT.

savoir faire *(sah-vwahr FAIR)* [French: to know how to act] The knowledge of how to behave in a social situation; tact; diplomacy. ⟨If part of Clinton's charisma and appeal has stemmed from his James Bondish *savoir faire* . . . what some people might find hardest to forgive aren't his falsehoods and inappropriate gropings, but his lollapalooza lapses of animal cunning.⟩—*Time*, September 21, 1998.

savoir vivre *(sah-vwahr VEE-vreu)* [French: to know how to live] Knowledge of worldly ways and social proprieties; good breeding; good manners.

sayonara *(sah-yoh-NAH-rah)* [Japanese] Good-bye; farewell.

scenario *(seh-NAH-ree-oh)* [Italian] An outline of the scenes of a movie, play, or ballet. By extension, a detailed outline of a plan of action.

schadenfreude *(SHAH-den-froy-deh)* [German: joy in harm] Gloating pleasure or malicious delight occasioned by someone else's misfortune.

schav *(shahv)* [Yiddish, from Polish] In Jewish and eastern European cooking, a sorrel soup usually served cold with the addition of sour cream, chopped egg, etc.

schema *(SKEH-mah)* [Greek] Concept; design; plan; strategy.

scherzo *(SKERT-zoh)* [Italian: a jest] In music, a humorous or playful composition, an alternative to the minuet, often the second or third movement of a string quartet, sonata, or symphony. ⟨He has composed a polka for elephants for the Ringling Brothers, a *Scherzo à la Russe* for Paul Whiteman, *Ballet Scenes* for Billy Rose, an *Ebony Concerto* for Woody Herman and his jazz band.⟩—*Time,* July 26, 1948.

schlag *(shlahg)* [German: a strike; a blow] Whipped cream. ⟨The Vienna-style coffee drinks, with plenty of *schlag,* are superb—made with the gold-standard Italian espresso, Illy Caffe, which is actually better than what you get in Vienna.⟩—*The Atlantic Monthly,* October 1994.

schlemazl See SCHLIMAZEL.

schlemiel, shlemiel *(shleh-MEEL)* [Yiddish, from Hebrew] In slang, an awkward, inept, or clumsy person; a bungler; one who is easily deceived. See also KLUTZ, SCHLIMAZEL. ⟨Benny Profane, self-styled *schlemiel* wanderer through the streets of Europe and America⟩—*The New York Times,* March 11, 1973.

schlepp, schlep *(shlehp)* [Yiddish, from German] In slang, to carry; to lug. To trudge; to move awkwardly or laboriously. ⟨a delicate man condemned now and forever to *schlep* his alter ego on his back whenever he goes⟩—*The Guardian,* February 13, 1999.

schlepper *(SHLEH-per)* [Yiddish, from German] In slang, a slow-moving, awkward, tedious person; a "drag." Also, a person who is unkempt or untidy.

schlimazel, schlemazl *(shlih-MAH-zl)* [Yiddish, from German and Hebrew] In slang, an awkward, inept person who is plagued by bad luck. Also written as *schlimazl, shlimazl.*

schlock *(shlok)* [Yiddish, from German] In slang, junk; worthless goods; anything of cheap or inferior quality. Trashy. ⟨Fifteen years ago, driven by disgust with the *schlock* filmmakers were churning out, he quit his job as a management consultant to make movies.⟩—*Time,* November 23, 1998.

schlockmeister *(SHLOK-my-ster)* [Yiddish, German] One who sells or deals in worthless goods; a junk dealer.

schmaltz *(shmahlts)* [Yiddish] Rendered chicken fat; grease. By extension, anything overly sentimental, especially in music or popular theater; mushy emotionalism. The adjective is *schmaltzy,* while "to *schmaltz* it up" is to add pathos or sentimentality to something. ⟨This theater music is written in Gypsy style, with characteristic changes of tempo and plenty of *schmaltz.*⟩

schmooze, schmoose *(shmooz)* [Yiddish, from Hebrew: reports; gossip] In slang, to converse idly; to chat. Chatter; idle conversation. Also, a heart-to-heart talk. ⟨"We *schmooze,*" Davidson said. "When we're on charters or on Tarmacs, . . . we talk hockey."⟩—*The New York Times,* April 17, 1999.

schmuck *(shmuk)* [Yiddish: penis] In slang, a contemptible, repulsive, or obnoxious person.

schmutz *(shmuts)* [German, from *schmutzig:* dirty] Dirt; a smudge. ⟨Suddenly, she stops short, whirls around, and asks her campaign adviser, Jim Spencer, "Do I have *schmutz* on my face?"⟩—*Time,* August 24, 1998.

schnapps *(shnahps)* [German, from Dutch] Any strong, dry alcoholic liquor, such as AQUAVIT, kirsch, or Dutch *genever* (gin). ⟨They celebrated the occasion with *schnapps* and smoked eel.⟩

schnook *(shnook)* [Yiddish] In slang, a stupid person; a dope; a sad sack; a pathetic case. ⟨Those who looked truly and stupendously dumb were the poor *schnooks* who had to stand on camera and talk about the fact that they didn't know very much about what was happening.⟩—*Time,* August 31, 1998.

schnorrer *(SHNOR-er)* [Yiddish, from German] In slang, an habitual or professional beggar; one who lives at the expense of others; a moocher; a sponger; a cheapskate.

schnozzle *(SHNAH-zl)* [Yiddish, from German *Schnauze:* snout] In slang, a nose.

schola cantorum *(SKOH-lah kahn-TOH-rum)* [Latin: school of singers] Originally, a choir school within the Vatican that provided music for religious services. Used nowadays as the name for some choral organizations.

schtik See SHTICK.

schul See SHUL.

schuss *(shoos)* [German: shot] In skiing, a straight run down a steep slope at high speed. To execute such a run. In American slang, a *schussboomer* is an expert downhill skier.

scintilla *(sin-TIL-ah)* [Latin] A spark; a trace. ⟨There is not a *scintilla* of evidence to suggest these people are unfit for work.⟩

séance *(say-AHNSS)* [French: session; sitting] A meeting of people seeking to communicate with spirits of the dead through a medium or spiritualist. Also, a meeting of an organization or a class.

sec *(sehk)* [French] In describing wines: dry, not sweet.

Seder *(SAY-der)* [Hebrew: order] A ceremonial meal at which Jews commemorate the Exodus from Egypt, and eat special foods that symbolize that event. ⟨As millions of Jewish families hold Passover *Seders* this week, in many households the ritual celebration of deliverance from Egypt will be followed by talk of a new predicament.⟩—*Time,* April 28, 1997.

segue *(SEHG-way)* [Italian, from Latin: to follow] A smooth and uninterrupted transition from one section of music to the next or, more generally, from one subject to another. In any good medley of popular show tunes, one familiar song *segues* smoothly into another.

seicento *(SAY-chen-toh)* [Italian: six hundred] The 17th century, i.e., the years designated in the 1600s.

seiche *(saysh)* [Franco-Provençal] A rhythmic oscillation that occurs occasionally in the water of a lake, landlocked sea, bay, etc., causing fluctuations in the water level.

semper fidelis *(SEM-pehr fee-DAY-lis)* [Latin] Always faithful: the motto of the U.S. Marine Corps.

semper paratus *(SEM-pehr pah-RAH-tus)* [Latin] Always prepared: the motto of the U.S. Coast Guard.

sensei *(sen-SAY)* [Japanese: teacher; master] A JUDO or KARATE instructor.

sepoy *(SEE-poy)* [Urdu, from Persian] Formerly, native Indian soldiers in the service of the British during the British occupation of India. ⟨after the abortive *Sepoy* Mutiny against their British rulers in 1857⟩—*The Guardian,* May 17, 1999.

seppuku *(SEH-poo-koo)* [Japanese] See HARA-KIRI.

seraglio *(seh-RAHL-yoh)* [Italian: enclosure] The section of a traditional Muslim house where women live in seclusion; a HAREM. ⟨He had marked the founding father's satirical, if now prescient, reference to critics' warnings that Americans studying their presidents might some day have "to blush at the unveiled mysteries of a future *seraglio.*"⟩—*The New York Times,* January 7, 1999.

serai *(seh-RYE)* [Turkish, from Persian: abode; palace] An inn; a stopping place for caravans.

serape *(seh-RAH-peh)* [Mexican Spanish] In Latin America, a blanket used as a shawl or a cape.

seriatim *(seh-ree-AH-tim)* [Latin] In a series; one after another. ⟨Conservative governments in Britain have produced sex scandals *seriatim,* and though readers of the popular press gobbled up salacious MINUTIAE, they seldom punished the sinners at the polls.⟩—*The New York Times,* February 8, 1998.

shako *(SHAY-koh)* [Hungarian] A military hat, usually cylindrical, with a visor and a plume on top.

shalom *(shah-LOHM)* [Hebrew] Peace. Hello. Good-bye. So long.

shaman *(SHAH-mahn)* [Russian: he who knows] A man, said to have the power of communicating with the spirit world, whose role is to protect others against invisible forces or hostile spirits; *shamans* usually have great prestige and power in their communities. The term originated among Siberian tribes.

shamus *(SHAY-mus)* [Possibly Irish, from the given name Seamus, or from Yiddish *shammes*] In slang, a policeman or a detective.

sharif, sherif *(sheh-REEF)* [Arabic] A Muslim prince or ruler who claims direct descent from Muhammad through Fatima, his daughter.

shegel See SHEKEL.

shegetz *(SHAY-gits)* [Yiddish] An often disparaging word for a non-Jewish man or boy; a Jewish male whose behavior and attitudes are seen to be more gentile than Jewish. See also SHIKSA.

sheik, sheikh *(shayk)* [Arabic: old man; an elder] In Islamic countries, a chief or leader of a tribe, village, or family; a venerable man. ⟨And this six-door nine-seater swallows gas fast enough (about 12 miles per gal.) to warm any oil *sheik*'s heart.⟩—*Time,* March 8, 1999.

shekel, shegel *(SHEH-kl)* [Hebrew] A silver coin of the ancient Hebrews; a unit of paper money in modern Israel. In slang, coins or money.

shiatsu *(shee-AHT-soo)* [Japanese, from Chinese] A Japanese form of massage that includes the use of acupuncture.

shibboleth *(SHIH-boh-leth)* [from Hebrew: freshet] A test word, used by the people of Gilead during the wars of biblical times to identify their enemies, the Ephraimites, who could not pronounce the sound *sh* except as *s*. Currently, any distinctive pronunciation, mode of conduct, or dress associated with a particular group that reveals class, nationality, political affiliation, etc. Also, an outworn principle or slogan that is still considered necessary by some members of a group.

shiitake *(shee-ee-TAH-keh)* [Japanese] In Japanese and Chinese cooking, a large, dark-brown or black mushroom, often sold dried.

shiksa *(SHIK-sah)* [Yiddish] A non-Jewish woman or girl; a Jewish woman or girl whose behavior and attitudes are seen to be more gentile than Jewish. See also SHEGETZ.

shikun *(shee-KOON)* [Modern Hebrew] In Israel, a planned housing development designed for specific ethnic groups or for members of a single profession.

shish kebab *(SHISH keh-bahb)* [Turkish] Small pieces of meat, skewered and broiled, usually over charcoal.

shivah, shiva *(SHIH-vah)* [Hebrew: seven] In Judaism, a seven-day period of mourning observed after the funeral of a family member. To "sit *shivah*" is to observe such a period.

shlemiel See SCHLEMIEL.

shlimazl See SCHLIMAZL.

shofar *(SHOH-far)* [Hebrew] A ram's horn used as a wind instrument, blown in biblical times as a signal in battle, now used in synagogues during the high holy days of the Jewish year.

shogun *(SHOH-gun)* [Japanese, from Chinese: lead the army] Originally, the title given to military commanders in Japan from the 8th through the 12th centuries. From then until 1868, the *shogun* (whose office was hereditary) was the actual ruler of Japan, under whom the emperor was a figurehead. ⟨"Edo period" denotes the 2½ centuries . . . [of] an absolute regime, founded there in the early 17th century by the military lord, or *shogun*⟩—*Time,* December 14, 1998.

shoji *(SHOH-jee)* [Japanese] A panel made of a light wooden frame covered with translucent paper, used as a screen or partition between rooms or within a room in a traditional Japanese house.

shtetl, stetl *(SHTEH-tl)* [Yiddish, diminutive of German *Stadt:* city] Formerly, a Jewish village or small town in eastern Europe, often a regional market center; a semirural, semiurban community of peddlers, shopkeepers, and artisans. ⟨When Nathan Kaplan writes from Chicago to find out more about his *shtetl,* Romaniuk offers to help.⟩—*The Guardian,* March 22, 1999.

shtick, schtik *(shtihk)* [Yiddish, from German: pranks; antics] A contrived or studied routine or performance, usually comic, or a piece of "business" used by an actor; the use of exaggerated devices or gestures to draw people's attention. A bit of cheating; a devious trick. Also, one's particular interest, talent, or public image in life. Also written as *shtik*. ⟨Einstein's *shtick* was mathematics—the diplomat's is persuasion.⟩

shul, schul *(shool)* [Yiddish] A synagogue.

shvitz *(shvihts)* [Yiddish] Sweat, or a place where one goes to sweat, as a steam bath. To perspire from the heat or from nervousness. ⟨A 90-foot-long marble colonnade . . . contains the rooms for the *shvitz*.⟩—*The New York Times*, August 19, 1999.

shvitzer *(SHVIT-zer)* [German] A person who perspires heavily. By extension, a show-off, a braggart.

sierra *(see-EH-rah)* [Spanish, from Latin: serrated] A chain of hills or mountains with a prominent series of jagged peaks.

siesta *(see-EHS-tah)* [Spanish, from Latin *sesta*: the sixth hour] In Spain and Latin American countries, a nap or rest period in the middle of the day or the first part of the afternoon.

simpatico *(sim-PAH-tih-koh)* [Italian] Sympathetic; congenial. ⟨She found the whole family to be unusually *simpatico*.⟩

sinecure *(SIN-eh-kyoor)* [Latin: without duty] A job or a title with few or no responsibilities. ⟨Positions on its board of directors are *sinecures*, and the boards don't hold management accountable in the way American versions now do.⟩—*Time*, March 1, 1999.

sine die *(SEE-neh DEE-ay)* [Latin: without a fixed day] A phrase used to indicate that no date has been set, as in "the court adjourned *sine die*."

sine qua non *(SEE-neh kwah NON)* [Latin: without which, nothing] Indicating something essential; a necessary element or condition. ⟨The ability of each player to listen to the others in a quartet is a *sine qua non* of fine ensemble playing.⟩

singspiel *(SING-shpeel)* [German] A play with both spoken dialogue and musical sections; an OPERETTA.

sirocco *(sih-ROH-koh)* [Italian, from Arabic] A hot south wind that blows into countries on the northern shore of the Mediterranean, sometimes humid, sometimes dry and heavy with North African dust.

sitar *(see-TAHR)* [Hindi] A musical instrument of India, similar to a lute, with an onion-shaped bowl and a long, broad neck that carries four strings to be played, and eleven tuned to the scale in use so that they may resound individually in sympathy when one of the four strings sounds its scale tone.

sitzmark *(SITS-mark)* [German] The imprint left by a person, particularly a skier, who has fallen backward in the snow.

skirl *(skerl)* [Old Norse] The sound of a bagpipe. To play the bagpipe.

skoal *(skohl)* [Danish: bowl] To your good health: an exclamation used as a toast in Scandinavian countries.

slalom *(SLAH-lom)* [Norwegian] In skiing, a steep, zigzag racecourse or race laid out between pairs of poles or gates, requiring sharp turns of varying difficulty. Any similar course, as one used to test the maneuverability of automobiles.

smorgasbord *(SMOR-ges-bord)* [Swedish: sandwich table] A buffet table that presents a great variety of hot and cold dishes. By extension, any situation that offers many choices. ⟨Here, in the sunny Southern Caliphate, they make up a *smorgasbord* of least-favored nations.⟩—*The New York Times Book Review*, July 18, 1993.

snorkel *(SNOHR-kel)* [German] A tube that carries air from the surface to a submerged swimmer or submarine, allowing the swimmer or the submarine to remain underwater.

sobriquet *(SOH-brih-kay, soh-bree-KAY)* [French] A nickname; a humorous or teasing appellation. ⟨A team known more by its *sobriquet* than its official name⟩

soi-disant *(swah-dee-SANH)* [French] An often disparaging term meaning so-called; self-styled; pretended. ⟨During the discussion, his *soi-disant* old friend failed to support his position.⟩

soigné, soignée *(swahn-YAY)* [French: (well) cared for] Well-groomed; carefully and elegantly turned out, done, or designed.

soiree, soirée *(swah-RAY)* [French, from Latin] A party or social gathering held in the evening, especially one given for a specific purpose, such as "a *soiree* of poetry readings."

sombrero *(som-BREH-roh)* [Spanish, from *sombra:* shade] A tall hat with a very wide brim, made of straw or felt, worn by men in the desert areas of Spain, Latin America, and the southwestern United States.

sonata *(soh-NAH-tah)* [Italian, from *sonare:* to sound] A musical composition for an instrumental soloist, usually consisting of several movements, with or without accompaniment.

sonatina *(soh-nah-TEE-nah)* [Italian] A musical composition similar to the SONATA, but shorter.

son et lumière *(sonh ay lüm-YAIR)* [French: sound and light] An outdoor nighttime spectacle, often a retelling of an historic event, that combines lighting effects, sound effects, narration, and music. Typically, a building of historical importance, such as a castle, would be used as background.

sopaipilla *(soh-pye-PEE-yah)* [American Spanish] A small pastry made of a yeast dough that is deep-fried and dipped in honey.

sorbet *(sohr-BAY)* [French, from Arabic] Sherbet.

sordino *(sohr-DEE-noh)* [Italian] See SOURDINE.

sotto voce *(SOT-oh VOH-cheh)* [Italian: under the voice] A very quiet manner of speech; a whisper. ⟨She spoke *sotto voce,* to avoid being overheard.⟩ ⟨civil servants in Parliament and Government that they can sometimes—*sotto voce*—be heard to deride⟩—*The Guardian,* May 20, 1999.

soubrette *(soo-BREHT)* [French, from Provençal] In a play or opera, the character of a lady's maid or maidservant who is young, pretty, and vivacious, as well as often sly and manipulative. An actress who plays such a role. ⟨Chaplin, the offspring of a vaudevillian and a music-hall *soubrette,* first appeared on stage at the age of eight.⟩

soufflé *(soo-FLAY)* [French: puffed; blown] A light, baked dish with a fluffy consistency, made with beaten egg whites combined with yolks and other ingredients ranging from cheese to chocolate. *Souffléed:* puffed up; lightened.

souk See SUK.

soupçon *(soop-SONH)* [French: a suspicion] A minute quantity; a hint of, as a slight taste or mere suggestion of a particular flavor.

sourdine *(soor-DEEN)* [French, from Italian] A mute; a device that fits on or into a musical instrument and changes its tone quality.

sous-chef *(SOO-sheff)* [French: under-chef] In a hotel or restaurant kitchen, the second in command.

soutane *(soo-TAHN)* [French, from Italian] A cassock worn by members of the Roman Catholic priesthood.

soviet *(SOH-vee-eht)* [Russian: a council] In the former Soviet Union, a local governing council elected by the workers of a community; the basis of the Russian system of government; any of the legislative bodies that exist at various levels of government.

sovkhoz (singular); **sovkhozy** (plural) *(sov-KOHZ, sov-KOH-zee)* [Russian] In the former Soviet Union, a strictly state-run enterprise, such as a farm or a factory, often located on a large estate that once belonged to a wealthy private owner. *Sovkhozy* were less numerous than KOLKHOZY.

spahi *(SPAH-hee)* [Algerian French, from Persian] A cavalryman in the Algerian French service.

spécialité de la maison *(spay-see-ah-lee-TAY deu lah may-ZONH)* [French] In a restaurant, a specialty of the house; the best or most important dish on the menu.

sprechstimme *(SPREKH-stim-meh)* [German] A vocal style halfway between speech and singing; rhythmic recitation on higher or lower pitches with no attempt to reproduce all the notes of a melody. Also called *sprechgesang*. ⟨a choir that has mastered both traditional singing parts and *Sprechstimme*⟩—*The New Criterion,* May 1999.

spritz *(shprits)* [German] A brief spray; a squirt.

spritzer *(SHPRIT-ser)* [German] An effervescent drink, often one made with wine and seltzer. ⟨Lunch consisted of crab salad and a refreshing lemon *spritzer.*⟩

spumante *(spoo-MAHN-teh)* [Italian: foaming] Bubbly; sparkling, as in a sparkling wine.

squaw *(skwaw)* [Algonquian] A North American Indian woman or wife. An informal and offensive term for any woman or girl.

staccato *(stah-KAH-toh)* [Italian] In music, short and detached, cutting each note off before it has sounded for its indicated duration. Abruptly, with sharp emphasis, as in "the *staccato* sound of gunfire." ⟨Speaking before a packed lecture hall in his *staccato*-like voice, punctuated by rapid inhales, he cast a spell, making each listener believe he was speaking only to him or her.⟩—*Time*, March 29, 1999.

status quo *(STAH-tus KWOH)* [Latin: state in which] The present state of things; without any changes. ⟨Many citizens will come forward to defend the *status quo*.⟩

steppe *(stehp)* [Russian, Ukrainian] A vast, temperate plain, as one of the extensive grasslands of Siberia and eastern Asia, that exists in three vegetation zones: the forest, or wooded *steppe;* the prairie, or tillable *steppe;* and the nontillable *steppe,* which is semidesert.

stetl See SHTETL.

stilyaga (singular); **stilyagi** (plural) *(stil-YAH-gah, stil-YAH-ghee)* [Russian] In the former Soviet Union, a young person who dresses and acts in the style of an American fan of heavy metal, punk rock, etc.

stipple *(STIP-pl)* [Dutch, from *stippelen:* to dot] To paint, draw, or engrave using dots or little touches instead of lines.

strafe *(strayf)* [German, from *strafen:* to punish] To attack people on the ground with machine-gun fire from an airplane. In slang, to punish; to criticize severely. ⟨Melvin writes romantic novels—62 so far—and *strafes* the lives of all who amble into his gun sight.⟩—*Time*, December 15, 1997.

streusel *(STROO-zel)* [German: a sprinkling] A topping made of breadcrumbs, sugar, cinnamon, flour, butter, and chopped nuts, to be spread over a coffee cake and baked.

stupa *(STOO-pah)* [Sanskrit] In Buddhist architecture, a memorial monument to Buddha or a Buddhist saint, sometimes containing relics or sacred texts; often, a circular base covered by a flattened hemisphere, with a post or a decorative spire rising through the center.

Sturm und Drang *(shtoorm unt DRAHNG)* [German: storm and stress] Used to characterize the turbulent period of a young man's life when childhood is past and manhood has not quite been achieved. Originally, used to describe the emotional life of the main character in Goethe's novel *The Sorrows of Young Werther* (1787). ⟨Thus the second decade of the American Negro's freedom was a period of conflict, of inspiration and doubt, of faith and vain questionings, of *Sturm und Drang.*⟩— *The Atlantic Monthly,* August 1897.

subpoena *(sub-PEE-nah)* [Latin: under penalty] A summons to appear at court as a witness, or to provide certain records or documents. ⟨Records *subpoenaed* from the Christian Coalition contain a carefully scripted set of questions and answers.⟩— *The Guardian,* May 23, 1999.

sub rosa *(sub ROH-zah)* [Latin: under the rose] Secretly; confidentially. In meetings of some ancient societies, a rose on the table symbolized that all present were sworn to secrecy about the business to be discussed.

succès fou *(sük-say FOO)* [French: crazy success] An extraordinary success; a great triumph, especially in a theatrical or other performance.

succubus *(SUK-yoo-bus)* [Latin] A demon in human female form that is said to attack men sexually in their sleep; an evil spirit. A prostitute. See also INCUBUS.

sui generis *(soo-ee JEH-neh-riss)* [Latin: of his (its) own kind] Said of a person or thing that is unique. One-of-a-kind.

suk, souk *(sook)* [Arabic] In Arab countries, a market or BAZAAR. Also written as *suq*. ⟨Built above the Old Port, "the Basket" is a warren of stepped streets and narrow passageways whose *souk*-like markets are more North African than French.⟩—*Time,* June 15, 1998.

sumi *(SOO-mee)* [Japanese] Black ink made from vegetable soot and glue and formed into sticks. The user scrapes the material off the stick and mixes it in water for use in calligraphy.

sumi-e *(SOO-mee-eh)* [Japanese] A style of monochromatic ink painting, brought from China in the mid-1300s by Zen Buddhists.

summa *(SOO-mah)* [Latin] A formal summary of a large work, or a broad summary of an entire field of knowledge, especially in philosophy, religion, or science.

summa cum laude *(SOO-mah kum LAU-deh)* [Latin] With highest praise; used on diplomas to denote the highest of three honors for academic achievement, as in "she graduated *summa cum laude* in religion and social work." See also CUM LAUDE, MAGNA CUM LAUDE.

sumo *(soo-moh)* [Japanese] A highly ritualized form of wrestling in Japan in which one opponent attempts to force the other out of the ring, or to touch the floor with some part of his body other than his feet. Contestants weigh as much as three hundred pounds, and carry on a family tradition in the sport. *Sumo* is said to have originated in Japan in the 1st century B.C., and it became a professional sport in the 1600s.

sushi *(SOO-shee)* [Japanese: it is sour] In Japanese cooking, small, shaped pieces of food made with cold, boiled rice dampened with rice vinegar and topped with raw fish or shellfish. Also, a long roll made by wrapping seaweed around vinegar rice and small strips of fish, vegetables, etc.; usually cut into bite-size portions. See also SASHIMI.

sutra *(SOO-trah)* [Hindi, from Sanskrit: thread; clue] In Hinduism, a collection of moral aphorisms that are intended to guide the conduct of life. In Buddhism, any of the sermons of Buddha.

suttee, sati *(suh-TEE)* [Hindi, from Sanskrit: virtuous woman] Formerly, the act of self-sacrifice by a Hindu widow on the funeral pyre of her husband. ⟨When the king died, she did her wifely duty and threw herself on his funeral pyre according to the Hindu tradition of *suttee.*⟩—*The New York Times,* June 5, 1999.

svelte *(svehlt)* [French, from Italian] Slender and graceful; willowy; lithe. Also, suave; pleasantly urbane. ⟨an actress who was both *svelte* and extremely poised⟩

swami *(SWAH-mee)* [Hindi, from Sanskrit: lord; master] A teacher of the Hindu religion. Also, a person of great knowledge or authority whose advice is sought by many; a PUNDIT.

sympathique *(sam-pah-TEEK)* [French] Used to describe someone who is likable, congenial, responsive, or generally appealing.

tabbouleh, tabouli *(tah-BOO-leh)* [Levantine Arabic] In Middle Eastern cooking, a salad of BULGUR, olive oil, and lemon juice mixed with parsley, mint, and tomato.

tabi *(tah-bee)* [Japanese] A type of sock that has a separate pouch for the big toe, worn often with ZORIS.

tabla *(TAH-blah)* [Hindi, from Arabic] A small, cylindrical wooden drum from India with a laminated leather head that allows the drummer, playing it with the hands, to vary the sound of the drum at will.

tableau vivant *(tah-BLOH vee-VANH)* [French: living picture] A silent representation of a famous painting, scene, or historical event by performers who are appropriately costumed and posed. ⟨one segment of the audience presented a *tableau vivant* of the city's society matrons, a vanishing breed as the younger generation adopts a more businesslike lifestyle.⟩—*The New York Times,* November 7, 1997.

table d'hôte *(TAH-bleu DOHT)* [French: host's table] A complete meal of preselected courses, served in a restaurant at a fixed price. See also À LA CARTE, PRIX FIXE.

taboo, tabu *(tah-BOO)* [Tongan, Fijian: forbidden] A restriction or ban placed on something that is considered by custom or religion as unacceptable, and is not to be touched, used, or spoken. Any prohibition based on social convention or custom. Forbidden by society as improper. ⟨breastfeeding from birth is seen as *taboo*⟩—*Time,* May 17, 1999.

tabouli See TABBOULEH.

tabu See TABOO.

tabula rasa *(TAH-boo-lah RAH-zah)* [Latin: scraped tablet] A clean slate; a mind not yet exposed to or affected by experience. Anything that exists in its original state of purity. ⟨You have messed up a nice clean *tabula rasa* with your own defective personality.⟩—*The Guardian,* April 21, 1999.

taco *(TAH-koh)* [Mexican Spanish] In Mexican cooking, a TORTILLA, sometimes deep-fried, bent into a U-shape and filled with meat, beans, vegetables, etc., and seasonings.

tae kwon do *(tye kwon doh)* [Korean, from Chinese] A Korean martial art, based on KARATE, that uses powerful leaping kicks and a variety of aggressive jabs, punches, choking moves, etc. to disable an opponent. See also JUJITSU.

tagliatelle *(tahl-yah-TEL-leh)* [Italian] In Italian cooking, egg noodles cut into long ribbons.

tahini *(tah-HEE-nee)* [Levantine Arabic] In Middle Eastern cooking, a paste or spread made from ground sesame seeds. Also called *sesame butter.*

tai chi chuan, t'ai chi ch'uan *(ty chee CHWAHN)* [Chinese: fist of the Great Absolute] In China, a martial art that developed into a system of meditative exercise which uses slow circular and stretching movements and positions designed to improve balance.

taiga *(TYE-gah)* [Russian, from Turkic] The vast evergreen forests that cover subarctic regions in Russia and North America, reaching to the northern limit of tree growth.

tailleur *(tye-YEUR)* [French: tailor] A tailored suit or a tailor-made ensemble for a woman.

taipan *(tye-PAN)* [Chinese: great company] The owner or head of a foreign business establishment. ⟨The company was sold some years ago by the bank's new *taipan,* who saw it as too extravagant.⟩

tambourine *(tam-boo-REEN)* [French: little drum] A small, round drum often used by Spanish dancers. It has a single head of stretched skin and pairs of metal disks loosely attached around its frame to provide a jangling sound as it is shaken or struck.

tambura *(tahm-BOO-rah)* [Persian] A musical instrument consisting of several long strings stretched taut along a wooden fingerboard. The player tunes the strings to the tones necessary for a particular piece of music, then plucks them to supply a droning bass for other instruments such as the SITAR.

tandoori *(tan-DOO-ree)* [Hindi, Urdu] In Indian cooking, cooked or baked in a *tandoor,* a cylindrical clay oven, at very high temperature. 〈Curry blends and *tandoori* pastes can now be found in American markets.〉

Tannenbaum *(TAH-nen-baum)* [German: tanning tree; hemlock] The hemlock tree, the traditional German Christmas tree. It gets its name from the use of its bark as the chief ingredient in a tanning solution.

tant mieux *(tanh MYEU)* [French] So much the better.

tant pis *(tanh PEE)* [French] So much the worse.

Tao *(dau, tau)* [Chinese: the way; the road] In some Chinese philosophies, that by which all things exist or occur; the basic principle of all nature. The rational basis of human conduct; the morally correct path of human behavior.

tapas *(TAH-pas)* [Spanish: covers; lids] An assortment of small cocktail snacks or appetizers.

tarboosh, tarbush *(tahr-BOOSH)* [Arabic] A brimless cloth or red felt cap with a silk tassel, worn by Muslim men.

tatami *(tah-TAH-mee)* [Japanese] In Japan, a heavy, woven floor mat made of rice straw, approximately three by six feet; the size of a room is determined and described by the number of *tatami* required to cover the floor.

tattoo (1) *(tah-too)* [Tahitian] To mark the skin with indelible designs or patterns by pricking it and inserting pigments; a design or picture made by this method.

tattoo (2) *(tah-TOO)* [Dutch, from *taptoe:* the tap is shut] A tapping or drumming sound; a quiet drum or bugle signal calling soldiers to their quarters in the evening. An entertainment that includes drumming and/or music and marching.

taupe *(tohp)* [French, from Latin *talpa:* mole] A brownish gray color often tinged with other colors such as purple, green, or dark yellow.

tavola *(TAH-voh-lah)* [Italian] A table.

tchotchke, chotchke *(CHOTCH-keh)* [Yiddish, from Polish] A cheap trinket, ornament, or souvenir. A knickknack. Also written *tsatzke.*

teapoy *(TEE-poy)* [Hindi] A small, three-legged table suitable for serving tea.

tempo *(TEM-poh)* [Italian: time] The speed or pace of a piece of music, regardless of its rhythm; the characteristic pace of any activity or occupation, as in "the frenetic *tempo* of life in the big city."

tempus fugit *(TEHM-pus FYOO-jit, TEHM-pus FOO-git)* [Latin] Time flies.

tepee *(TEE-pee)* [Dakota] An easily portable, single-family tent of animal hides stretched over a conical structure of light poles. It has a flap at its peak to close off cold or to release smoke from the campfire inside. Not to be confused with a WIGWAM, which is generally dome-shaped.

tequila *(teh-KEE-lah)* [Mexican Spanish, after a district in Mexico] A strong liquor made by distilling the fermented mash of the agave plant.

teriyaki *(teh-ree-YAH-kee)* [Japanese] Broiled fish, chicken, or beef that has been marinated in soy sauce, ginger, SAKE, and sugar. Prepared in this way, as in "salmon *teriyaki.*"

terra-cotta *(teh-rah KOT-tah)* [Italian: baked earth] A hard, kiln-fired clay, brownish red in color and often unglazed, used for pottery, sculpture, and as a structural material. Anything made of such material or having a similar color.

terra firma *(TEH-rah FER-mah)* [Latin] Solid earth; dry land, as distinguished from air or water. ⟨Once on *terra firma,* which was little more than an inhospitable chunk of wasteland, the crew slept.⟩—*The New York Times,* April 12, 1999.

terra incognita *(TEH-rah in-kog-NEE-tah)* [Latin: land unknown] Any unknown or unexplored region; a field of study or subject as yet unexplored. ⟨Modern medicine has unravelled mysteries, mapped the erstwhile *terra incognita* of even the most overlooked of organelles, forced disease after disease to retreat in disarray⟩—*The Guardian,* May 2, 1999.

terrine *(teh-REEN)* [French] An oval, earthenware baking dish with its own lid. A PÂTÉ of meat or vegetables cooked in such a dish.

thug *(thug)* [Hindi: rogue; cheat] A vicious ruffian, thief, or killer. Formerly, one of a confederacy of professional assassins in India who worshipped Kali, the Hindu goddess of destruction. ⟨the lads are chased into the outback by immigration officials, British S.A.S. operatives and a vengeful *thug* from Belfast.⟩—*Time,* May 17, 1999.

tic *(tik)* [French] A sudden, involuntary muscular spasm or twitch, often of the face. By extension, a personal quirk; a recurrent peculiarity of someone's behavior. ⟨His endless acerbic comments seem less like argument than a nervous *tic.*⟩

tochis See TOKUS.

todo el mundo *(toh-doh el MOON-doh)* [Spanish] All the world; everybody. ⟨Everyone—*todo el mundo,* tout le monde!—says so.⟩—*The New York Times,* March 11, 1988.

tofu *(TOH-foo)* [Japanese, from Chinese] In Oriental cooking, a white, mild-flavored curd made from soybean milk, also called *bean curd*.

tohubohu *(TOH-hoo-BOH-hoo)* [Hebrew] Confusion; chaos.

tokus, tochis *(TOOK-us)* [Yiddish, from Hebrew] A slang word for buttocks. Also written *tuchis*.

tontine *(tonh-TEEN)* [French, after 17th-century Italian banker Lorenzo Tonti] A type of collective life annuity in which individual profits increase as the number of subscribers decreases with each of their deaths; the last survivor takes the whole. The group of subscribers, or the share of one participant. A *tontine* has served as the organizing factor in novels of mystery or intrigue.

toque *(tohk)* [French] A woman's close-fitting, brimless hat. A plumed velvet cap with a brim and full crown, worn in the 16th century. See also CLOCHE.

torchère, torchiere *(torsh-YAIR)* [French: tall stand for a candelabrum] A tall floor lamp with a reflecting bowl of glass or metal that directs the light upward.

toreador *(toh-ray-ah-DOR)* [Spanish] A bullfighter.

torero *(toh-RAY-roh)* [Spanish] A bullfighter, especially a MATADOR. ⟨In the dangerous art of the *torero*, the degree of brilliance in the performance is left to the fighter's honor.⟩

torte *(tort, TOR-teh)* [German, from Italian] A rich cake made with butter, eggs, and ground nuts, containing little or no flour.

tortilla *(tor-TEE-yah)* [Spanish: little cake] A staple of Mexican cooking; a pancakelike unleavened bread made from cornmeal or wheat flour, baked on an iron griddle or on earthenware.

tostada *(toh-STAH-dah)* [Mexican Spanish] A Mexican dish made by topping a fried TORTILLA with a variety of ingredients such as cheese, GUACAMOLE, refried beans, etc.

touché *(too-SHAY)* [French: touched] In fencing, the expression used to acknowledge a hit or a touch by the opponent's foil. In speech, an exclamation recognizing a telling remark or a valid accusation.

toupee *(too-PAY)* [French, from *toupet:* a tuft of hair] A wig or patch of false hair worn to cover baldness or a bald spot. Formerly, a tuft of false hair, especially at the top of a wig.

tour de force *(toor deu FORSS)* [French: feat of strength] A feat of exceptional skill, strength, ingenuity, or adroitness; an outstanding achievement or performance; a stroke of genius. ⟨In a scientific *tour de force,* Florey, Chain and their colleagues rapidly purified penicillin in sufficient quantity⟩—*Time,* March 29, 1999.

tournedos *(toor-neh-DOH)* [French] In French cooking, small rounds of beef tenderloin served on fried bread and often topped with mushrooms or FOIE GRAS.

tout de suite *(toot SWEET)* [French] At once; immediately; right away.

tout le monde *(too leu MONHD)* [French] All the world; everybody; everyone.

trattoria *(trah-toh-REE-ah)* [Italian] An informal restaurant or eating place that offers Italian food at moderate prices.

trecento *(treh-CHEHN-toh)* [Italian] The 14th century; a word applied to works of Italian art, literature, etc., of the 1300s. ⟨The dominant painters of the *trecento* were followers of Giotto.⟩

trek *(trehk)* [Afrikaans, from Dutch *trecken:* to pull or haul] Originally, in South Africa, to travel by ox wagon. More recently, to travel or migrate slowly or with difficulty. Any journey that involves hardship. ⟨A kitten survived a four-mile *trek* across the city of Worcester.⟩—*The Guardian*, May 17, 1999.

triage *(tree-AHZH)* [French: sorting] The process at any scene of disaster—battlefield, earthquake site, hospital emergency room—by which medical personnel decide which victims have the greatest chance of survival if treated promptly. Many modern hospitals have a *triage* office at the entrance to the emergency room. ⟨It is hoped that *triage* will be done by the most experienced clinician available.⟩

tricot *(TREE-koh, tree-KOH)* [French, from *tricoter*: to knit] A plain, machine-made knitted fabric, such as jersey, made of various natural or synthetic fibers.

triskaidekaphobia *(triss-kye-deh-kah-FOH-bee-ah)* [Greek] Fear of the number thirteen. ⟨The fact that Schoenberg was born on September 13, 1874, and was fervently *triskaidekaphobic* must have produced a sense of foreboding from childhood on.⟩—*The New Criterion*, May 1999.

tristesse *(tree-STEHSS)* [French] Sadness; melancholy.

troika *(TROY-kah)* [Russian: threesome] A Russian sleigh or wagon drawn by three horses harnessed abreast. A group of three persons, especially administrators or leaders, or three nations acting together to exert control or make policy decisions. ⟨[They] tell the inside story of how a *troika* of Chirac intimates . . . put him back in the saddle of power.⟩—*Time*, February 15, 1999.

troll *(trohl)* [Old Norse: demon] In Scandinavian folklore, an imaginary being; a giant or mischievous dwarf that lives in a cave or under a bridge. In modern slang, a derelict or homeless person who sleeps under a bridge or viaduct.

trompe l'oeil *(tromp LEU-yeh)* [French: deceives the eye] In art and decoration, an image that creates the illusion of reality through extremely fine and realistic detail. A painting or decoration produced in this manner. ⟨The city has encouraged comic-strip characters to venture into the streets, brightening up gray and windowless walls with colorful *trompe l'oeil* murals.⟩—*The New York Times*, September 15, 1996.

trousseau *(troo-SOH)* [French] The collection of clothing and household linens with which a bride begins married life. ⟨I received a *trousseau* of hand-embroidered Russian table and bed linens when I married.⟩

tsar See CZAR.

tsatzke See TCHOTCHKE.

tsimmes See TZIMMES.

tsunami *(tsoo-NAH-mee)* [Japanese] A catastrophic ocean wave, usually produced by an undersea earthquake or volcanic eruption, capable of destroying shorelines, harbors, buildings, and whole villages before it subsides. Not the same as a tidal wave. Also called *seismic sea wave*. By extension, anything of great size and unstoppable force. ⟨That year she was engulfed in another *tsunami* of publicity when she won the international competition for the opera house in Cardiff, Wales.⟩—*Time*, April 5, 1999.

tuchis See TOKUS.

tundra *(TUN-drah)* [Russian, from Lapp] A vast, flat, treeless plain of the Arctic regions, where the subsoil is perpetually frozen (permafrost). ⟨In Labrador, she came perilously close to losing her way in a *tundra* without landmarks.⟩

tutti-frutti *(TOO-tee FROO-tee)* [Italian: all fruits] A preserve, confection, ice cream, or chewing gum made or flavored with a variety of fruits.

tutu *(too-too)* [French] A ballet skirt made of many layers of net or tarlatan.

tzigane *(tsee-GAHN)* [French, from Hungarian] A Gypsy, especially one from Hungary. Of or pertaining to Gypsies.

tzimmes, tsimmes *(TSIM-mes)* [Yiddish, from Swabian dialect] In Jewish cooking, a sweetened stew or casserole of meat or vegetables, fresh and dried fruits, etc., often served at the Jewish New Year. By extension, a fuss, hullabaloo, or uproar. ⟨We also had *tzimmes* made with prunes, carrots and beef, lots of sour cream and homemade horseradish so strong it brought tears to our eyes.⟩—*The New York Times*, May 18, 1983.

über- *(Ü-behr)* [German] Over. Used as a prefix meaning over, super, above, or superior, as in *übertechnocrat*.

übermensch *(Ü-behr-mehnsh)* [German: superman] In Nietzschean philosophy, a superior being who represents the highest level of passion, creativity, and dominance.

uhlan *(OO-lahn)* [German, from Polish and Turkish] A lancer and cavalryman, originally of the Polish army, later prominent in the German army.

uhuru *(oo-HOO-roo)* [Swahili] Freedom; independence.

ukase *(YOO-kayz)* [Russian] Originally, an order or edict of the Russian czar. Any official decree or proclamation issued by absolute or arbitrary authority. ⟨their church—the one institution that could stand above the regime's unjust compromises and senseless *ukases*⟩—*Time,* May 3, 1999.

ukiyo-e *(yoo-KEE-oh-eh)* [Japanese: pictures of the transitory world] In Japan, between the 17th and 19th centuries, a style of painting and wood-block printmaking that depicted the commonplace tasks and pleasures of ordinary people.

ukulele *(yoo-koo-LAY-lee)* [Hawaiian: leaping flea] A small, guitar-shaped instrument with four strings and a fretted fingerboard, associated with Hawaiian music.

ulpan (singular); **ulpanim** (plural) *(OOL-pahn, ool-PAH-nim)* [Hebrew: instruction] A school for the study of Hebrew, particularly one providing immersion courses for recent immigrants to Israel.

ultimatum *(ul-tih-MAY-tum, ul-tih-MAH-tum)* [Latin] A final statement of conditions, terms, or demands, rejection of which may lead to a breaking off of friendly relations or to the use of force. Any last demand, proposal, or concession.

umiak *(OO-mee-ahk)* [Greenland Eskimo: womens' boat] A large, lightly framed open boat covered with animal skins and used by the Eskimos to transport goods and belongings. See also KAYAK.

und so weiter *(oont zoh VYE-ter)* [German] And so forth; ET CETERA.

ur- *(oor)* [German] A prefix meaning original or earliest, usually used in reference to cultural or historical matters; *urtext,* for example, is the original or primary form of a written work.

utile dulci *(OO-tee-leh DOOL-chee)* [Latin: useful and sweet] The useful with the pleasurable; taken from a line by the Roman poet Horace.

vade mecum *(VAH-deh MAY-cum)* [Latin: go with me] Anything carried for frequent or constant use, such as a manual or a guidebook. ⟨following this realization I discovered other absences in my essential cultural *vade mecum*⟩—*The Guardian,* February 28, 1999.

valet *(VAH-let, vah-LAY)* [French] A gentleman's manservant who takes care of clothing and other personal matters; a hotel employee who performs similar services for patrons; an attendant who parks cars at a hotel or restaurant.

Valkyrie *(val-KEE-ree)* [Old Norse: chooser of the slain] In Norse mythology, one of the beautiful war maidens who brings the souls of heroes slain in battle to Valhalla. ⟨Into any fray she bursts, a media Medusa, a *Valkyrie* for hire, Penthesilea fighting for Amazon rights.⟩—*Time,* December 12, 1994.

vanitas *(VAH-nih-tahss)* [Latin: vanity] A form of still-life painting depicting objects symbolic of death and the fleeting nature of earthly pleasures; a GENRE popular in the Netherlands in the early 1600s. ⟨And then there are the *vanitas* paintings. Human skulls and just snuffed lamps and candles put a moralizing spin on accumulations of posh goods.⟩—*The New Yorker,* December 6, 1999.

vaquero *(vah-KAY-roh)* [Spanish] A herdsman; a cowboy.

vaudeville *(VOD-vill)* [French, from *voix de ville:* voice of the town, or *vau de Vire:* valley of the Vire] Originally, a simple 16th-century love song that became a popular song with a new satirical text. Later, a popular entertainment consisting of a variety of individual comic acts and skits, songs, and dance numbers. ⟨She made the transition from second-class *vaudeville* to first-class Broadway musical theater.⟩

vedette *(veu-DEHT)* [French, from Italian: lookout] Formerly, a mounted sentinel, now a small naval launch used for reconnaissance. In informal French, a star performer; a famous ARTISTE.

veld, veldt *(vehlt)* [Afrikaans, from Dutch: field] The open country or grassland of South Africa, having few trees. ⟨When [he] saw the place last month, he said, "This is the bush *veldt*. This is my home."⟩—*Time,* April 20, 1998.

velours *(veh-LOOR)* [French: velvet] A plushlike fabric, similar to velvet, with a short, thick pile. It can be made of natural or synthetic fibers.

velouté *(veh-loo-TAY)* [French: velvety] A rich, smooth white sauce made with meat or poultry stock, sometimes thickened with egg yolk.

vendetta *(vehn-DEH-tah)* [Italian, from Latin *vindicta*: vengeance] A blood feud in which a murdered person's relatives take vengeance on the killer or the killer's family. By extension, any bitter and ongoing feud, quarrel, contest, or rivalry. ⟨Bhutto and her husband argue that the charges are part of a *vendetta* waged against them and the PPP by Nawaz Sharif and his rival Pakistan Muslim League.⟩—*Time,* April 26, 1999.

vendeuse *(vanh-DEUZ)* [French] A saleswoman; a female shop assistant.

venue *(VEHN-yoo)* [French] A designated place of meeting; the location or scene of an event. In law, the place where a crime is committed, or the county, etc., where the case arising from it must be tried. Change of *venue:* relocation of the place of trial.

⟨Defense lawyers argued in their motion for a change of *venue* that their clients' contacts with Puerto Rico are few⟩—*The New York Times,* January 13, 1999.

veranda, verandah *(veh-RAN-dah)* [Hindi, from Portuguese: balustrade] A large, open porch or balcony, usually roofed and partly enclosed, built along the outside of a house.

verbatim *(ver-BAY-tim)* [Latin] Word for word; in exactly the same words, as in "a *verbatim* record of the discussion."

verboten *(fehr-BOH-tn)* [German] Forbidden; prohibited. ⟨Companies that deal in tobacco, belch sulfur dioxide, support Planned Parenthood, finance risqué movies . . . the *verboten* list will be endless.⟩—*Time,* February 1, 1999.

verdigris *(VEHR-di-gree)* [French: green of Greece] A green or bluish PATINA that forms on copper, brass, or bronze after long exposure to the air. It consists mainly of copper sulfate, and may be used as a pigment or in a dyeing process.

verglas *(vehr-GLAH)* [French: glass ice] A thin, slick coating of ice on the ground or, in mountaineering, on rock.

verismo *(veh-RISS-moh)* [Italian: realism] In Italian opera and literature of the late 19th and early 20th centuries, a style characterized by the objective depiction of everyday life, using plain language and realistic dialogue. ⟨My, that runaway subway train crashed onto the platform with a certain vigorous *verismo.*⟩—*Time,* May 29, 1995.

veritas *(VEH-ree-tahss)* [Latin] Truth. See also IN VINO VERITAS.

vérité *(vay-ree-TAY)* [French] Truth; truthfulness. See also CINEMA VERITÉ.

vers de société *(vehr deu sohs-yay-TAY)* [French: society verse] Light verse characterized by wit, elegance, and gentle irony, designed for a small, sophisticated audience.

verso *(VEHR-soh)* [Latin] The left-hand page of an open manuscript, book, or piece of music, as opposed to the RECTO. It is usually even-numbered.

vertu See VIRTU.

vibrato *(vih-BRAH-toh)* [Italian] A variable, fairly rapid fluctuation in the pitch of a musical tone, produced intentionally on an instrument or by the human voice. ⟨He tends to play with a very fast *vibrato* that makes everything sound somewhat frantic.⟩

vignette *(veen-YEHT)* [French: little vine] A short, graceful literary work. Any small, charming, intimate scene or view. A small illustration or decorative design placed on the title page of a book or at the beginning of a chapter.

vigorish *(VIG-er-ish)* [possibly Yiddish, from Russian: profit; winnings] The fee paid on a bet, as to a bookmaker, or the interest paid to a usurer or moneylender. Sometimes shortened, informally, to *vig.*

villanelle *(vil-lah-NELL)* [French] A style of popular vocal music that spread from Italy to all of Europe in the 16th century; a favored form for songs by composers of the late Renaissance, and later by others in the 19th century. Also, a similar style of poetry. ⟨For her, difficult forms like the *villanelle,* the sestina and the tritina, enable the poet to achieve more than if he or she were just free-associating.⟩—*The New York Times,* April 13, 1999.

vin du pays, vin de pays *(venh deu pay-EE)* [French] A local wine, one that is available only in or near the region where it is produced.

vin ordinaire *(venh ohr-dee-NAIR)* [French: ordinary wine] A cheap table wine, often of unspecified origin.

virago *(vih-RAH-goh)* [Old English, from Latin] A ceaselessly scolding woman with a very loud voice; a shrew. The word is constructed on the Latin word *vir,* man, indicating that a *virago* is a woman who is like a man. ⟨[The play's] razor-tongued *virago* becomes more approachable not by the administering of a good spanking but after a raucous bout of paint ball.⟩—*The Guardian,* May 22, 1999.

virtu, vertu *(veer-TOO)* [Italian: merit, excellence] The quality of excellence, rarity, or beauty that resides in fine things, as in "objects of *virtu.*" Knowledge of or a taste for such objects, or the objects collectively.

virtuoso *(vur-choo-OH-zoh, veer-too-OH-soh)* [Italian] A person of extraordinary skill in one of the arts, especially in musical performance. ⟨In the 18th century, falsettists regularly alternated with castrati on the operatic stage, singing the *virtuoso* coloratura roles of Handel and Gluck.⟩—*Time,* June 7, 1999.

vis-à-vis *(veez-ah-VEE)* [French: face to face] In relation to or compared with, as in "outlay *vis-à-vis* profits." A person situated opposite another; a person in a corresponding situation, rank, or office.

vivace *(vee-VAH-cheh)* [Italian] In music, lively; brisk; vivacious.

viva voce *(VEE-vah VOH-cheh)* [Latin: with living voice] Orally; spoken; by word of mouth. In some European and British universities, the oral section of an examination.

vive *(veev)* [French] An exclamation meaning "long live," as in *vive le roi!:* long live the king! See also À BAS.

vizier *(vih-ZEER)* [Turkish, from Arabic] A minister of state or high official in some Muslim countries, especially in the old Turkish empire.

vogue *(vohg)* [French, from Italian *vogare:* to row] The prevailing fashion or mode, often preceded by "in"; popularity; general acceptance, or favor, as in "the current *vogue* for online stock trading."

voilà *(vwah-LAH)* [French] There! Behold!

voir dire *(vwahr DEER)* [Old French: the truth to say] An oath administered to a witness or juror who promises to speak the truth in an examination to determine his or her competence to testify; the examination itself. ⟨At the opening of the impeachment hearings, Henry Hyde read the resumés of the twelve house managers as a kind of summary *voir dire* of their credentials.⟩

vol-au-vent *(vohl-oh-VANH)* [French: float on the wind] In French cooking, a light, flaky pastry shell filled with a RAGOUT of meat, chicken, fish, or vegetables in a sauce.

volte-face *(vohlt-FAHSS)* [French, from Italian] An about-face; a turnabout; a complete change of attitude, opinion, or policy.

voodoo, vodou *(VOO-doo)* [West Indies Creole, from West African] A folk religion of the West Indies, especially Haiti, that combines African beliefs and superstitions with elements of Roman Catholicism. Derived from Dahoman slaves, *voodoo* rituals include ecstatic trances and magical practices. By extension, an informal term describing overly simple solutions or concepts that verge on the magical, as in "*voodoo* politics."

vorspiel *(FOR-shpeel)* [German: before the play] A prelude or overture to a musical work; an introductory scene to a play; a curtain-raiser.

vox populi *(voks POP-yoo-lye, voks POH-poo-lee)* [Latin: the voice of the people] Popular opinion or sentiment. ⟨more important, it was supremely responsive to the *vox populi*, and generally progressive.⟩—*The New York Times*, September 16, 1990.

voyeur *(voy-YEUR, vwah-YEUR)* [French: one who sees] A Peeping Tom; one who seeks sexual excitement by watching the sexual acts of others, usually secretively. ⟨His subject was private life . . . in which the artist is both agent and *voyeur.*⟩—*Time*, August 31, 1998.

wadi *(WAH-dee)* [Arabic] In arid areas of North Africa, Arabia, etc., the channel or bed of a stream that flows only after an occasional storm, or the stream itself; a dry watercourse; a valley. See also ARROYO. ⟨Another tough fight involved the Egyptians, who were battling an Iraqi corps in western Kuwait, on the east side of the *Wadi* al Baten, a vast dry riverbed⟩—*The New York Times*, February 27, 1991.

wahine *(wah-HEE-nee)* [Polynesian] In Hawaii and Polynesia, a girl or young woman.

waka *(WAH-kah)* [Japanese, from Chinese] A native Japanese verse form, one distinct from poetry written in other languages, or from verse written in Chinese by a Japanese poet.

wallah *(WAH-lah)* [Anglo-Indian, from a Hindi suffix: man] A person engaged in or in charge of a particular occupation or activity; used in combination, as in "the ticket *wallah.*"

wampum *(WAHM-pum)* [Algonquian] White and colored cylindrical beads, worked into necklaces, belts, etc., once used by North American Indians as currency. Informally, money; cash.

wanderjahr *(VAHN-der-yahr)* [German] Formerly, a period of travel and self-improvement undertaken by an apprentice at the end of his apprenticeship. More recently, a year's travel taken after completing one's education and before beginning professional life.

wanderlust *(WAHN-der-lust)* [German] An impulse or strong desire to travel and seek adventure; restlessness. ⟨About 95% of clients come to us with Kipling visions and *wanderlust* ideas of traveling⟩—*Time,* May 24, 1999.

wasabi *(WAH-sah-bee)* [Japanese] A plant of the mustard family; the pungent root is ground into a gray-green paste traditionally served with SUSHI.

wat *(waht)* [Thai: enclosure] In Cambodia and Thailand, a Buddhist monastery or temple, such as the famous *Angkor Wat* in western Cambodia.

weltanschauung *(VEHLT-ahn-shau-oong)* [German: worldview] A comprehensive view, philosophy, or image of the world and mankind's relationship to it.

weltschmerz *(VEHLT-shmehrts)* [German: world pain] World-weariness; romantic discontent; sentimental gloom over the state of the world.

wickiup *(WIK-ee-up)* [Fox: house] Among the nomadic Native American tribes in the western and southwestern United States, a loosely constructed hut made of brushwood or similar material. By extension, any rude hut. See also WIGWAM.

wie geht's? *(vee GAITS)* [German] How are you? How's it going?

wigwam *(WIG-wahm)* [Algonquian] A round or oval-shaped lodge or dwelling of the North American Indians, consisting of poles covered with hides, bark, etc. Informally, a place used for political meetings; New York's Tammany Hall was sometimes referred to as "the *Wigwam.*" See also WICKIUP.

windigo, witigo *(WIN-dih-go)* [Ojibwa: cannibal] In Ojibwa folklore, an evil giant who devours humans; one of a tribe said to inhabit an island in Hudson Bay.

wok *(wok)* [Chinese] A round-bottomed, bowl-shaped, steel cooking pan from China, designed for rapid cooking with a minimum of fuel.

wunderkind *(VOON-der kihnd)* [German] A wonder child; a child prodigy; a person who achieves success at a relatively early age. ⟨*wunderkind* director Sam Raimi has struggled to find a suitable vehicle for his awesome film-making talents.⟩—*The Guardian,* May 21, 1999.

xenophobe *(ZEN-oh-fohb)* [Greek] A person who is afraid of or distrusts strangers or foreigners. ⟨Calling Wilson a "blind, deaf Don Quixote" and Clemenceau a *xenophobe*⟩—*Time,* March 29, 1999.

Yahrzeit *(YAHR-zite)* [Yiddish, from German *Jahrzeit:* a year's time] In Judaism, the anniversary of the death of a family member.

yakitori *(yah-kee-TOH-ree)* [Japanese] In Japanese cooking, pieces of marinated chicken that are broiled and served on small skewers. ⟨Tourists will love the inexpensive neighborhoood *yakitori* shops and noodle restaurants.⟩

yarmulke *(YAHR-mull-keh)* [Yiddish, from Polish, Ukrainian] A small, round skullcap worn by males during Jewish religious ceremonies, and by some Orthodox or Conservative Jews during prayer and religious study. Also called a *kipa.* ⟨she stars in it wearing a pillbox-contoured designer *yarmulke*⟩—*The New York Times,* November 18, 1983.

yashmak *(YAHSH-mahk)* [Arabic, Turkish] The long, narrow face veil worn in public by some Muslim women. See also CHADOR.

yenta *(YEN-tah)* [Yiddish] A woman who gossips excessively; a busybody; a nosy, gossipy woman. By extension, any obsessive talker; a gossip. ⟨Smith said Gretzky is a "hockey *yenta*" who likes to keep informed of rumors and scuttlebutt through his extensive grapevine⟩—*The New York Times,* January 4, 1999.

yeshiva *(yeh-SHEE-vah)* [Hebrew: a sitting place] A Hebrew school, particularly for Orthodox Jews who are preparing to enter the rabbinate; a school of Talmudic studies. An Orthodox Jewish elementary school that offers both religious and secular courses.

yeti *(YEH-tee)* [Sherpa Tibetan] A mysterious, large, manlike beast, known as the "Abominable Snowman," that is said to roam in the Tibetan Himalayas. Similar creatures, said to inhabit parts of North America, are known as "Big Foot" or "Sasquatch." ⟨Bhutan's wilderness . . . conceals many rare species, including tiger, bear . . . and, some say, even the fabled *yeti*⟩—*Time*, December 21, 1998.

yin-yang, yin and yang *(yihn-yang)* [Chinese] In centuries-old Chinese religion and philosophy, the two basic principles whose interplay affects the fates of all beings and things. *Yin* is seen as Earth, female, passive, and dark; *yang* is heaven, male, active, and light.

yoga *(YOH-gah)* [Hindi, from Sanskrit: union] A Hindu philosophy that advocates mental and physical discipline, such as abstract meditation, designed to free the self from material concerns and promote spiritual union with the Supreme Being. A related system of breathing exercises and postures used to achieve mental and physical well-being or tranquillity.

yogi *(YOH-ghee)* [Hindi, from Sanskrit] A person who practices YOGA.

yogurt, yoghurt *(YOH-gert)* [Turkish] A smooth, creamy food prepared from milk that has been curdled by the action of certain bacteria.

yurt *(yoort)* [Turkic: home] A portable, circular, dome-shaped tent made of felt or animal hides laid on a framework of poles; common among the Mongol and Turkic peoples of central Asia.

zabaglione *(zah-bahl-YOH-neh)* [Italian] In Italian cooking, a light, foamy, custardlike dessert made with beaten and warmed egg yolks, sugar, and marsala wine.

zaddik, tzaddik (singular); **zaddikim, tzaddikim** (plural) *(TSAH-deek, TSAH-dee-kim)* [Hebrew: righteous] The leader of a Hasidic group. A person of extraordinary piety or virtue.

zaftig *(TSAHF-tikh)* [Yiddish: succulent] A slang word used to describe a woman who is pleasingly plump, or full-bodied and shapely.

zaibatsu *(zye-BAHT-soo)* [Japanese: wealthy CLIQUE] In Japan, the vast capitalist empires or financial cliques, usually controlled by a single family, that developed after 1868 and flourished during World War I. Originally organized by a small number of private investors with close ties to government officials, *zaibatsu* owned and operated companies in many areas of economic activity. Mitsui and Mitsubishi were among the largest and best known.

zakuski *(zah-KOO-skee)* [Russian] In Russian cooking, appetizers or HORS D'OEUVRES. ⟨At a farewell dinner, I paced myself so well, nibbling *zakuski* between gulps, that I never even considered a jump.⟩—*The New York Times,* June 28, 1998.

zapateado *(zah-pah-tay-AH-doh)* [Spanish: clog shod] A Spanish FLAMENCO dance performed by men, characterized by rhythmic stamping and STACCATO heel tapping.

zarzuela *(zahr-ZWAY-lah)* [Spanish] A style of Spanish operetta that originated in the Palace of La Zarzuela in Madrid in the 1600s and is still popular in the 20th century.

zeitgeist *(TSYT-ghyst)* [German: spirit of the time] The general feeling or point of view that is typical of a particular era, as the revolutionary *zeitgeist* of Germany in the time of Hegel. ⟨the basic idea that the world may become any man's oyster . . . is the *Zeitgeist* which impels our students to a profound reverence for acquisitiveness.⟩—*The Atlantic Monthly,* September 1932.

zendo *(ZEN-doh)* [Japanese] In Zen Buddhism, a room or a place set aside for meditation.

zenith *(ZEE-nith)* [French, from Arabic] On the celestial sphere, the point exactly above the observer, as opposed to the NADIR. The highest point; the culmination.

ziggurat *(ZIG-ger-aht)* [Assyrian] Among the ancient Assyrians and Babylonians, a temple in pyramidal form that resembled a series of terraces, with a broad ramp winding around the outer structure from bottom to top. ⟨the space beneath Foster's grandiose *ziggurat* remains popular with people who could not care less about the digitalised sums that come and go through fibre-optic cables.⟩—*The Guardian,* April 11, 1999.

zingara (f), **zingaro** (m) *(TSING-gah-rah, TSING-gah-roh)* [Italian] A Gypsy. See also TZIGANE.

zombie *(ZOHM-bee)* [Kongo or Kimbundu: god] In VOODOO cults, a dead body said to be reanimated by witchcraft, but lacking a will or the ability to speak. By extension, someone whose behavior or reactions are listless, expressionless, or seemingly automatic. ⟨That said, though, Grossman's child-*zombie* scenario sounds too far-fetched.⟩—*Time,* May 10, 1999.

zori *(ZOR-ee)* [Japanese, from Chinese] A Japanese straw or rubber sandal with a flat sole and a thong between the first and second toes.

zuppa inglese *(TSOO-pah een-GLEH-zeh)* [Italian: English soup] An Italian dessert, similar to an English trifle, made with layers of plain cake liberally sprinkled with rum and covered in custard.

zwieback *(ZWY-bak)* [German: twice baked] A small loaf of bread that has been sliced and oven-toasted until browned and very dry. Similar to the French biscotte.

zydeco *(ZY-deh-koh)* [Louisiana French] Dance music from the French-speaking area of Louisiana and east Texas, based on Cajun music and the blues; a vigorous, rhythmic style performed mainly by fiddle, guitar, and accordion. ⟨It's a festival built on time-tested music with Louisiana roots: jazz from traditional improvisation to modern modalities, *zydeco* and Cajun songs, gospel, blues, rhythm-and-blues and rock.⟩—*The New York Times*, April 27, 1999.